# BOYS OF '66

# BOYS OF '66

## The England team that won the World Cup- then and now

## MARTIN TYLER

**HAMLYN**

Edited by **Richard Widdows**
Designed by **Janette Place**
Jacket designed by **Phil Bush**

Additional contributions and material by **Brian James**, **Phil Soar** and **Richard Widdows**

Published 1981 by The Hamlyn Publishing Group Limited
London ● New York ● Sydney ● Toronto
Astronaut House, Feltham, Middlesex, England

© Copyright 1981 STW Publishers Limited
ISBN 0 600 34660 9

Phototypeset by Pearl Island Filmsetters (HK) Ltd
Printed in Italy

# CONTENTS

# Introduction

It is fifteen years since England won the World Cup. Spiced by the opposition of West Germany, it was more than just a sporting success—it touched the emotions of the whole country. The names of twelve heroes, the Boys of '66, were on a nation's lips. No England team has emulated that performance, nor looked likely to do so. The World Cup of 1966 remains the only major trophy won by the island which invented the game. So what has happened to those eleven footballers and one manager since? Some have remained prominent, others have drifted into anonymity which seemed impossible that steamy afternoon at Wembley, but perhaps the most remarkable thing about the men is the speed at which their lives continue to change. I finished writing this book in March 1981. In the next three months I was astonished to see six of my twelve subjects leave the jobs they had held at the time I interviewed them: Gordon Banks' fears were fulfilled when he left Telford, Geoff Hurst became the sixth manager in four years to depart from Chelsea, Bobby Moore resigned from Oxford City, Alan Ball returned to Southampton, Martin Peters left the Sheffield United managership after a missed penalty in the last minute of the last game of the 1980-81 season caused the club's first-ever relegation to the Fourth Division, and Nobby Stiles went down with Preston North End. So, of the seven men actively involved in the game when I interviewed them, only Jack Charlton retained his job at the end of the season. I apologise to the reader if some of the problems I have had in keeping up with this remarkable course of events are apparent.

I hope that the product of my interviews and the considered recollections of the Boys of '66 not only remind the reader of occasions he or she would like to remember but also reveal things not known before—like the fact that Geoff Hurst left the victors' dressing room just to check that the scoreboard really did read 4-2, that his third goal had gone in before the referee's whistle blew.

For their time, consideration and patience I thank all the Boys of '66. I hope the end product is worthy of what they achieved.

**Martin Tyler**

*The boys of '66, plus coach Harold Shepherdson and trainer Les Cocker, team up with Sir Alf for his testimonial dinner at the Café Royal on 30 July 1974—eight years to the day after the World Cup final and three months after Ramsey had been sacked as England boss. More than 500 attended, including 62 of the 101 players he selected to play. A gold-plated replica of the Jules Rimet Trophy was among the many gifts the former manager received.*

# THE WINNING OF THE WORLD CUP

The story of the boys of '66 has its roots in the events of an Ipswich spring morning in 1963. England's football team had a new manager, Alf Ramsey, who proclaimed to a reporter that England would win the 1966 World Cup. History does not record the tone of the remark, but casual or trumpeting it was to haunt Ramsey for the next three years.

Time has dimmed the significance of Ramsey's confidence, if confidence rather than bravado it was. England had never before, and for that matter have not since, progressed beyond the quarter-finals of a World Cup tournament. Much subsequent analysis denigrated England's success because it was achieved on home ground, yet when Ramsey made his most famous remark that advantage was not seen to be the overwhelming one it is today. Only two countries had previously won the trophy at home—the last, Italy, nearly 30 years before. Since 1963, of course, three out of four World Cups have been won by the home side.

Ramsey's statement, repeated soon afterwards at a London press conference, was taken seriously for only one reason: Ramsey's own reputation for the remarkable.

Alf Ramsey had joined Ipswich Town as manager in 1955 after a distinguished career as full-back for Southampton, Spurs and England. At the end of his first full season with the Suffolk team they won the Third Division South Championship. Four years later Ipswich, unsung and unfashionable, made off with the Second Division Championship and reached, for the first time in their history, the First Division.

What followed has passed into the legend of the game. In their first season at the highest level, 1961–62, Ipswich won the League Championship, only the fourth team in history to win both divisions in consecutive seasons and the only club to win the League Championship in their first ever Division 1 season. They did it with a team that had few discernable stars, but with a pattern of play that perplexed all their rivals. That pattern was created by Alf Ramsey.

That summer England reached the quarter-finals of the 1962 World Cup in Chile, losing 3-1 to Brazil, the eventual winners. Walter Winterbottom had been England's manager for 17 years, and the time for change had arrived.

In Lamb's words: 'Come the moment, come the man.' Two years earlier Ramsey's name would not even have been considered. Two years later (by which time Ipswich were back in the Second Division) he might not have been the overwhelmingly popular choice. Even in 1962, the FA did not regard his appointment as a foregone conclusion. Others were seriously considered, Jimmy Adamson of Burnley reputedly being the front runner. But in the end it went to Ramsey, who officially took up his appointment on 1 May 1963.

Ramsey accepted the job on his terms, insisting that he would pick the team himself, the first England manager to rid himself of the FA selection committee.

The first game at which he had any contact with the England team was on 27 February 1963, when they lost 5-2 in Paris in a European Nations Cup fixture, and on 6 April they lost again, at home to Scotland.

It is in the context of all this that his public pronouncement that England would win the World Cup has to be remembered and judged. It was an astonishingly brave prediction so far ahead of the date. It said, effectively: 'Have faith in me. And if I fail you can have my head.'

Three of those who went to play in the 1966 World Cup final were chosen by Ramsey for his first official game

*Alf Ramsey, almost hidden from view, is introduced to the Queen by his captain before the first game of the finals on 11 July 1966, against Uruguay. His bold claim, made three years before, that England would win the trophy, is about to be put to the test. On the left is John Connelly, whose last cap came in this match.*

as manager, a 1-1 draw against Brazil on 8 May 1963. Goalkeeper Gordon Banks, beaten by a swerving free-kick from Pepé, was winning his second cap. Bobby Moore, West Ham's precocious defender, had been a surprise late selection for the 1962 World Cup squad and then played in every game. Bobby Charlton, first chosen in 1958, had already established his pedigree without being convincing about his best position. Charlton played against Brazil at outside-left.

But Ramsey's main priority at the outset was to establish a firm base at the back. And the blend which was to give England an unblemished record for the first 442 minutes of the World Cup was first unveiled against Scotland at Wembley in April 1965.

First caps were awarded to Jack Charlton, a tough but rather obstreperous centre-half with Leeds United, who was beginning late in his career to prove that he was more than just Bobby's older brother, and Nobby Stiles of Manchester United. Short of stature and of sight, Stiles hardly wore the look of a thoroughbred, but Ramsey foresaw the midfield balance his defensive abrasiveness and hard tackling would bring.

In goal Banks had performed consistently in his two years under Ram-

sey and was holding off the challenge of Tony Waiters, the raw Peter Bonetti and the veteran of the 1962 World Cup, Ron Springett.

George Cohen from Fulham, a fitness fanatic, caught the eye of the crowd with his pumping runs down the touchline—still a new tactic for full-backs—but Ramsey appreciated the value of his speed and strength in quelling the opposition. On the other flank Ray Wilson's quality had marked him down as the nation's best left-back, even though his bread and butter work was conducted in the comparative obscurity of the Second Division with Huddersfield Town; only ten months before the match against Scotland, at almost 30, he had finally been upgraded into the higher echelons with a transfer to Everton.

At the centre of England's defensive castle stood Bobby Moore, whose progress under the new manager had endured a hiccup or two but who was on course to become an on-field extension of Ramsey.

Further forward Ramsey's options were less clear cut, but one player seemed certain to be in the vanguard of England's attack in 1966.

Jimmy Greaves was established as the best goalscoring forward England had produced since the war, possibly of all time. It was always assumed by the public at large, even to the eve of the final, that Greaves must form part of Ramsey's plans. Even as late as 1965, Geoff Hurst was a comparative unknown, and certainly unconsidered by the press and public as a potential World Cup forward. Even his one claim to public acclaim, West Ham's second goal in the 1964 Cup final, had a touch of the absurd about it—the ball rebounding off the crossbar onto the back of Preston goalkeeper Alan Kelly's head and shoulder and into the net.

Elsewhere, Roger Hunt had marked his England debut with a goal against Austria in 1962. He gathered goals by the shoal for Liverpool, yet his claims did not appeal to the southern public, to whom his tireless effort appeared to be a substitute for genuine touch.

For the time being, Ramsey was still searching for wingers to fit his basic tactical pattern. Peter Thompson, for years a public favourite both inside and outside Liverpool, shuttled in and out of favour. One of the most talented wing players of his generation, he too often dwelt on the ball and cut inside to suit ·Ramsey's simpler plans.

But Thompson was not the only wing option. In the 18 months prior to the final Terry Paine, Derek Temple, Bobby Tambling, Gordon Harris, Ian Callaghan and John Connelly were all given their chance. None really succeeded, but their presence must give the lie to the common lament that Ramsey preferred to play without wingers. He did not; he simply couldn't find what he wanted.

In May 1965 a new face entered the World Cup debate, when 19-year-old Alan Ball was chosen for his first cap against Yugoslavia in Belgrade. He could attack down the touchline but possessed the restless energy that gave Ramsey a possibility of operating without recognised wingers.

Though both full-backs had attacking natures and offered genuine width, that facet of their game pro-

*Uruguay's Ladislao Mazurkievicz comes under pressure from Jack Charlton. Like so many World Cup openers it proved a turgid match, with the nervous Uruguayans, conscious that a draw against England and three points off France and Mexico would do, concentrating on defence—'played with ten full backs' as Ray Wilson puts it. They achieved their goalless draw —and criticism mounted on Ramsey to make changes.*

*England's first goal of the finals—a 30-yard special from Bobby Charlton which Mexico keeper Calderon can only watch into the net—came almost halfway through their second game. The side showed two changes from the Uruguay game: Paine and Peters replacing Connelly and Ball, later a hero in the final.*

vided few dividends for England; no England goal in the 1966 World Cup came directly from those sources.

If a single game can be pinned down as the moment at which Ramsey's tactical options and the players at his disposal finally gelled, it was against Spain in Madrid on 8 December 1965. His team that day was Banks, Cohen, Jack Charlton, Moore, Wilson, Stiles, Ball, Bobby Charlton, Eastham, Baker and Hunt. Replace Eastham and Baker with the West Ham pair of Peters and Hurst and you have the World Cup winning team.

With no recognised winger in the side, Ramsey opted for a 4-3-3 formation with a packed (for those days) midfield and Baker at times playing with his back to the goal as a diminutive target man. Ramsey was to say later: 'It had become apparent that we didn't have the wingers who could get past defenders, take the ball to the goal-line and pull it back. Defences had tightened up so that if a winger did get past a full-back he was always confronted by another covering player. We had to think of something else.'

The Spaniards reacted to this winger-less side as Ramsey hoped. The full-backs were lured out of position, leaving gaps behind them for Ball, Cohen, Wilson and Bobby

Charlton to exploit. Within eight minutes Baker had scored from a Wilson cross, and Hunt made the result safe with half an hour left. Spanish keeper Iribar was magnificent, and the England forwards missed several chances; otherwise the game might have resembled a bull-ring slaughter rather than a football match. Spanish manager José Villalonga said afterwards: 'They were phenomenal, far superior both in their experiment and their players.'

From this point Ramsey's tactics and side were nearly settled. It was only the most effective goalscoring combination which he had yet to discover—and here the only apparent question was still who would partner Greaves up front.

As Ramsey was gradually piecing together his jigsaw, the puzzle of the tournament's make-up was also taking shape. England didn't need to qualify. Nor did Brazil, as holders. But 14 other places were open.

Uruguay, Chile and Argentina had few problems in their South American groups. Mexico, far too good for the USA and Central America but rarely good enough to trouble the rest of the world, came through as usual. From the East, the totally unknown North Koreans defeated Australia in a play-

off for the single African and Asian place, though they were undoubtedly helped by the withdrawal of nearly all the African competitors in protest against FIFA's refusal to give Africa a guaranteed spot.

In Europe the failures were, at times, more notable that the successes. Czechoslovakia, beaten finalists in 1962, went out when they lost in Bratislava to Portugal, who thus qualified for their first ever appearance in a final series. Scotland had the misfortune to draw Italy and Poland in the same group, and effectively lost their chance when Poland scored twice in the second half to win 2-1 at Hampden on 13 October 1965. As a result, they needed a draw in Naples on 7 December 1965 to earn a play-off, but failed after the League refused to cancel its fixtures on 4 December and several managers of English clubs (including Scots Matt Busby and Bill Shankly) refused to rest key players.

The upshot of it all was that a Scottish team which theoretically had available the talents of Denis Law, Jim Baxter, Willie Henderson, Ian St John and Willie Stevenson failed yet again to qualify for the finals. It was a bitter pill for team manager Jock Stein, who gave up the job soon afterwards with a personal pledge, on

which he finally relented, never to take it on again.

Wales beat Russia in Cardiff in their qualifying group but could not plunder enough points elsewhere, while Northern Ireland were only a point away from a play-off after winning three and drawing two of their six matches in group five. Switzerland edged through ahead of the Irish. Yugoslavia went out in the group headed by France, largely because they had dropped three points to Norway, and Bulgaria beat Belgium 2-1 after a play-off in Florence, a surprising twist to a series of matches which saw Belgium win two games 5-0. West Germany had little difficulty in overcoming Sweden and Cyprus, while Hungary qualified comfortably at the expense of East Germany and Austria.

And so, as the teams gathered in England in early July, the battle-lines were being drawn. England's final run-in to the competition—a rapid tour of Finland, Norway, Denmark and Poland which produced four wins and an aggregate of 12-1—inevitably made them one of the favourites. Prior to the opening match against Uruguay they had lost only one of 21 internationals—a 3-2 defeat by Austria at Wembley on 20 October 1965. It was a

*Scorers Charlton and Hunt trudge off the pitch after the Mexico match. Their expression, that of losers rather than winners, reflects the laboured nature of their win against a side described by Hugh McIlvanney in 'The Observer' as having 'about as much right to be in the World Cup as the Isle of Man has to be represented on the Security Council.' Two points and a pot of goals were expected, and fears were expressed now about England's ability to live with the big boys in the last eight.*

remarkable record by any standards.

Brazil, winners of the past two World Cups, still remained the team to beat, though their tour of Europe before the finals had been anything but convincing. Too many of their players had been around too long, and if they were to win, it would be because of the genius of Pelé and Garrincha and their ability to score enough unexpected goals to offset the inevitable defensive frailties. These two sides apart, the field was open. West Germany, Italy and Russia all had their backers, and there was some grudging respect for Argentina, winners of the 'Little World Cup' competition in 1964.

Preparations had been going on in England since September 1963. The World Cup organising committee had its headquarters at the White City, scene of the 1908 Olympic Games and where, oddly, the Uruguay–France match was to be played. The committee had wanted to use Highbury, but the pitch was 16 feet too short for FIFA regulations. Everton's Goodison Park faced the same problems— being 12 feet too short and six feet too narrow, but costly alterations were made.

Elsewhere in Britain the stadia virtually picked themselves, though Newcastle's St James' Park had to be abandoned (because of difficulties with the local council, who still own such a famous ground) in favour of Ayresome Park, the home of less fashionable Middlesbrough.

Most improvements were paid for by the organising committee, which eventually received a grant of £400,000 from the government. The biggest problem, in space terms, was that of press accommodation. Goodison had to be provided with 700 press seats and Wembley eventually held 1,000 journalists. Seating for numerous television commentators was even more of a problem but equally necessary— the audience for the final was estimated to be 400 million.

A 'season ticket' for 10 games (including the final, a semi-final and a quarter-final) cost £25.75 for the very best seats and £3.87 to stand. As another sign of how relatively simple and uncommercial football was only 15 years ago, the organising committee could not find a single sponsor or advertiser for their ticket

and sales brochures, one million of which were distributed in 1965. The total ticket sales at all 32 matches was eventually 1,600,000 out of the total printed of 2,100,000, a remarkably high 80 per cent average.

Total gate receipts in 1966 were £1,550,000. Villa Park attracted the biggest attendance in terms of percentage of tickets sold with 96 per cent capacity; Ayresome Park and (surprisingly) Old Trafford were the smallest with just over 50 per cent.

The symbol of the tournament was World Cup Willie, designed by Reginald Hoye to exploit commercial licences for the organising committee. Looking rather dated today, Willie was the first symbol of its kind readily identifiable to the British people, a fact which no doubt explains its remarkable durability in the heady period of mini-skirts and 'swinging London'.

One other feature of the build-up was rather less well received: the theft of the Jules Rimet Trophy from the Stampex Exhibition at Central Hall, Westminster, on Sunday 20 March 1966. A week later the Cup was sniffed out under a hedge in South-East London by a mongrel, Pickles, who became almost as famous as the players in the competition. The theft had been followed by ransom demands in which a part of the trophy was detached and sent to Joe Mears, chairman of the FA. Later the police did make an arrest. The relief at the FA when the Cup was recovered was understandably enormous. The only comparable precedent—the loss of the first FA Cup in 1895—had a far less happy ending; that particular trophy has never been seen since.

Alf Ramsey set up camp at Lilleshall in June, with 27 players, five of whom would be deleted from the final squad. Two of the party had staked late claims; the West Ham pair of Geoff Hurst, who had performed a major role in England's 4-3 win in Scotland, and Martin Peters, whose wide-ranging talents were employed by Ramsey for the first time against Yugoslavia in May.

The pruning was done before the four-game tour of Finland, Norway, Denmark and Poland. All the players rightly believed that the numbering of the final 22 was significant: 1. Gordon Banks (Leicester);

2. George Cohen (Fulham); 3. Ray Wilson (Everton); 4. Nobby Stiles (Manchester United); 5. Jack Charlton (Leeds); 6. Bobby Moore (West Ham); 7. Alan Ball (Blackpool); 8. Jimmy Greaves (Spurs); 9. Bobby Charlton (Manchester United); 10. Geoff Hurst (West Ham); 11. John Connelly (Manchester United); 12. Ron Springett (Sheffield Wednesday); 13. Peter Bonetti (Chelsea); 14. Jimmy Armfield (Blackpool); 15. Gerry Byrne (Liverpool); 16. Martin Peters (West Ham); 17. Ron Flowers (Wolves); 18. Norman Hunter (Leeds); 19. Terry Paine (Southampton); 20. Ian Callaghan (Liverpool); 21. Roger Hunt (Liverpool); 22. George Eastham (Arsenal).

Of the four warm-up games, the last was much the hardest, Ramsey having decided that he must have a genuinely tough match before the tournament began. As a result, he

*LEFT: Roger Hunt celebrates his 28th birthday by tapping in the rebound from Jack Charlton's header in the 38th minute against France. England, with Callaghan in for Paine, failed to take several chances against a French side looking to attack, and Banks had to be at his best to make the two points safe.*

*BELOW: Number two for Hunt as he heads home Callaghan's 75th-minute cross. France were down to 10 men at the time—Simon was off receiving treatment after a crippling foul by Stiles—while Herbin had been a passenger for most of the game. England's injury problems concerned Greaves, with a gashed shin.*

picked what must be assumed to have been his first choice side for that game in Katowice. So, six days before the World Cup began, his team was different from the eventual World Cup winners in just one position—Greaves played while Hurst, who had a fumbling match against Denmark, did not.

The England party re-assembled at the Hendon Hall Hotel—ideally cast close to the Empire Stadium—at lunch-time on Friday 8 July. The tournament's opening match was scheduled to kick-off at 7.30 the following Monday. The tradition of the hosts contesting the first game was maintained with England playing Uruguay at Wembley.

This seemed a good choice. Uruguay were one of the three countries who had won the World Cup twice, along with Italy and Brazil. They had staged the first World Cup and won a remarkable game against Brazil in Rio in 1950 to steal the Cup from under the noses of the biggest football crowd in history, and did not lose a single World Cup game from the inception of the tournament until a semi-final in Lausanne in 1954. Unfortunately, the successors to this proud tradition were not to enhance it.

The Uruguay–England game contained all of the things that were perceived to be wrong with the 1966 World Cup and, more significantly, that have been wrong with the game since. The goalless draw on that bright, sunny evening was the first of a succession of four identical results in the opening games of the World Cup (Mexico v Russia in 1970, Brazil v Yugoslavia in 1974, West Germany v Poland in 1978). The tension in both teams made relaxed, controlled football virtually impossible—there was simply too much to lose.

The visitors had no thought other than to gain a draw—their cavortings at the final whistle showed their delight with what they had achieved. For much of the game, Uruguay played with a 10-man defence. Their play was usually skilful but, for all that, entirely lacking in ambition. Against it, the England defence was rarely troubled. The midfield created opportunities competently and controlled the game well, but the England forwards could do little against the Uruguayan blanket. Troche was a thoroughly competent sweeper, patrolling behind a back line of four, with Silva and Cortes in front of them

*While the rest of the squad train at Roehampton, Greaves nurses the injury sustained the day before against France. At this he stage he thought he could be fit for the Argentina game two days later, despite his three stitches. If not there was only one other front runner available—Geoff Hurst.*

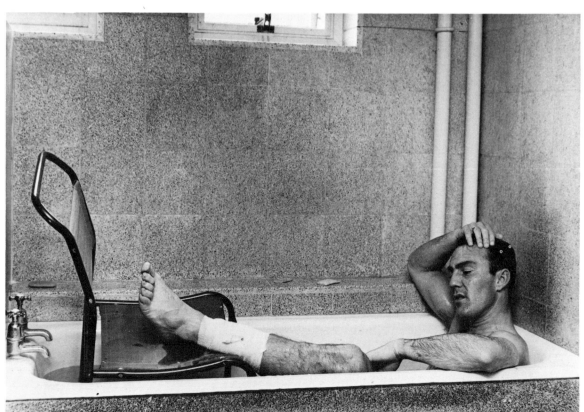

to provide cover well before any brave and determined opponent reached the danger area. England won 16 corners and had 15 shots worthy of the name, but few were real chances; a Connelly shot hit goalkeeper Mazurkievicz on the chin, a 25-yard Bobby Charlton effort was just a foot over and, near the end, a Jack Charlton header from a Greaves cross sailed just a foot wide with the defence nowhere.

The danger, increasingly, was that Uruguay would break away, notch a single goal and close up for the rest of the game. Nobody in the 87,000 crowd ever relaxed from contemplating this awful possibility, and indeed Uruguay came close on more than one occasion—particularly from a 30-yard Cortes free-kick which evaded defenders and attackers alike. Even the fouling was cynical rather than whole-hearted. The neat Uruguayans would do enough with unbalancing body-checks or obstructions to halt England's progress, but not enough to incur any major penalty.

After the game Ramsey said he was satisfied with the performance if not the result and reiterated his view that England would win the tournament, a view not widely shared by his listeners. The game had, by and large, lessened the convictions of more impartial observers. The lack of a single, really creative midfield player plus the inability of any of the forwards (Greaves included) to break down the tight marking was going to ultimately cost England dear; that was the general tenor of press comment the following day.

The next two games in England's group were instructive. France and Mexico drew 1-1 at Wembley two days later, and Uruguay then beat France 2-1 at the White City on the Friday. The incongruity of playing a World Cup match in a stadium which had hardly ever been used for football in its 60-year history while, within 10 miles, there were 12 perfectly good, ready-made football grounds, was not lost on the public. Under the circumstances, the officially declared attendance of 45,662 was astonishingly high.

The France–Mexico result was a great boost to England, effectively neutralising their own draw. Neither side looked like serious contenders but, equally, no-one could expect France to play so badly again. As England had climbed uphill since that 5-2 thrashing in Paris in 1963, so France had obviously declined. Only Robert Herbin, a red-headed midfield player, really caught the eye. Mexico scored first in the 49th minute through their centre-forward Borja, while France equalised 10 minutes later through Hausser, snapping a quick shot in off Calderon's post.

The Uruguayans had also been encouraged by France's performance and, expecting to beat them, the South Americans approached Friday's game with an entirely different attitude from the stifling one of the previous Monday at Wembley. Oddly, the defence seemed less assured and France took a surprise lead after 15 minutes when Herbet was rugby tackled and De Bourgoing scored from the penalty. But by half-time the defensive frailties of the French had also let them down and Rocha and Cortes had taken advantage to put Uruguay 2-1 ahead.

The result was a good one for England. France were effectively out and so a win against Mexico on Saturday 16 July would come close to guaranteeing England's place in the last eight. Ramsey changed his line-up, not unexpectedly, giving Paine a run in Connelly's place and bringing Peters in for Ball. Though England won the game 2-0, it was ultimately no more satisfying than the Uruguay match. The forwards laboured just as unconvincingly against an even more unadventurous, if less skilful, defence; as Hugh McIlvanney said, '. . . their formation could hardly have been more negative if they had dug foxholes.'

Unlike Uruguay, Mexico appeared to have no chance, or even desire, to score goals, but this hardly helped the English cause. It was not until the 35th minute that the 93,000 crowd had something to cheer, with Hunt getting the ball in the net for England for the first time in the series. Sadly, the referee disallowed the goal for, it was assumed, a push by Peters as he headed the ball back into the middle. Two minutes later the incident had been forgotten as Bobby Charlton scored perhaps the most memorable goal of his career; he picked the ball up near the centre-circle, ran forward 10 yards, moved slightly to his right

15

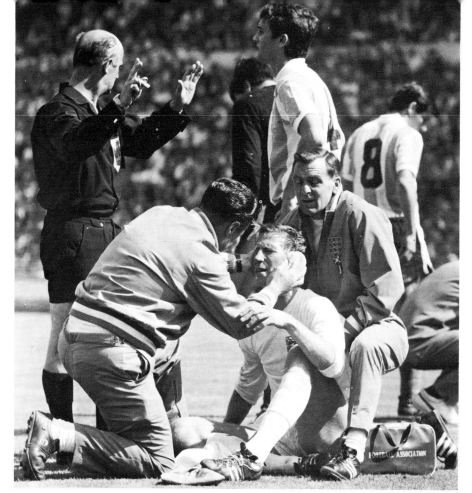

*Referee Kreitlein ignores the pleas of Perfumo as Jack Charlton, tended by Shepherdson and Cocker, recovers from the latest in a series of senseless Argentinian fouls. The quarter-final proved the least palatable of England's six games, plagued by fouls and endless bookings—including both Charltons.*

and hit it with his right foot into the far corner from 30 yards. The second-half saw a more relaxed performance, though barely more penetrating. Peters had another header cleared off the line and then, after 75 minutes, Greaves took a fine pass from Bobby Charlton, shot left-footed at keeper Calderon and Hunt had an easy job to make it 2-0 from the rebound. It was a win, and it virtually put England through, but it left unanswered one basic question—could England score against better opposition?

Ramsey had now tried Connelly and Paine (concussed for much of the Mexico game) and was to try Callaghan against France in the hope of finding a way round the back of sides determined to defend in numbers. None of the three orthodox wingers were to give Ramsey what he wanted —though one game in that sort of atmosphere is hardly a fair trial—and he would turn away from them for the quarter-final against Argentina.

Mexico completed yet another inconsequential appearance in a final series with a well earned 0-0 draw against Uruguay at Wembley on 19 July. They were much the better side, coming closest to scoring when Cisneros hit a post, and at least went home with the knowledge that in 1970 they would have home advantage.

England, meanwhile, were back at Wembley on the evening of Wednesday 20 July for their final group game; 98,270 people presumably turned out hoping for a more confident performance, since France had to win by two clear goals to cause an upset. Their chances were rendered virtually nil after only 10 minutes when their key player, Herbin, left the field for treatment and came back as a passenger. Nonetheless, Herbin provided the closest chance of the first half-hour when the England defence left him alone for a free header which he only just missed. Greaves was offside when he put the ball in the net after 30 minutes—he was not to score a goal in the competition—and there was some doubt eight minutes later when Hunt stabbed in an easy chance by

16

the foot of the post after Jack Charlton had headed a centre back across the face of the goal. But the arguments on this occasion were nothing compared with those after England's second goal, in the 75th minute.

Stiles, who ironically had been sent flying by the referee, a Peruvian with the unlikely name of Yamasaki, at the start of the match and had since been booked, clearly fouled Simon with an unnecessary late and unsavoury tackle. The referee ignored it, allowing Callaghan to cross for Hunt to score his second goal of the game. Simon had taken over Herbin's role of creater in the second half, to very good effect, and Stiles's foul was bad enough for some FA Council members to question his inclusion in the team despite the fact that the referee had not even blown for a foul.

Stiles gives his version of the episode in a later chapter but Ramsey is thought to have put his views forcefully, probably to the point of resignation, over his right to pick the team. Stiles stayed and so did Ramsey. Stiles responded to the extra responsibility imposed by his manager's support and did not again give any cause for concern about his tactics or attitude, and against Portugal in the semi-final he was to give an almost faultless performance.

So England were through, taking Uruguay with them as predicted. But it had been a depressingly poor group, a means to an end as A-levels are a way to university. Whether England could rise above their lacklustre displays remained to be seen but the early skills, delights and surprises of this World Cup were unquestionably found elsewhere.

The biggest shock came at Middlesbrough on Tuesday 19 July, where a mere 18,727 spectators saw one of international football's greatest upsets —when North Korea beat Italy 1-0. Coming to England as an unknown quantity, and disappearing again afterwards into equal obscurity, the North Koreans added enormous interest and colour to the whole series. They had skill, speed and strength, but obviously suffered from one factor they could not control: genetics—none of the side was taller than 5 ft 8 in.

Having lost 3-0 in the group's opening game to Russia, the Koreans improved with a 1-1 draw against

Chile, setting the scene for that historic confrontation at Ayresome Park. Italy, having beaten Chile 2-0 but losing 1-0 to Russia, were still clear favourites to go through. But they lost Bulgarelli with torn knee ligaments after half an hour, and, worse, a goal 10 minutes later from Pak Doo Ik; the standing joke of the time was that journalists could not understand the Korean names and

*ABOVE: In the 36th minute Kreitlein could stand no more. Argentina captain Antonio Rattin, who had been booked and had complained throughout the match about every decision, moaned once too often, about the latest caution, and was sent off. After farcical scenes lasting nearly 10 minutes he eventually went.*

*LEFT: It took England until the 77th minute to break down the 10-man opposition, a magnificent glancing header by Hurst from a superb cross by clubmate Peters (in background).*

17

would simply write down the menu from a Chinese restaurant near the ground before filing their reports. Italian counter-attacks proved fruitless and a casual observer outside the ground would have thought that Middlesbrough had won the FA Cup when the final whistle blew.

If the surprises and the joy were at Middlesbrough, the football and the controversy were in the North-West, where Brazil, Portugal, Hungary and Bulgaria, easily the strongest of the four groups, were playing out their games at Goodison Park and Old Trafford. The six games produced a see-saw effect: Brazil, the favourites, won their first game and then lost the next two—a failure Ramsey had predicted after watching the holders on their European tour. Hungary, second favourites, lost their first game but won their next two.

Brazil started with a reasonably convincing 2-0 win over Bulgaria. The two goals, one in each half, had an odd symmetry. Pelé was fouled by

Yakimov, in his creative moments one of the best players in the whole tournament, and scored the first from the free-kick, while Garrincha, from 25 yards, got the second from another free-kick after *he* had been fouled. The following night Portugal beat Hungary 3-1 in an entertaining game at Old Trafford. But the Hungarians then contributed hugely to one of the tournament's most thrilling encounters against Brazil at Goodison Park on 15 July.

Though Pelé, out with an ankle injury, was not playing, 57,000 turned up in the Merseyside rain to see a remarkable game. Within three minutes Bene had opened the whole match up with a swerving run along the right wing; past one, two, three Brazilian defenders he went before clipping the ball inside a hesitant Gylmar for one of the few truly individual goals of 1966. Within a quarter of an hour Brazil were level, Tostao scoring with his left foot past Gelei to give us a glimpse of what was to come in 1970.

*Herr Kreitlein, looking like some Nazi fugitive, is escorted from the pitch after being extricated from a bunch of incensed Argentinian fans and players at the final whistle. The unmistakable shape of Ken Aston, head of the referees' committee, tries to smooth things over.*

But the night's real hero was a Hungarian, Florian Albert, who had assumed the mantle of his great predecessors of 1953 and was running the game from the centre. In the 64th minute he started the move which led to the best goal of the whole World Cup. His perfectly flighted ball to the right wing found Bene, who went to the goal-line and cut the ball back perfectly into the path of Janos Farkas. He volleyed the ball with his right foot into the back of the net from 12 yards without breaking his stride. It was the sort of goal schoolboys dream about. A few minutes later Bene was pulled down in the area and Meszoly made it 3-1. It was the first time Brazil had lost a World Cup game at any level since the quarter-finals in Switzerland in 1954. Their opponents that day in Bern—Hungary.

It is a common exaggeration that Brazil were eliminated from the 1966 World Cup because Pelé was kicked out of the competition. It is certainly true that he was brutally treated in the game with Portugal at Goodison on 19 July. After half an hour defender João Morais chopped viciously at Pelé twice in the same dribble, ending the series for both player and country. It remains a mystery why referee George McCabe did not send Morais off, but Pelé had to leave the field for nearly 10 minutes and when he returned it was only to limp on the left wing. Nonetheless, this was Brazil's last group game and they were 2-0 down to goals by Simoes and Eusebio by the time Pelé went off. In truth, they had lost their World Cup against Hungary, not against Portugal. Rildo got one back for Brazil in the second half, but Eusebio made it safe with another for Portugal. Hungary then went on to beat Bulgaria 3-1 at Old Trafford and these two entertaining teams were thus through to the quarter-finals.

The remaining foursome, group 2, was perhaps the most predictable. Switzerland played like makeweights from the start, losing 5-0 to West

*Alf Ramsey tries to stop Alberto Gonzales taking home Cohen's shirt after the game. 'Mind you, the Argentine guy had almost had the shirt off my back during the game,' says George. 'The left sleeve was about a foot longer than the other at the finish.' Minutes later Ramsey would light an international fuse during a press interview with his notorious 'animals' reference—a remark that was to rebound on both English and Scottish clubs in subsequent seasons.*

*Hugs all round after Bobby Charlton's shot had put England one up against Portugal in the semi-final. Simoes and Augusto look back in anger at their defence.*

was now coached by Juan Carlos Lorenzo, later to find lasting notoriety with Independiente, Lazio, Boca Juniors and Atlético Madrid. In the end, Luis Artime won the game for Argentina with his two goals to Martinez's one for Spain; suddenly Argentina had become one of the teams to be feared.

They added to this reputation in rather a different way during their next game, against West Germany at Villa Park on Saturday 16 July. The match ended 0-0 but was most notable for Jorge Albrecht's violent tackling, which ended with a knee in Wolfgang Weber's groin and Albrecht's marching orders. The Argentinians were later to develop a complex conspiracy theory around the consequences of their behaviour which went something like this: their players were sent off against West Germany and England, the eventual finalists. The referee for their game against England was a German, while neighbours Uruguay had two men sent off against West Germany when an Englishman, Jim Finney, refereed. As extra evidence of complicity they use the argument that England played all their games at Wembley to suggest the whole competition was a set-up from the start. The only problem with this careful construction is that film of the Argentinian tackling still exists.

Their game with West Germany ended 0-0. The only other notable incidents apart from the sending-off were full-back Roberto Perfumo's two headers against his own bar. The rest of the matches in the group went their predictable way, and West Germany and Argentina ran out easy qualifiers with five points each and no defeats.

As the quarter-finals approached Alf Ramsey, despite his outward imperturbability, was still facing major problems. The situation was both good and bad. The defence had yet to concede a goal and looked to have come to a peak of understanding at the right time. None of the other seven quarter-finalists had kept a clean sheet in the group games.

But up front the side was not creating many chances and not scoring enough from those that it did. England had managed only four goals so far, which compared poorly with Portugal's nine and Hungary's seven—and those came against rather stronger

Germany and picking up no points and only one goal in their three games. With West Germany's power seemingly certain to guarantee them qualification, the group's critical game was between Argentina and Spain at Villa Park on 13 July.

The Argentinians had suffered a thoroughly unsettling run up to the competition. FIFA had refused to allow them to include their best home produced players, Sivori and Maschio, for the not entirely unreasonable reason that both had been capped by the countries whose clubs they had been transferred to. Two managers—Minella and Zubeldia—had resigned in the previous 12 months and the team

opposition. Greaves had not scored a single goal; Hunt, though he had scored three, was still being criticised; the wingers, Ramsey judged, had all failed. And now he faced an Argentinian side which could be relied on to add cynicism to that packed defence against which England had so struggled when Uruguay employed it.

Moreover England faced the quarter-final without the opportunism of Jimmy Greaves, injured against France. Hurst was the obvious, and only, replacement. Alan Ball was recalled in place of Callaghan. The press saw this as a forward for a forward, while doubting that Hurst could replace the incomparable Greaves, and a winger for a winger. Because Ball wore the number 7 shirt and played on the right it was assumed, even after the tournament was over, that he was a sort of winger and that England had played a genuine 4-3-3. It is strange to recall that, only 15 years ago, the vast majority still saw numbers as designating very precise positions (Peters, with a number 16 on his back, was a constant enigma). The reality was rather different.

Ball actually performed as a forward-running right-side midfield player in a formation much closer to 4-4-2, and it is probably fair to say that circumstances forced Ramsey's tactical hand rather than the other way round.

With four men in midfield, Ramsey expected to be able to win more of the ball there. Alan Ball, his most priceless asset being sheer energy, certainly did move forward on the right whenever the opportunity presented itself (most memorably for England's third goal in the final) but clearly he was not expected to play exclusively along the touchline. Four men in midfield meant, of course, abandoning the winger. That in itself forced a change of tactics on Ramsey. Rather than having a player go round the defence and knock the ball back for two central forwards, Ramsey now had to reach those forwards by more direct means. By chance, Ron Greenwood had actually provided him with the answer by moulding Geoff Hurst as a target-man, though at this stage the ploy was nothing like as refined as in 1970, when Hurst had developed it much further, and in 1966 the term was not even in general use.

It is easy with hindsight to see how all this developed but at the time it was anything but clear. The absence of Greaves was seen as a fatal flaw though, when all was said and done, Hunt had so far scored three goals and Greaves had scored none. Bill Shankly's oft-repeated justification for Hunt's selection was not just a truism: 'Yes, he misses a few—but he gets in the right places to miss them.'

The Argentinians were unhappy that they had to play at Wembley, where they had never won, because

*Ten minutes from time and Charlton does it again, converting Hurst's sweet pass with a spectacular shot to virtually seal England's place in the final. Eusebio's penalty three minutes later produced a tense climax to a game that had none of the negativity and niggling of previous games; Portugal, in fact, didn't concede a foul until the 57th minute. England's win was built on a tight performance from a defensive unit that had remained unchanged throughout the competition, and they reached the final having conceded just one goal—a penalty for hand-ball.*

England had so much experience there. In fact the venues for each and every game had been established well in advance with the winner of group one playing the runners-up of group two at Wembley, the runners-up in group one playing the winners of group two at Hillsborough and groups three and four splitting similarly at Goodison and Roker. Certainly this gave England the possibility of playing all their games at Wembley, but the Argentinians were not noted for their vociferous objections when FIFA granted the same chance in 1978, when they were also allowed evening kick-offs throughout to maximise the television audience.

All this was just part of a jittery preamble to what Hugh McIlvanney later described as 'not so much a football match as an international incident.' Of the game itself there is not too much worth recalling. Argentina showed themselves to be technically the better and more skilful side and, even when their opponents had been reduced to 10 men, England still struggled to make any impression. The outcome revolved round two incidents: the sending-off of Argentinian captain Rattin and the goal that decided the match.

Argentina approached the game in a manner that later became all too familiar to followers of Juan Carlos Lorenzo's sides. The petty fouling was constant, the body-checking almost automatic. When tackled themselves, the Argentinians would roll around the turf in simulated agony, perhaps a trick they had picked up from one or two of the West Germans in their Villa Park encounter. Matters were not helped by West German referee Rudolf Kreitlein's fussy attitude—it was never discovered exactly how many Argentinians he booked but it must have been more than half the team and, as Brian Glanville commented in the *Sunday Times*, '...at last, possibly because he had no pages left in his notebook, he abruptly ordered Rattin off.'

Antonio Rattin was Argentina's key figure on the pitch, strolling around midfield, distributing the ball to whichever of his team seemed to have most space with a rare but convincing arrogance. He had already been booked for fouling Bobby Charlton when he tried to intervene to stop Artime being added to the list of Argentinians recorded for posterity. To everyone in the ground he appeared to be abusing the referee, but Rattin himself later insisted that he was only asking for an interpreter to help calm things down.

Herr Kreitlein was not convinced either and clearly decided he would have to despatch Rattin to the dressing-room if the game was to have any chance of finishing at all. At this point all hell broke loose as Rattin refused to go; Kreitlein was surrounded by Argentinian players and officials and at least four members of the South American team clearly indicated that, if Rattin went, so would they. Harry Cavan, FIFA's commissar (a strange word for FIFA to use) at this game and Ken Aston, famed for being in charge of the infamous Chile-Italy game four years before and now head of the referees' committee, both joined in as the arguments and protests went on for nearly 10 minutes.

In the end, Rattin went, the first man ever to be sent off at Wembley— and the game recommenced in an even more cynical mood than before. As the second half went on England looked, if anything, even less like scoring than before. Only one shot from Hurst, magnificently saved with a flying leap from Roma, had given the 91,000 crowd hope. It was in the 77th minute that what had by then become the unexpected actually happened. Wilson short to Peters on the left, a carefully flighted cross and there was Hurst, almost ghosting through to the near post, to deflect the ball just enough so that it entered the netting on the far side of Roma. The perfect West Ham goal.

The chaos that had marred the match continued after the game. Ramsey prevented his players from exchanging shirts and, in an interview, declared famously: 'We have still to produce our best football. It will come against the right type of opposition, a team who come to play football and not act as animals.' Some Argentinian players and officials had threatened the referee, who was protected by a police posse, others urinated against the tunnel wall. FIFA subsequently imposed the maximum fine on the Argentinian FA and threatened to refuse them entry to the next World

Two of the semi-final stars: Banks again proved almost faultless, saving the day with a magnificent tip-over to deny Coluna in the dying seconds; Stiles spiked the threat of Eusebio, cutting off his options rather than marking him tight. If any of the team had ever doubted their ability to win the trophy it disappeared in this match—perhaps the finest, in footballing terms, of the tournament. The fans, too, sensed a new belief; no provisos this time about the quality of the opposition or playing 10 men.

*The early blow: Helmut Haller jumps for joy as his 13th-minute shot squirts past Banks and an England error is punished for the first time in the competition— after 'the only mistake I ever saw Ray make,' according to Cohen. 'In many ways it was a defender's dream ball...from deep,' says Wilson. 'And I just mistimed it badly... went up a little early. The lad Haller checked his run...and I knocked it straight to him.' Banks explains that 'when he hit it there was a bit of confusion between me and Big Jack... when I realised it was coming through it had gone past me. I didn't even get a touch.'*

Cup (nearer home in Mexico) unless 'certain assurances were given'.

Rattin was suspended for his country's next four internationals, Ferreiro and Onega for three, the latter for spitting at Cavan. The FA were also asked to reprimand Alf Ramsey for his remarks. History surely showed that all of this was just a footnote to what really mattered— Geoff Hurst's goal. For the 13 minutes that remained after it, the crowd chanted 'We want two'; but as Brian Glanville remarked, they should have been very glad of one.

The other Europe-South American clash was, if anything, even more brutal. The game between Uruguay and West Germany at Hillsborough was effectively decided in the 10 minutes after the break. First Uruguayan sweeper Troche, for a foul on Emmerich, then Silva, for a physical assault on Haller, were sent off. Against nine men, West Germany had a much easier job than had appeared remotely possible in the first half and Held, Beckenbauer, Seeler and Haller made the score 4-0.

The match of the round was undoubtedly at Goodison. With virtually the whole of England sitting at home watching the game at Wembley, the most astonishing thing that happened on their television screens that afternoon was not the Rattin incident,

but the flash from Liverpool after 30 minutes: Portugal 0 North Korea 3.

The Koreans had come at Portugal like demons from the start, Pak Seung Zin scoring in the game's very first attack. Li Dong Woon soon made it two and Yang Sung Kook three. At this point the stage really was set for the greatest upset in history, but it says much for Portugal that they composed themselves and by half-time Eusebio had scored twice, once from a penalty, to make the score merely remarkable rather than absurd. The second half was one-way traffic: Eusebio scored twice more, including another penalty, and José Augusto made it five.

At Roker Park, Hungary's meeting with Russia failed to capture the public imagination. Only 27,000 tickets were sold and even fewer turned up to see Russia win 2-1. Hungary had not beaten Russia since 1954 and were to lose again because of their achilles heel throughout the tournament—goalkeeping. After only six minutes, Gelei dropped a simple shot from Malofeev and Chislenko was there to put Russia ahead. Immediately after the start of the second half Porkujan was left unmarked to put Russia two up and the game was effectively over, Bene's goal being a mere consolation.

Thus the semi-finalists comprised

four European nations. Russia and West Germany met at Goodison on Monday 25 July, much to the annoyance of the Liverpool crowd who had, not unreasonably, wanted to see England play there. At the time Everton were Cup holders and Liverpool League champions, so the city believed it had better claim to be the heartland of English football than the wastes of North-West London. Only 36,000 turned out to see the match (though 44,000 tickets had been sold) and those who stayed away missed a brutal game, highlighted in Germany's first goal almost on half-time.

Schnellinger crashed into Chislenko on the left touchline, leaving a clear gash on the Russian's leg. Italian referee Lo Bello ignored the incident and let Schnellinger go on to cross the ball to Haller, who scored with a beautiful right-foot shot. On the restart, Chislenko, incensed by all this, attacked the nearest German, who happened to be Sigi Held. Off went Chislenko, Lo Bello blew for half-time and Russia were virtually out of the World Cup. Chislenko was the fourth player sent off against the Germans in the series.

In the second half Beckenbauer scored with an almost lazy 20-yard shot which the 37-year-old Lev Yashin was blamed for conceding, though he was probably unsighted. Porkujan's goal three minutes from time came too late to influence the result.

While the Russia-West Germany game was to disappoint viewers everywhere, the other semi-final proved an entirely unexpected treat. The abiding memory of the game is that the referee did not have to blow his whistle until the 23rd minute, and then only for a harmless obstruction on Eusebio. The Portuguese did not concede a free-kick until the 57th minute, which might well qualify as some kind of international record. There was not one unpleasant, dangerous or, as far as one could tell, intentional foul throughout the whole game. Quite how this extraordinary event emerged from what had gone before must remain one of football's insoluble mysteries—but much of the credit must clearly be given to Portuguese manager Otto Gloria and the attitudes he had instilled in his team after the group games.

In such a rarified atmosphere of freedom England's football flourished. From the start, the England-Portugal game, played at Wembley on Tuesday 26 July, was clearly going to be a contest between the unyielding English defence and the free-scoring Portuguese forwards. So it proved, with England fashioning quick and dangerous breaks.

After 31 minutes, Ray Wilson

*It took England just six minutes to equalise when Moore, after being fouled by Overath, took a quick free-kick and Hurst, timing his run to perfection, beat the German defence with this well-placed header. It is perhaps the least appreciated of England's goals because it came early and has been swamped by the drama that followed. But it got England back in the game when it could so easily have got away from them. England had been behind for the first time in the finals—and they had proved to themselves they could fight back. But so could the Germans...*

RIGHT: The combined efforts of Schnellinger and Tilkowski fail to stop Peters' low lashing drive putting England 2-1 ahead in the 78th minute. 'I'm glad the bugger never come to me,' says Jack Charlton, who was standing only feet away, 'because I'd have kicked it over the bar.'

BELOW: Peters wheels away in triumph—after what he and everybody thought would be the winning goal.

pushed a long ball hopefully forward, Hunt chased but was beaten to it on the edge of the area by keeper Pereira. That should have been the end of the attack but, instead of gathering the ball, Pereira decided to attack it feet first. It bounced off his legs straight to Bobby Charlton, who stroked it with his right foot straight into the goal. One-nil to England. Rather than tackle direct Stiles regularly jockeyed Eusebio, always trying to position him in such a way that, should be break past the Manchester United man, there was another defender to make the tackle. This was to prove Stiles' game every bit as much as it was Bobby Charlton's.

The second goal, after 79 minutes, was far more creative than the first. A careful build-up ended with Cohen putting the ball at Hurst's feet near the bye-line. He beat Hilario and then pulled the ball back perfectly for Bobby Charlton to finish in a style equal to the build-up. Several Portuguese players congratulated Charlton —who had been having a marvellous game in midfield as well as in attack— as he ran back to the centre-circle. But the game was not yet over. Within three minutes Jack Charlton had handled a Torres header on the line, the referee had given a penalty, Eusebio had scored his eighth goal of the tournament—and Banks had conceded his first. It would have made a marvellous final.

Portugal got some small reward when they won the third-place match at Wembley on the following Thursday, beating Russia 2-1. Eusebio struck his ninth goal, yet another penalty, and Torres got the other. But like most third-place games, it did not linger in the memory for very long. Too many thoughts had already turned to the final.

England had never lost to Germany and had beaten them twice 1-0 as recently as May 1965, in Nürnberg, and February 1966, at Wembley. That, plus home advantage, was clearly enough to make England favourites. The West German side virtually picked itself, Horst Höttges coming back as right-back in place of Friedel Lutz, who had briefly replaced him for the semi-final. Beckenbauer had apparently received a second caution in the semi-final, but FIFA chose not to confirm it and he was able to play.

For England, however, there was still a massive question—would Greaves play? A gashed shin had provided the excuse for his absence from the previous two games, but this was clearly no longer relevant. Hurst, who had scored against Argentina and so effectively made the second goal against Portugal, was hardly going to be dropped at this stage, which left Roger Hunt the more vulnerable.

It is unlikely, however, that Ramsey seriously considered straying from the manager's dictum of never changing a winning side. He clearly preferred the certainty of Hunt's efforts to the possibility that Greaves might, at last, show some of his old form. He formally announced the team at 11 on the morning of the match, Saturday 30 July. Most of the players knew the previous evening, but for Greaves it was a bitter pill.

Here was the climax of his personal story—or should have been—the most important game England would ever play, and surely the whole of Greaves' career had led up to this pinnacle. The look of virtual disbelief on his face as Geoff Hurst scores his third goal (page 73) tells the story. One cannot help but believe that he is thinking: 'That should have been me.' A wholly natural emotion from a man who chose to start his family holiday rather than have the disappointment thrust in his face again at the post-match banquet.

As far as the English press were concerned West Germany were just the sacrificial lambs. Not a single commentator seemed to give them a serious chance—a surprising blindness. This of course, dismayed manager Helmut Schoen not at all. In Beckenbauer he knew he already had one of the greatest players in the world; in Seeler, Held and Haller three thoroughly reliable goalscorers; and in Emmerich the strongest shot in the competition and an unpredictable element on the left which could easily turn the contest. The Germans had moved to the Homestead Court Hotel at Welwyn Garden City in preparation for the game. They remained confident as the rain fell and the minutes ticked away to 3 pm.

Because of the colour clash, England wore their second strip of red shirts and white shorts for the first time in the competition. Watching a re-run of the entire game 15 years later, one is struck not by the fanatically nationalistic fervour of the crowd of 96,924—that was to be expected—but of their good nature towards the Germans. There was none of the booing of national anthems and general abuse that characterise the Wembley international of the early 1980s.

West Germany started nervously. Goalkeeper Hans Tilkowski, a relatively weak link, was knocked out in an early England attack attempting to punch clear from Hurst. Nonetheless, the German defence looked sound with Willi Schulz an ever-dependable sweeper and Karl-Heinz Schnellinger deputed to mark Alan Ball closely.

Schoen had decided that, after Charlton's performance against Portugal, he had to be reined in and Beckenbauer was given the task of doing so—a decision for which Schoen was criticised afterwards. Eventually the most significant effect of this decision was not that it contained Charlton, but that it tended to contain Beckenbauer, thus costing the Germans perhaps their most creative match-winning influence.

When the first goal came it was a complete surprise. After 13 minutes Wilson, who had not made a single mistake that anyone could remember throughout the whole tournament, was presented with an easy clearance from a Held cross. Perhaps he just had too much time, but the ball flew unerringly straight from his forehead to the feet of Helmut Haller, standing just a dozen yards from Banks' left-hand post. Thirty million Englishmen watched as Haller appeared to pivot in slow motion and place the ball past Banks' right hand—not with a particularly firm shot. One-nil to Germany. It was scant reassurance that, since the war, the World Cup had not been won by the side which scored first in any of the four finals.

The crowd began to fear the Germans closing up shop, trying to hold on to their lead. To their credit they tried no such thing. Within six minutes England were level. Overath tripped Moore and the England captain took the free-kick immediately, floating the ball in from the left for Hurst to drift past the defence and head in at Tilkowski's right-hand post. It was in the style of the winner against Argentina, and another beautifully executed West Ham goal.

From this point onwards the game fluctuated. Hunt missed an easy chance for England, Overath had a 25-yard shot well saved by Banks. As the second half wore on Ball became more and more the key man, running Schnellinger off his feet, gaining the ascendency on the right side of the field. After the game Ball's was the favoured name for the unofficial 'man of the match'—a remarkable achievement when he had been playing alongside the first man to score a hat-trick in a World Cup final.

With just 12 minutes left it was Ball, appropriately, who provided the breakthrough. His shot was pushed out for a corner by Tilkowski, he took the kick himself and the ball dropped for Hurst. With more hope than conviction, Hurst struck a low shot, from outside the penalty area. The ball span off Höttges' left foot, up and into an unmarked space containing Peters and Jack Charlton. The West Ham man got there first and it was 2-1.

*LEFT: A minute to go...and a ragged England wall faces Emmerich's free-kick. The marking is all at sea as Weber (far right) edges inside the box...*

*BELOW: Weber's well-taken shot eludes Wilson's foot and Banks' hands to level the scores. Most of the England team are convinced that the free-kick was a bad decision and that Schnellinger handled—Moore is still appealing. 'If noboby had touched that ball it would have gone for a goal-kick, maybe a throw-in,' says Banks. 'The ball hit his arms and it dropped to Weber.'*

*1-LEFT: Hurst thumps Ball's pass past the lunging Willi Schulz 10 minutes into extra time. The scorer's verdict is an understandably terse 'yes, it was'. Note the position of referee Dienst.*

*4-ABOVE: A frame from the film 'Goal!' again shows the view of the Russian linesman, and of Ball, perhaps the player best placed to pass a judgment, after he had cut the ball back to Hurst. 'I don't think the linesman could have seen it because I was in a better position than him. I was right on the line...but to be honest I couldn't tell whether it was a goal or not.' The evidence of moving pictures is little more helpful than the photographic material.*

*5-RIGHT: The helplessly beaten Tilkowski is still falling as the ball bounces up and Roger Hunt spreads his arms in a reflex response to a goal. 'It looked to me to be at least a foot over the line. I'd scored lots of goals on rebounds and my normal reaction would be to go in...'*

2-BELOW: *The ball crashes against the underside of the bar and rockets downwards. This angle exaggerates the distance Bakhramov was from the line.*

3-ABOVE: *For and against. While this print (from an Italian agency) 'places' the ball a couple of feet from the line, it also shows that the linesman had a clear view, if not from the best position.*

6-ABOVE: *'...but I was so certain that I turned away.' Weber, in fact, headed clear. 'The ball definitely crossed the line,' says Bobby Charlton. 'I was there and I saw it with my own eyes. It* was *over.'*

By rights that goal should have won the World Cup. And eight minutes later the game ought to have been over when Hunt, Hurst and Bobby Charlton broke clear with only Schulz between them and Tilkowski. But Hunt underhit the pass and Charlton, off balance, pulled the shot wide. That gave the Germans just enough hope for a counter-attack, which was to pay dividends with only 30 seconds left. Seeler clearly made a back for Jack Charlton and the Englishman was rightly aggrieved when the fussy Swiss referee Gottfried Dienst gave a free-kick against him. Emmerich took the kick, the ball bounced round the England area, appeared to come down off Schnellinger's arm (though careful viewing of film of the incident suggests any hand-ball was entirely accidental) and landed at the feet of Weber beside the right-hand post. The centre-back took the chance magnificently, sweeping the ball into the net past Banks.

So the World Cup final went to extra time for the first time since 1934. Ramsey came out and told his exhausted players that they had won the game once; now they must, and could, do it again. No doubt Helmut Schoen was giving similar inspirational messages to his team...but no-one asks the losers. Bobby Moore said later, when asked about the sheer tension that was gripping the stadium and, indeed, the whole country at that point: 'No, I'd be wrong to say we felt it. We didn't really. At that point it was not much more than another football match, another 30 minutes to be got through. We were exhausted remember, and we'd played so many matches in the past few weeks. All the mental strain had been got out of our systems beforehand. There was no sense of the history of the moment. The crowd was a long way away.'

So the game went to an extra 30 minutes—and produced the most controversial goal in international history. Ten minutes into the first period only Ball would have had the energy to collect a long pass from Stiles, and, crossing from the right, found Hurst just inside the area. Hurst turned on the ball and hit it quickly. The speed of the shot fooled Tilkowski, the ball hit the crossbar, came down almost vertically and the backspin carried it out of the goal. It all happened so fast that nobody knew whether the ball had crossed the line. What referee Dienst did was to ask his Russian linesman Tofik Bakhramov what he thought, and he said one word: 'goal!'

At the time the referee seemed to be passing the buck—he was closer than the linesman. Many of the England players felt that the linesman was not well placed to judge, but our photographs show that he could well have had the clearest view of the ball hitting the ground.

Interestingly, none of the 20 or so photographs of the incident, nor the two feature films of the competition, gives a clear view of the ball actually touching the ground. On the television film Tilkowski's body is still in mid-air and obscures the vital evidence; only one camera position then. Bobby Charlton and Roger Hunt, the two England players with the best vantage points, both strongly affirm today that it was a genuine goal.

In Germany, however, it is still raised today as a matter of dispute, with the position of the shadows in the pictures usually being mentioned, and clearly it was unfortunate that the deciding moment of the match will always be clouded in uncertainty. There is less argument that England remained the better side, and Hurst's 'Roy of the Rovers' finale devalued some of the German protest.

England had carefully played out the remaining 20 minutes, though Seeler had only just failed to head home yet another equaliser in the last 60 seconds. The referee was literally looking at his watch when the ball fell to Bobby Moore in the England penalty area. Jack Charlton takes up the story of those last few seconds.

'In the last five minutes of extra-time I'd got so anxious it wasn't true. It's a terrible thing playing in a game and watching the referee running about, a watch in his hand. I think it had cost us at the end of normal time. I also felt that we'd enough of the ball to take it into the corners to relieve the pressure. We shouldn't have been under such pressure then. In those last five minutes of extra time we probably had about three or four good breaks...every time we went to try to score another goal. But we lost possession on the edge of their box, and they kept coming back at us. So

*ABOVE: The goal that settled it: Overath's chase is in vain as Hurst smashes home Moore's long pass in the dying seconds of extra time.*

*LEFT: Another view of the goal that brought the first hat-trick in a World Cup final. Overath wasn't the only player in pursuit: 'I was shouting at Geoff because he should have given the ball to me,' explains Alan Ball. 'We were two against one...I was screaming to him to square it, and I'd have walked it in. I was just about to curse him...and then I was yelling "great goal!"'*

I was screaming my head off to take the bloody ball into the corner. All we really needed to do was to keep possession.

'Then I remember Bobby Moore choosing to pull down a really difficult ball in our box. Away to my left. He pulled the ball down on his chest, and controlled it...at a time in the game when my first inclination would have been to see if I could have humped it out of Wembley. Which was the difference between me and Bobby Moore. I was brought up that if you were in danger around the edge of the box, you get the bloody thing out.

Get it away as far as you can. Don't take any chances. Bobby was brought up at West Ham where he was encouraged to have the ball, to play football—in any area of the field. I never would.

'So he pulled this ball down. He stopped it. He looked up, and then he started to move with the ball. I was shouting to him, hump it into the corner...'cos I had one eye on him, one eye on the referee with the watch in his hand, looking at it. The crowd were going crackers, and I was thinking, "He's got to blow any second, don't bloody lose possession there."

I ran across behind him in case he made a mistake, which was standard practice when I used to play with Bobby Moore.

'So I was in the perfect position to see him play the best ball I've ever seen in my life...for Geoff Hurst. He looked up and he saw Geoff start to run. It was a superb ball. And then I watched Geoff run away with the ball. It was like watching someone disappear over the horizon.'

Hurst's finish matched the quality of Moore's service, and the mood of tension snapped into uncontrollable celebration. 'When I received the ball from Mooro my first thought was to go for the corner flag, just to waste time. But it seemed such a long way away that I ran on towards goal. I could hear someone behind me [it was Overath] so I thought, well, if I hammer it really hard then at worst it'll go in the crowd and that'll take up 30 seconds, and he's bound to have

blown by then. So when I got to the edge of the area I just belted it—and in it went.'

To the tens of millions at home the goal was even more remarkable, for they could see the whole field on their television screens and were aware that several fans were already on the pitch. It provided Kenneth Wolstenholme with the best remembered and best-timed line of his career in commentating as Hurst headed for goal. 'And there are fans on the pitch. They think it's all over...IT IS NOW!'

It is sometimes said that the English are great losers but self-conscious and embarrassed in victory. Not so on the night of 30 July 1966. The nation joyfully drank, sang and shed a tear in triumph, saluting the achievement of one manager who had seen an outrageous prediction fulfilled and 11 players who would carry the proud label of World Cup winners for the rest of their lives...

*The celebrations begin. 'The one thing you obviously get, when you sit back and think about it,' says Bobby Moore, 'is the tremendous satisfaction of achieving what you set out to do...and of reaching the highest pinnacle in the career you've chosen.' Nobody can ever take that away from the boys of '66.*

# GORDON BANKS

**Born Sheffield, 30 Dec. 1937; Sheffield Schools, Millspaugh Steelworks, Rawmarsh Welfare; joined Chesterfield Oct. 1955 and turned pro 1957; League debut 29 Nov. 1958 v Colchester (home, 2-2); transferred to Leicester May 1959 for £6,000; 2 Under-23 caps 1961; full debut 6 April 1963 v Scotland at Wembley (1-2); remained first choice for 9 seasons, losing only 9 of his 73 England games...**

I arrived at the door of the sumptuous home via taxi, tube, the Inter-City train service, two buses and a brisk walk, mainly uphill past a marker that told me I was 14 miles from Stafford and 13½ from Nantwich.

England's goalkeeper in the 1966 World Cup final trod the necessary few steps from the open fire in his luxurious lounge, itself bigger than the goal area he used to command, to welcome his visitor.

But it was a toss-up which of us had made the more arduous journey. Gordon Banks was collecting the painful legacies of his career of breathtaking bravery.

Years of diving on to his right side, in the manner of that most imprinted of saves from Pelé in the 1970 World Cup, had left him at the age of 43 with the need for an artificial hip. The footballer who had re-written a simile—as safe as the Banks of England—had undergone major surgery in the early weeks of 1981. The sapping after-effects had come as surprise even to a man well acquainted with the hospital bed.

The warmth of his greeting and the comfort of his home could not disguise the difficulties that life has brought to Banks, a lesson to those who romantically believe that winning a World Cup medal is a passport to happiness everlasting.

Yet for more than six years after England's win at Wembley Banks continued at the very height of his great power. As the 1972–73 season began he remained England's first-choice goalkeeper, and though he was 28 when he gained his proudest medal, he made more international appearances after the World Cup than before it. In March 1972 he played a crucial role in Stoke City's captivating win in the League Cup

final; his own hands having ensured that Wembley place by performing one of his most remembered saves, a plunge to his right to turn aside a thunderous semi-final penalty from Geoff Hurst. In May 1972 came a belated award as the football writers' Footballer of the Year.

Five months later the procession of honours came to a horrible halt. Travelling home from receiving treatment at Stoke's Victoria Ground on 22 October, Banks pulled his car out to overtake a line of traffic on the B5038 between Whitmore and Trentham and collided with a van. A shattered windscreen removed the sight of his right eye. Only delicate surgery prevented serious damage to the left.

He had been looking forward to his Sunday lunch, and to watching the television highlights of what would prove to be his last game in League football, at Liverpool, where he had left the field in anger. 'I'd had a bad reaction from the referee, Roger Kirkpatrick. We were winning 1-0, and coming off at half-time Tommy Smith had gone over to the referee and was tearing into him. Everybody knows Tom!

'Come the second half, we're holding out quite well. I get the ball and roll it along the ground. Pick it up. Run and kick the ball. And he awards an indirect free-kick for steps. Now that rule was brought in to stop time-wasting, not to specifically count the number of steps a goalkeeper uses to kick the ball away.

'Let's face it—every keeper at that time couldn't help but take more than four steps. So I've got penalised, and they score a goal from the free-kick. Which virtually has handed them what I thought was an equaliser on a plate.

'There was only five minutes to go when one of the Liverpool players had now beaten one of our men, who had made a challenge on him. The Liverpool player had half-stumbled, the ref had waved play on. We now take possession and clear it, but he then blows his whistle for a free-kick against our player who'd committed the foul. To me it was a diabolical decision. They score off it. They score a goal from the free-kick. To me he'd handed Liverpool two points.

'What annoyed me more, right at the end of the game, was Tommy Smith, now walking off the pitch with his arm round the referee. Of course I lost my head. Gave the referee a lot of stick myself, which of course got a lot of headlines on the Sunday.'

It was a sad farewell to League football, and an unnecessary one if only medical science had experienced the precedent of a goalkeeper with hampered vision. After a number of friendlies and games following his rehabilitation, including a minor representative call-up by the ever-loyal Ramsey, Banks retired to the comparative obscurity of a job coaching Stoke City's youth team.

During the 1973–74 season I worked with him on ITV's *Penalty Prize* competition, in which a number of adoring youngsters kept sufficient composure in the face of their idol to qualify for the 'shoot-out' before the Wembley League Cup final, when Wolves beat Manchester City. The emotional reception when Banks took his place between the posts for the pre-match competition almost matched the roar at winning the World Cup itself. It seemed certain that his injuries from the accident had decreed that appearance as a final bow before an always appreciative public.

But three years later the hunger of soccer in the United States for 'name players' brought a request for Gordon Banks to play again. His disability came as no drawback to the clubs who were desperate for any publicity to drive the stories of baseball and American football off the sports pages. Banks joined Fort Lauderdale Strikers —where they were happy to label him the 'great one-eyed goalkeeper'.

At the end of his first season, 1977, his superb performances brought the accolade of a place in the League All-Star team. In 26 games he conceded a mere 29 goals, success that surprised him but also made him

wonder whether his retirement in England might have been premature.

'I didn't know how it was going to turn out when I got there, to be honest. I'd only played a handful of games over in England, even though I'd trained. Mind you, I went on to work very hard before that season. I had balls fired at me every day. So by the time the season started I felt quite confident.

'But I still didn't know when it came to competition, how I would cope. I hadn't played any competitive games really since the accident. I thought to myself, "what are the Americans going to think if I have a bad time, the one-eyed goalkeeper!" But I was very, very surprised at the standard I attained.

'Looking back on it now, had I known what was going to come out of constant training in terms of readjustment of the other eye, taking over the balance and the distances of things, then I would have said, "no problems". I would have asked for a year and I would have been back playing. But nobody knew. A professional goalkeeper has never been in that situation. Of course by the time I'd played my two years in America it was too late then for a comeback.'

The souvenirs from Fort Lauderdale take their place in a caringly designed trophy room in the Banks household where the World Cup winners medal is proudly mounted.

'The first thing that comes to mind about the final is the nervousness on the morning. I think I remember getting a pretty good night's sleep. I'm one who could always got my head down even on the eve of a great occasion such as that.

'I was conscious of the importance of the day, and the surprise really of being there. I wouldn't have said that there was a player in that side that actually thought for one minute in the first game at Wembley that we'd ever reach the final. Oh, they wanted to! Don't get me wrong. And they were going to give one hundred per cent whatever. But I don't really think deep down we thought it, because we weren't a conceited bunch. I think everybody was a down-to-earth fellow. I don't think we ever lost control of ourselves. I wanted to feel as though we were approaching it as just another international match.'

*The save that sealed Banks' place among the all-time greats of goalkeeping. Pelé's powerful downward header is almost home while Banks, who was covering the near post, is not yet halfway across his goal. The save itself is made from here as Banks flings himself to flick the ball upwards to the safety of a corner. 'I'm looking where I'm falling because I knew I was near the post. And I thought it had gone in.' So did the crowd— whose elation turns to disbelief—and Pelé, who describes it as the best save he has ever seen.*

*Banks and Jeff Astle emerge for the second half of the 1970 World Cup game with Czechoslovakia at Guadalajara. Gordon kept a clean sheet, as he had against Rumania. Two days later he went down with food poisoning—he now believes it may have been deliberate— and so missed the vital quarter-final against West Germany, which England lost 3-2.*

For Banks there was much experience to draw on. The World Cup final represented his 33rd England appearance, the donning of his 33rd new international jersey, this one to be swapped with Hans Tilkowski after the game. His pre-match warm-up in the toilet area by the dressing-room had also by now become a ritual, conducted far from any team-mates who might receive a painful blow from the series of stretches and the windmill action of alternate toe-touching.

'If I remember rightly on the day, there were one or two of the lads not as boisterous as they would normally be for international matches. This would be the nervous system probably holding them back, and I think one or two of us said something like "bloody hell, is this a morgue in here" to try to break the tension and relieve the atmosphere.

'When it was time to go we were lined up in the tunnel, and I threw a ball up against the wall just to get a feel of the thing. I shook hands with one or two of the German players. I think I was about second or third in line but I wasn't looking up the tunnel. Then when I finally turned round I could see it was raining. The sun was out but it was raining.

'I was a little bit annoyed about that because I knew that even if it stopped straight away, I was going to have to put gloves on. In my day a goalkeeper always felt more secure *without* gloves. It didn't worry me to the extent that it was going to make my game suffer, but I know that deep down I would have been a good deal happier if it had been a dry pitch.'

Banks soiled his gloves on the pitch, fearful of their dryness against a wet ball, and called for as much handling in the kick-in as possible, particularly to catch crosses. One ritual had to be observed, Jack Charlton striking a ball into the net.

Thirteen minutes into the game, however, Banks was to be beaten far less willingly, by Helmut Haller—the first time in the tournament England had conceded a goal in free play.

'The ball was coming across and I shouted to Ray Wilson to leave it. Whether he didn't hear me or whether he thought there was someone behind him I don't know.

'It was going out for a goal-kick. But Ray elected to make sure. Haller, who had been running with him, checked out—and Ray's header landed straight at Haller's feet.

'When he hit it there was a bit of confusion actually between me and Big Jack, though Jack didn't know this because he was in front of me, facing Haller. As soon as the shot was hit, I could see that the ball was going towards Jack. So I went across, and then Jack must have thought that I'd covered it, because Haller didn't really hit it all that hard. And I thought Jack was going to stop it, so I momentarily relaxed. Then he let it go, thinking it was coming through to me.

'By that time it had gathered a bit of pace. When I realised it was coming through, it had gone past me. I didn't even get a touch. But had I known Jack was going to leave it I would've saved it. We looked at each other at the time, but we never really discussed it afterwards.'

From the keepers' viewpoint the match never allowed any relaxation in concentration. Banks remembers the awareness of the pace of Held and Haller, the threat of Uwe Seeler—'a livewire who was always causing us problems because he was darting here and there'—and the potential shooting power of Emmerich, whose deflected free-kick pegged England back on the very brink of victory.

'First of all the ball was pumped forward and Big Jack made what I call a very fair and honest challenge for the ball. I was right behind Jack and I could see that he had both hands by his side, and he leaned forward and he won the ball.

'I could see that someone would be having a whack at the free-kick so I wanted four in the wall, even though it was at a bit of an angle. But what they had done was to push extra men into the box. After the deflections the ball was hit across the face of the six-yard box, and Schnellinger was making a run in for any rebound. If nobody touched that ball it would have gone right out for a goal-kick, maybe even a throw-in.

'There's no way that it was deliberate, but the ball hit his arm, which took all the pace off it. So it really gave them an advantage because as we know now it dropped to Weber, who knocked it in. It was right in front of me, and really it should have been a free-kick to us.

'When I look back on it, and I'm not bragging, I really felt I was unlucky not to stop the goal. What happened was that the ball was now on the floor, and Ray Wilson was going across to block it. And I realised that if the shot was coming along the floor, Ray would stop it.

'So now I dive another three feet higher than Ray's leg, thinking that if he lifts it I stand a chance of getting it. As it happened Weber got underneath it—whether deliberately or just because he was stretching for it—and it went another couple of feet over me.'

For a goalkeeper the prospect of extra time did not carry the physical pain of a further half hour of strenuous running; but it was as tough mentally. 'Like everyone else I was deflated. Alf came down, and he missed that goal, you know. He'd been in the box, and he was in the lift on his way to be with us for the celebrations when the Germans scored.

'But I remember his words distinctly and they've often been quoted: "You've won this Cup once, now you've got to go out and win it again." And we knew he was right. We couldn't throw it out the window just because they'd scored in the last few minutes.'

One incident in the semi-final against Portugal epitomises the total respect that the goalkeeper commanded within the team. A decisive foray off his line followed by a clearing punch left Nobby Stiles in a breathless heap in his own penalty area with an ear 'like a cabbage'. As Banks helped him Stiles was in such disarray that he didn't know which of his aching parts to hold. But the keeper's quick question of concern was brushed aside by a 'Well done, that's the way to do your job,' as Stiles limped back into the fray.

On the last blast of Herr Dienst's whistle in the final, Gordon Banks declared his joy by flinging high the arms that had protected England's goal so valiantly, then collapsing to the ground. After the joyous embracing he sought out a tearful Tilkowski for the special communication that keepers reserve for each other in every match—an emotional exchange unhindered by the German's tiny smattering of English.

'The joy of actually winning was immense. It was a marvellous day, made that more special by the Queen being there. I think there would have been a tremendous amount of sadness among the players if we'd lost in front of the Queen and playing in our own country.'

If there was one blight on the day for Banks it came at the post-match banquet at the Royal Garden Hotel in Kensington, where Lev Yashin, the veteran Russian, received the official vote as the tournament's best goalkeeper. 'I'm not being conceited, but I found it hard to accept because they hadn't reached the final. A lot of the lads were shocked and turned to look at me when it was announced.'

When the formalities were finally over and the players could unwind with their wives, ironically in Banks' case the German-born Ursula, his party spent the remainder of the evening in the hotel relaxing with George Cohen, slightly disappointed that the breadth of the social invitations had broken up the squad while the evening was still relatively young.

'One of our biggest assets, I thought, was that we were all really like a team. Like a League club. And everybody got on well with each other. Obviously there were differences in temperament. Three or four of the lads would enjoy playing cards. Then you had George Cohen, who liked to go and read in his room on his own. Ray Wilson, in particular, I used to like his company. He used to make me laugh, and I always had a bit of a joke myself as well.

'To be honest we look back now and regret financially that we didn't all stay in London for a week or two weeks after the final. We had many, many invitations which would have given us the chance to capitalise on our success. I know in my own mind that on that Sunday I was glad to get home, and I know all the lads were, because we had been away working and training for that long with all that pressure. But financially it was a great mistake.'

If Banks needed preparations for the traumas that were to follow later in his life, one rude awakening arrived less than a year after he had collected his World Cup medal. Matt Gillies, his manager at Leicester, was being pressed by an ambitious young goalkeeper called Peter Shilton, whose pleas for first-team recognition were becoming increasingly insistent.

Gillies yielded and asked England's automatic choice and undisputed num-

*Banks celebrates Stoke's 3-2 win over West Ham in the League Cup semi-final second replay at Old Trafford in 1972— a result that put the club in its first ever major final. Banks' form was a big factor in the success, notably a magnificent save from Geoff Hurst's thundering penalty in the second leg of the semi-final, when the aggregate score was 2-2.*

ber one if he would consider a transfer.

'I was flabbergasted. I was the current goalkeeper. I'd just played in the World Cup final. I'd been to four FA and League Cup finals in six years with the club. And the manager says what would I think about moving on because "I think we've had the best out of you". It staggered me because I was feeling that I was just getting to my peak.

'I just couldn't believe it. At home I would try to put myself in his place and even then I still couldn't figure out what kind of a manager would want to sell a World Cup player. And of course, once he'd said it as far I was concerned Leicester City Football Club meant nothing to me. I could've said that I didn't want to go, I was on a contract, but for that man to have actually said those words to me at that particular time . . . I couldn't get away from the club quick enough. And it didn't matter where I was going.'

Tony Waddington's Stoke City were the grateful recipients of Leicester's generosity, obtaining Banks for a mere £50,000, and in the Potteries he more than doubled his total of England caps. Ironically Peter Shilton, who fulfilled the trust placed in him by Gillies, also made the same move seven years later—but for more than six times the fee.

The Banks transfer caused no change to his stature with Ramsey, and when England left for Mexico in 1970 to defend their world crown, it was clear that Peter Bonetti and Alex Stepney, the other two keepers in the squad, were there to back up the undisputed number one. Events in that tournament, even more than in 1966, were to confirm the greatness of Gordon Banks.

If in the video age he has left one special moment to be replayed through the ages to the goalkeepers of subsequent generations it arrived in Guadalajara, when England faced Brazil, favourites to succeed them as world champions. Banks has always believed that the context of his now legendary save from Pelé's fearsome header has created its value.

'I'm sure I equalled that save in League games, but this one is special when you put it in a World Cup finals game against a team of Brazil's stature and against a player of Pelé's greatness. Had we been losing 3-0 it would not have had the same impact, either, but it was nil-nil, and we were playing really well on the day.

'Carlos Alberto hit an unbelievable ball with the outside of his right foot. It literally curled round Terry Cooper and dropped right into Jairzinho's path. He could motor too, but he took the ball towards the goal-line, and there was no way he could shoot from there. But I had to take up my position at the near post because Tostao had made a run there. That's

*Steering a shot past the post in that 1972 final, against Chelsea. Banks had been in two Wembley club finals with Leicester, the last one a decade before, and lost them both. This time, partly thanks to his fine keeping and a rare goal from 1966 squad member George Eastham (in the background here) it was third time lucky. Gordon was later voted Footballer of the Year—only the second time in 25 years that the award had gone to a goalkeeper.*

*ABOVE: The tangled remains of Banks' car after the head-on crash with a van on 22 October 1972. Two months later he was convicted of dangerous driving.*

*RIGHT: Banks had 108 facial stitches but nothing could save the sight of his right eye, wrecked by two glass splinters. He received over 5,000 cards, telegrams and letters from concerned fans.*

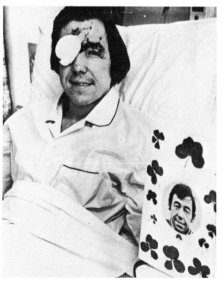

why I had so far to go across to make the save.'

The sequence of pictures on the wall of Gordon Banks' trophy room (*see page 37*) testify to the belief that the outcome just had to be a goal. Faces in the crowd turned in an instant from expressions of delight to disbelief; Pelé, whose timing of the leap to meet Jairzinho's cross was totally in keeping with the perfect rhythm of the move, believed he had scored.

So too did the man who catapulted to his right, and who somehow used the power on the ball, which was bouncing up from the driven downward header, to propel it over the bar.

'Once I'd lifted my arm to cover the bounce of the ball, I'm looking where I'm falling because I knew I was near the post. And I thought it had gone in. And of course the crowd erupted, and I still thought they'd scored. I was conscious, I think, of the quality of the save because of the distance I had covered to get to it.'

It was no fault of Banks that England were finally beaten 1-0, a close range blast from Jairzinho that sped past him. But it still seemed that the construction of the tournament could lead to an opportunity for revenge. In the final.

England's next critical task was the quarter-final against the old adversary,

West Germany, in León, the occasion for which Banks' importance will always be remembered...by his absence. Today he is cynical about the gastric illness that forced his late withdrawal and thrust Peter Bonetti, cruelly short of match practice, into the centre of the subsequent defeat. Banks now gives credibility to the theory that he had been poisoned deliberately.

'At first when that idea was mentioned I thought it was a load of bunkum. But after a while I couldn't understand why I was the only one ill because we were all eating the same food and drinks. And I'm normally very good when it comes to foreign food. Also I was so violently sick. And though Bobby Charlton and Keith Newton just had a touch of something, I was the only one. So the more I look back the more I believe my food could so easily have been tampered with.

Banks was so weak that he couldn't even attend the match as a spectator. 'I saw the goals later on television and I felt they were really down to my sickness that had thrust Peter Bonetti right at the last minute into the game. And to be honest with you, he couldn't possibly have been prepared. Nobody could have been.'

Preparation was not in Gordon Banks' mind when he returned to pick up his life in British football after spending the summers of 1977 and 1978 proving in the United States that his mastery of his trade could survive the most harrowing of disabilities. He still feels no bitterness about the cruel stroke of fate that led to the loss of his eye.

What bitterness he does feel relates to broken promises, the details of which he refuses to make public. Broken promises that forced an unexpected spell of unemployment.

A chance meeting with Lawrie McMenemy led to a week's specialised coaching for Southampton's goalkeeping staff, and McMenemy's help brought the possibility of more work around the League clubs in that capacity. But, against the advice of the Southampton manager, he accepted a full-time general coaching

*The first game after the accident: Gordon turns out for an All-Stars side in a charity match near Stoke in January 1973, when he played up front and scored in a 5-2 win. The real thing was more difficult; while Fort Lauderdale later made good use of his ability—he was NASL Goalkeeper of the Year in 1977— and promoted him as 'the great one-eyed goalkeeper', he could find no place with a League club in England after his dismissal by Port Vale.*

post with Fourth Division Port Vale. The accessibility to his home of the Burslem club and the lure of a regular income proved too great.

'Lawrie said don't take it, and really he was right. There was no money to spend, and the players at the time I didn't feel were quite good enough. My plans backfired in my face where I believed the only chance we'd got was to get them quite fit, and marking a lot tighter.

'And I was working on this sort of thing when there was a bit of a players' revolt. They thought I was working them too hard, which I couldn't understand because I wasn't giving them any more training than I did when I was playing. So the club decided to clear out all the staff.

'It's funny really, because at the time they called me into the office I thought they were going to offer me the manager's job...and instead they gave me my cards!

'It comes back to a theory that I've been shouting for quite a while now. I feel that more and more people with experience are getting pushed out of the game, and people with less experience are getting jobs. For the life of me I can't understand why it is.'

The frustrations of the sack were partly assuaged by a continuing involvement in the game as manager of Telford United in the Alliance Premier League, but mostly by the support of his family.

The loyalty of Ursula survived the pain of a much-publicised liaison between her husband and another woman during his spell in Florida. 'I was fortunate I got my senses right. I put my house in order. Whatever caused it Ursula understood, and she stood by me when it would have been easy for her to dismantle things.'

That security has been mightily appreciated as the operation to his hip made more difficult the task of managing the side at Telford. That job would come to an abrupt end in March 1981 when Banks was sacked before accepting a post as the club's promotions manager.

'I don't think a physical disability has anything to do with me not getting a League job. I can see really as well as anybody. And it doesn't affect my thinking about the game. It doesn't affect my vast experience and knowledge. Whether or not I would have been accepted when I finished playing had I not had the accident...well, nobody can answer that question.'

It was a sad note on which to leave, but the talk continued as I accepted a lift to Crewe station.

'All my money is tied up in my house. If I had to start a business I'd have to sell it. I don't obviously want to do that, and anyway football has been my whole life. With the unemployment situation as it is now I shudder to think what I might do. It would be a gamble obviously if I had to go into a shop or something. And if I lost I would finish up all the years that I played without anything. It seems incredible really.'

*Telford's change... the Alliance Premier League's club's chairman welcomes Banks on his appointment as manager—once the seat of Geoff Hurst—on 3 January 1980. 'I've applied for jobs in the League, and I've had a couple of interviews, but I didn't get them. I feel that if this job doesn't work my chances to get back in the game are very limited.' Telford finished 13th in the APL's first season, and in March 1981 Banks was sacked as team manager.*

# GEORGE COHEN

**Born West Kensington, London, 22 Oct. 1939; West London and London Schools; joined Fulham 1955 as left-half and turned pro Oct. 1956; League debut at 17 v Liverpool 2 March 1957 (home, 1-2), but not a regular till well into next season; 8 Under-23 caps 1959–63; full debut v Uruguay at Wembley 6 May 1964 (2-1); missed only 4 of 28 England games to World Cup...**

It had been almost ten years since I had last spoken to George Cohen ... since I had been a member of a willing if less than successful first-team squad with Isthmian League Corinthian-Casuals, whose pre-season training one summer had been galvanised by one of the boys of that summer of '66.

England's right-back at Wembley had just parted company with Fulham, where his 15 years of service had ended as a frustrated youth team coach. As a group of players whose ambitions outstripped our abilities we hung on every word of encouragement and instruction. His cry of 'scabby ball' at a mis-hit pass punctuated every practice match. George would then exhibit the correct technique with a strength totally out of keeping with a man carrying savage knee damage that had brought a premature end to his own playing days.

I phoned George Cohen at his home just outside Tunbridge Wells, where he now conducts his own business as a land and property developer. I was flattered that he remembered me as a journeyman striker with scarcely more than a peripheral role in those training sessions a decade earlier. He hadn't been aware of my subsequent excursion into journalism, but he was pleased to arrange a meeting to talk about the World Cup. How, he wanted to know, were the other members of the squad that I'd seen?

Tunbridge Wells has never been a hotbed of football gossip. Many of George Cohen's present business associates have a knowledge of the game that extends to an awareness that England did win the World Cup, but not to a realisation that Cohen took part in the proceedings.

Yet his present circle of friends know what most of football does not:

that today George Cohen still calls on the fighting spirit that first of all made him a top-class footballer and then drove him through months of pain in a brave but fruitless bid to repair that injured knee.

His battle against a distressingly serious illness began late in 1975. 'I had symptoms of colitis, which is very debilitating. And I think it showed up very quickly because I'd been so fit over the years. I went to see my GP, a wonderful man, the real village doctor by the name of Dennis Law! He told me that he thought there was something radically wrong, and he sent me to a surgeon in Tunbridge Wells. It didn't worry me much at the time, but then things got very bad and I lost a considerable amount of weight very quickly.'

The verdict was immediate surgery, and the knowledge of the gravity of the illness undermined even the strongest of wills. 'The extent of the problem was very difficult to take ... very difficult to take, indeed. The treatment I had to have prior to the operation led to the most uncomfortable three weeks of my life. It was a type of treatment that was physically something of a degrading experience, but it was carried out by a team of ancillary nurses who were absolutely marvellous with me.'

Cohen's weight had tumbled from 13 to 11 stone, but though the surgery in February 1976 slowed his decline, it did not halt it.

'I went a year to eighteen months feeling very well. I think my general level of fitness helped the recovery. But then I started feeling ill again. Again the same symptoms. Again I started to lose weight. Feelings I can only describe as a constant bad dose of the 'flu. It was soul-destroying. It was a tremendous effort even to pick up a pen. So I had to go through the same routine again, and this time my morale was about as low as it could possibly get.'

George underwent a second operation, a colostomy. Eighteen months later he needed further treatment, followed by an agonising period when his body reacted adversely to the withdrawal of the drugs that had been essential to his treatment. His gratitude to the medical staff who have attended him in Tunbridge Wells and in the Royal Marsden Hospital in Sutton reflects their part in his physical survival.

He clearly places his recovery from the mental anguish at the door of his wife Daphne, who has made light of a situation that would disturb many less devoted companions. Another influential factor has been his own sense of humour, which keeps him cheerful despite depressing days when 'you wonder how much longer you can keep pissing into the wind.'

Despite his name George Cohen is not strictly Jewish, though his recent investigation into his family tree has

discovered roots from immigrant Russian Jews. As a man who admires Jack Benny and George Burns, his humour has a definite ethnic flavour, and he peppered our conversation with wisecracks that wouldn't be out of place in Golders Green: 'Jack Charlton had wonderful long legs. And a terrific nose. I often said with his nose and my name, we'd have made a fortune.'

Yet many of his 1966 team-mates clearly saw him as the more serious type—perhaps because he loved nothing more in the breaks from matches and training than retiring to his room, which he shared with Terry Paine, for a good read. 'I loved Dennis Wheatley. I think I read all his books except one solely about witchcraft, which I started but couldn't get into. Frank Yerby was another favourite. If I wasn't training or doing something that Alf had set up for us, reading was the perfect relaxation for me prior to a match.'

The importance of the World Cup to Cohen's career was magnified by the lack of success of his club. Fulham

*A polite handshake with the Queen before getting down to business with Uruguay. 'Every player has his hopes and fears, and I wanted to be the best player in the competition. It didn't work out that way…I didn't have a particularly wonderful World Cup. Waiting his turn is Gordon Banks, with whom Cohen played 27 of his 37 England games—the same number as he shared with full-back partner Ray Wilson.*

gained promotion from the Second Division in 1959, but many of his 408 League appearances were spent battling to keep the side in the First. Comedian Tommy Trinder kept Fulham's name in the spotlight—but mostly as a music-hall joke. The warmth of the public feeling for the inhabitants of homely Craven Cottage offered scant consolation to a professional as ambitious and dedicated as George Cohen.

But that dedication made him the ideal personality for Alf Ramsey; his athleticism was perfectly suited for the demanding role of a defender of whom much was expected as an attacking force in a set-up without natural width. Jack Charlton used to rib him about his centres at the end of those buccaneering runs being more dangerous to the crowd than to the opposing goalkeeper, but there was plenty of truth in Cohen's riposte that more went behind because he crossed more balls than any other player.

At his abiding memory of the World Cup final, the eyes again twinkled with humour. 'My memory is of the most diabolical left-footed shot I've ever attempted. I think it went into the fifth row of the crowd.

'Seriously though, it was a feeling of finality...that this is the one... that this is going to be your greatest experience, and by Christ I hope I play well. Every player has his hopes and fears, and I wanted to be the best player in the World Cup. I really wanted to be, you know?

'It didn't work out that way. I didn't have a particularly wonderful World Cup. But throughout it I always had that feeling—Christ, I hope I don't play badly.'

George Cohen certainly did not play badly, and he was essential to the format of a defence which proved to be the foundation of the triumph.

'We were a very well balanced team and the defence was beautifully balanced. Gordon was undoubtedly the world's greatest goalkeeper at the time. Ray wasn't a power player, but he was a superb left-back. I always felt he could go out there and do his job in a collar and tie. He was that neat. Bobby wasn't good in the air and he didn't have any great speed, but his reading of the game made him such a great player. His judgement about situations was always one

hundred per cent correct. And Jack of course compensated in the air. And he had those wonderful long legs. And of course that nose...'

To that defensive blend George Cohen added the power and speed of his own game. If anyone did beat him down the touchline the side would be in trouble, but his pace more than matched those who set out to create that kind of difficulty for England.

In the final West Germany were more than aware of the threat of Cohen's sprinting in an attacking role. 'In fact in the final Sigi Held spent most of his time looking at me straight in the eye, wondering when I was going to go on a run. Whenever they had lost possession and we were looking to go forward, he kept me in his sights, and Held of course was a very fast player himself. Quite frankly it was a bit disconcerting. At first I wondered what he was doing, looking at me like that, but after about fifteen minutes it dawned on me that in fact he wanted to know what I was doing.'

The years of daily weight-training,

*George with hat-trick hero Hurst at the dinner on the evening of the final—but the shy retiring image masks a personality of wit and perception. 'I'm a very emotional person, but I'm very quiet with it. I keep my feelings to myself—though I may have been extrovert in my style of play.'*

*Reg Matthewson lends support as Cohen clears against Middlesbrough during his first-team comeback at Craven Cottage on 21 December 1968. It was a year before—to the day—that he had first damaged his knee as Fulham took on Liverpool in their vain fight against relegation, and in that time he had endured numerous breakdowns and disappointments, playing only 45 minutes of League football. Fulham lost this one at home 3-0—on their way to a straight drop into the Third Division.*

running, skipping and jumping up terraces served George well in extra time. 'I knew that another half an hour would make me tired, but that it wasn't going to be desperate. I was sure that the likes of Overath and Held were in far, far worse shape than I was. They had crucified themselves coming up towards the end of normal time.

'But I had always taken my training very seriously. I wasn't a natural footballer. I had to work at a lot of things, but I recognised that my greatest asset was my strength and my speed, which I'd developed to a point where I was almost even time in my sprinting.

'A very curious thing happened to me just recently when I was at the hospital for a regular check-up. The specialist was saying that my right kidney was much better than when he had seen me a year earlier. It's much larger than the left one, he said, but that one of course has been dead for many, many years. It's quite possible that I only had one kidney when I played in the World Cup final! I told him that he'd made me virtually useless now in the transfer market...'

The contrast between George Cohen's sense of humour and his serious side was never more apparent than at the moment when the referee's final whistle indicated that the World Cup was finally won. Embarrassment rather than exultation predominated. 'Nobby jumped on me. It looked like copulation. I don't know what he was doing, but I didn't enjoy it very much! It wasn't surprise as much as embarrassment. After all we were only fifty yards away from the Queen at the time. When he was that close to me I could hear a whistle. It was the intake of breath between his teeth!

'I'm a very emotional person, but I'm very quiet with it. I keep my feelings to myself, though I may have been extroverted in my style of play. When we scored in the final, I preferred to get back into a position where I could start the game again and save those few extra yards of running to congratulate people. At the final whistle I just thought, "Thank God for that, we've won...and what a fantastic experience".'

George Cohen played just seven more times for England before his career evaporated in one excrutiating moment on 21 December 1967. Fulham were playing Liverpool. 'Their goalkeeper struck a long clearance that I moved forward to reach before Peter Thompson. I was conscious too that Johnny Haynes was drifting into

space forward to my right. The ball dipped suddenly as it arrived, what with all the top spin, and I was in mid-air as I tried to knock it towards Johnny. I didn't connect properly and there was a rotation in my right knee. I was screaming in pain before I hit the ground.'

His efforts to beat the injury matched his dedication when he was fully fit, and the following season he even returned to the first team for half a dozen games. But numerous disappointments and set-backs bit into his home life. 'I wasn't easy to live with. My wife may love me but even she couldn't cope. I got very irritable with the uncertainty of it all. I was very single-minded about football. I had one direct path and that was the game.'

At 29 George Cohen was finished with football. While Fulham were the beneficiaries of one of the first £100,000 insurance pay-outs, he had to be content with a warm-hearted testimonial involving many of the 1966 side, and a job on the coaching staff. In 1971 a disagreement with manager Bill Dodgin led to his resignation, though the pair remain close friends.

'I wanted to stay in the game as a manager. I didn't want to be the second lieutenant...I wanted to be the captain. Earlier there had been talk of me going to Orient, Watford and Reading, but nothing happened.

'Sidney Brickman, this very dear friend of mine, whom I'd met some ten years before I packed up, had often mentioned working for him. I'd never really thought of property speculation as my sort of scene, but I thought I'd give it a go. So Sidney placed me with his architect at Camden Town. I could always draw at school, I got 'O'-level in art, and I understood what I was looking at. I learned planning law, and building rates, and what to look for in buying a piece of land or property.

'The architect from Henry Osborne Associates would come out with me and look at pieces of land. He would ask me what I thought, and why. And from that I've become an unqualified expert.'

The Jewish background, however distant, must have left an innate business sense in George Cohen. Shortly before his first operation in 1976 he established his own concern, and in the business of purchasing land, building and developing the property he now deals with sums of money far larger than he would have done had he become a First Division manager.

*The camera picks out George in the Fulham stands as he watches his pals entertain Oxford on 29 March 1969 — the day after he was told by doctors that he would never play top-class football again. This last time the knee had lasted six months before packing in yet again ...and at 29 Cohen became coach to the youth team, a job he did for two years before leaving the club he had served his whole career—a unique record among the boys of '66.*

*On site at one of his company's developments in Tunbridge Wells. Cohen began by learning the basics after leaving Fulham in 1971—he describes himself with characteristic modesty and humour as 'an unqualifed expert' —and is a successful land and property developer. Now serious illness, which started in 1975, threatens his hard-earned position.*

George took me out to his latest development, a plot of land close to Tunbridge Wells' own 'millionaires row'. Like most businessmen he has been hit by the recession; like all self-employed entrepreneurs his health is vital to his operation. Here in affluent Kent stands one monument to 1966. Sidney Brickman built a public house on the Broadmead estate and called it the *Sir Alf Ramsey*. Inside, George Cohen's welcome is clearly not just because he is a local property dealer. The decor is a shrine to England's success, but only recently has his own home displayed the same kind of nostalgia.

'My medal is in a glass case which embarrasses me somewhat. My wife insisted that after all these years we display it along with a few caps and some Inter-League medals that I won. But it's in the past.'

He couldn't remember whether he still had his red number two shirt from the final; it might have gone to charity, he thought. The only shirt he was sure he did not have was the one an Argentine wanted to swap at the end of the bitter quarter-final. Ramsey, who was on the verge of describing England's opponents to the world's press as behaving like 'animals', ran on to the field to stop the swap.

The Cohen international shirts are now mostly shown off by his two sons—one of whom, Andrew, is showing signs of introducing a second generation into League football. As a right-sided forward his schoolboy prowess interested first Fulham and latterly Charlton Athletic.

One of the main regrets of the restrictions placed on George's life by his illness is that he cannot fully participate in the rough and tumble of a relationship between father and sons. As an instinctive athlete he is frustrated that he can no longer turn out in charity matches. However, his contact with the professional game is not totally lost because he occasionally scouts for Middlesbrough.

'If anybody remembers me now its because I attacked down the wing. I would like to be remembered as a person whom the wingers found difficult to beat.'

Fate has also found George Cohen hard to beat. He complains happily about being overweight, inwardly acknowledging what a good sign that is for his health. And if he doesn't dwell on the past, it's because more than most of us he has great cause to appreciate that there's a present...

# RAY WILSON

Born Shirebrook, Derbyshire, 17 Dec. 1934; Shirebrook Central Sec. Mod. School, Langwith Boys Club, Langwith Junction Imps; joined Huddersfield early 1952 and turned pro August 1952; progress delayed by national service, then string of injuries; switched from wing-half to full-back by manager Bill Shankly; League debut v Luton 15 Oct. 1955 (home, 0-2); England debut at Hampden 9 April 1960 (1-1); lost place to Mick McNeil start of 1960–61 season; regained it a year and 10 games later to become automatic choice; transferred to Everton June 1964 for £40,000; team's most-capped player in 1966...

Leeches House Funeral Home overlooks the M62 in that part of West Yorkshire where the summer wind has a raw edge, and where winter comes early and stays late. You reach it, off the roundabout above the motorway, by an anonymous slip road. There are no signs. But as the funeral director says, his is a business that does not respond to advertising. Even if you are the holder of a World Cup winners medal.

It's several years now since Ray Wilson got used to the predominant smell in his working life being embalming fluid rather than embrocation. He has cultivated a distinguished grey beard which, with the pin-stripe suit of proper sobriety, has helped mould his physical appearance for a role in which age is an advantage.

Yet he still appreciates the interviewer's amazement at the incongruity of a magnificent left-back, supreme in his day, choosing a career that is married to death and family grief.

At 31 Ray Wilson was the oldest of the boys of '66, which provides a clue for his finding security away from football. The game that made him recognised did not make him rich, because his career spanned the abolition of the maximum wage in 1961.

Most of his 13 years of loyal service to Huddersfield Town, in the Second Division, were when the relationship between club and player was akin to master and slave. The only way to better oneself by forcing a transfer was to cause trouble; and Ray Wilson was not that type of professional.

'I played at the time when the money wasn't about. I felt privileged to be playing soccer and to be paid for it. Even when I went to Everton I never asked for a rise. When we'd just won the World Cup, I just went in and signed my new contract. I think that year they did give me an extra tenner a week. That took my basic up to £60, though things were geared at Everton for bonuses to win things. And we did get to two cup finals when I was there, and we were rarely out of the top six in the First Division. So we got more money that way.

'But one of my sons has had three or four different cars before he's 21, whereas I couldn't even think of getting one until I was around 27. All I really got out of football was the money to buy my own house when I finished playing.'

The Wilsons chose to return to the Huddersfield area as Ray's playing career wound down, precipitated by a damaged right knee that today prevents even jogging as a form of exercise. Less than 12 months after winning his 63rd and final cap (in the 1968 European Championship third-place play-off with Russia in Rome) Wilson was given a free transfer by Everton.

Because of the family's love affair with the Pennines, he opted for one more season close to home with Fourth Division Oldham Athletic, though several other local League clubs, including Rochdale and Stockport, were also interested in signing him. 'I'd had my day really, but it was one more year's wages, and I wasn't in a position to turn them down.

'It might have been worse for me if I hadn't had a season in the reserves before leaving Everton...if I'd gone straight from First Division football

*Ray Wilson had already won 30 of his 63 England caps as a Second Division player when he joined Everton from Huddersfield Town in June 1964 for £40,000, then a British record for a full-back. He played in two FA Cup finals with Everton, but he never won a League Championship medal—the club's two recent titles were won the year before he arrived and the season after he left. With the retirement of Brazil's Nilton Santos in 1963 he was generally considered to be the best left-back in the world.*

to Oldham. But I had a spell in the reserves before leaving, and I think that helped. It's not as though I was 27 or 28 when I had to drop out of it. I was 34, and just about ready for it.'

What followed represented the usual dilemma that affects a professional athlete at the end of his active career. Ray Wilson was fortunate to have an option: either he could take his chances in the snakes and ladders world of football management or pay serious attention to an offer from Edward Lumb, his father-in-law, to go into his business. To an ex-footballer with no qualifications the contrast between his previous lifestyle and arranging funerals for a living seemed immaterial. It offered the prospect of a steady income.

'After I left Oldham I went to Bradford City. I was in charge of the young lads there, and in midweek I played in the reserves. I only played a couple of League games for them. A nice lad called Jimmy Wheeler was manager at the time, and he was one of the reasons I decided not to stay in the game. In terms of effort, worry and work, he put in everything.

'But the more he did, the more he tried, the worst it went. He got the sack after losing four of the first five games in the '71–72 season, and then I took over. But I didn't want to leave this area. And I knew that there was no way I could be manager at Bradford City for 20 years.

'So I said I'd help the club out until they could find someone else. It was strange really, because I didn't find the job difficult at all. It all turned round for us on the field. It was smashing. Everything went really well. We won five of our first seven games.

'But I'd made my mind up. I'd talked to my father-in-law. He was going to retire in a couple of years, and we'd agreed that I would come into the business properly, taking my embalming course and learning the trade correctly. It was a wrench because the club was doing well, and Bradford City offered me very good money to stay. But I'd made my decision, and now I'm very glad that I did.

'My father-in-law put no pressure on me. I just discussed it with my wife. And the type of business was not relevant. It was the right opportunity. The chance was there, and it just seemed a shame not to give it a go really. I'd worked with him in the summers when I was with Huddersfield, so I wasn't foreign to it as such. And I did realise that it could be very unpleasant. The job takes a lot of getting used to.

'The physical side? You know very early whether you can cope with that. Fortunately I could. And so that's the easy part of the business for me now. The main difficulty, especially when I'm really busy, is meeting people when they're at their lowest ebb all the time. That certainly gets to me. People say that funeral directors get used to it. But I can assure you that they certainly don't. I certainly feel the pressures, especially when I get a long run of mixing with grief-stricken people. Then I desperately need a couple of days break.

'Many of the lads I played with joke about the job, but it doesn't seem that strange to me. I enjoy it and I get a lot of satisfaction from it. In terms of being successful, it's only average. It's a small business. I run it on my own. And it's increasing gradually. We live quite comfortably but no more than that.'

Comfortable is also the overriding feeling of being in Ray Wilson's company. The eyes twinkle at the recollection of a moment, an instant reminder that he is younger than the professional image he now needs to create. He still retains the humour of the dressing-room, where clearly he was both respected and popular. The more time I spent with him, the easier it became to see him coping with the delicate nature of his present occupation.

'I'm quite sensitive. I appreciate people's feelings. It sounds as though I'm blowing my own trumpet, but I'm sincere. I've always got on quite well with people. I like people to like me. I seem to have a certain rapport that people seem to be quite easy in my company. I think you can feel that after a while, can't you? Winning the people over is very, very important. I've improved at that of course because when you go into this business you really do go in at the deep end.'

His home now is a farmhouse at Barkisland, far enough off the beaten track to be unable to get newspapers delivered. He describes himself as a 'one-pub man', around which his social life is built. The matter-of-fact temperament of West Yorkshire folk makes sure that there is no regular fêting of his fame and background.

It's only passing strangers who occasionally bring up the subject of the World Cup, and not all of them pick out England's left-back of 1966, who now stands unrecognised on his occasional visits to the terraces of Huddersfield Town, the club he served so splendidly for so long.

'The memory of winning the World Cup is now like a warm glow. Because I'm not in the game any more, the recollections are not so much of the games, but of the people, and of those special times. Although I'd made up my mind not to be a manager, it was still hard to get off my behind after playing soccer for 20 years, and not really being able to do anything else.

'You miss the comradeship. When you've spent 20 years living, sleeping and getting in the bath a couple of times a day with lads of your own age who have a different sense of humour to other walks of life—that's what I've missed. I certainly haven't missed the game itself.

*Back in business... just 14 days after the World Cup final. Wilson tackles Liverpool's Peter Thompson (a member of England's squad of 27 in 1966) during the Charity Shield match at Goodison —a game Everton lost to a goal by Roger Hunt. Wilson's strong, reliable tackling was probably the most outstanding part of his game. 'I always felt he could go out there and do his job in a collar and tie,' says full-back partner George Cohen. 'He was that neat.'*

53

'As far as the World Cup was concerned, it was a nice finale for me. I'd been at Huddersfield for so long that the move to Everton came as a surprise. And earlier in 1966 we'd won the Cup, so it was a great year for me.

'With England I always roomed with Bobby Charlton—from my first tour. We had almost ten years together. And I can remember on the morning of the final, me and Bobby went shopping. Which was unusual for me because I was one who usually stayed in bed as long as possible on a match day. Bobby wanted to do some shopping. So we just went out —into Golders Green, actually.

'By that time we'd got attuned to the nerves. I always liken it to playing a five-set tennis match. I found the opening more nerve-racking. You're the home side. The host nation opened the finals, and none of the other qualifiers played at the same time. So the attention was really on us when we played Uruguay. And they played with ten full-backs!

'After that it became like playing one continuous match. Even when we weren't actually playing we were watching the other games. You didn't have time to think about nerves. It was very unlike the FA Cup final, where you waited five or six weeks after winning your semi-final before going to Wembley, and even the hardest lads would play like tanner-ball players to avoid injury.

'And we were very confident of beating the Germans. I don't mean to discredit them, but they'd never beaten us at that time. And especially after playing Portugal in that super match in the semi-final—we were quite relaxed about it.'

Ray Wilson never had his name taken in a Football League match for committing a foul—an astonishing record for a full-back who made over 400 appearances. And his first ever League caution came after the World Cup, the following September, for violence of the tongue in disputing a penalty at Leeds. He recalls: 'I don't think I ever gave many fouls away. The most was when I played against Stanley Matthews in his comeback game for Stoke City. I coughed twice and the referee blew.'

The timing that was the essence of not only his sure tackling technique but his all-round defensive strengths deserted him for once in the 13th minute of the World Cup final. A slip, universally accepted as his only mistake of the competition, led to Helmut Haller taking advantage of his poor header to give West Germany the lead. As George Cohen, his full-back partner in 27 internationals, would say later: 'That's the only mistake I ever saw Ray make. That's how good a player he was.'

Time has not dulled Wilson's memory of the episode. 'It was a terrible error really. It was a long, angled ball played towards me. In many ways it was a defender's dream ball—what I call a Fourth Division ball. From deep, way out. And I just mistimed it badly. I went up a little early. I was on my way down, and

*Aided by Everton colleagues Alex Scott and Sandy Brown (right), Ray kicks off a new Liverpool take-away service. Wilson says he often found the public side of being a top player an embarrassment.*

I didn't get the same power to my header. The lad Haller was crafty enough to check his run going in with me, and of course I knocked it down straight to him. He didn't strike it very well but he slotted it in.

'You don't tend to feel the magnitude of the mistake at the time. Perhaps if I'd been younger it would have possibly destroyed me. But it wasn't so long before we got back on level terms. And afterwards we always made the joke that usually the team who scored first in a World Cup final lost, so that I'd just been making sure we'd win!

'In many ways I didn't think it was a very good football game, when I think in terms of the previous match against Portugal. I thought when we'd got in front 2-1 that was certainly it. We had quite a few chances after that to seal it.

'They were really tired. I always used to feel throughout my England career that at Wembley visiting sides would set off like bombs, and you could sense they would go after about an hour's play. But when West Germany sneaked that equaliser, you tended to feel that they were in the driving seat. But the more I think back on it the England side at that time was really geared to picking themselves off the floor. The one thing about us then is that we could play not particularly well and still get a result.'

Even though he now admits to feeling his age in the sapping stresses of extra time, Ray still had two more years of international football ahead of him, and he played in 12 of England's 16 games after the World Cup. Then only the onset of osteoarthritis in that right knee, rather than any diminishing of his talent, cost him not only his England place but also his professional playing career.

But as he took the first serious exams of his life to prepare for his career away from the game, he still put on his boots in an unlikely Sunday morning setting with a local club,

*From dressing-room to funeral parlour: Ray at work in his business near Huddersfield. 'Many of the lads I played with joke about the job, but it doesn't seem strange to me. The main difficulty is meeting people when they're at their lowest ebb all the time. That certainly always gets to me.'*

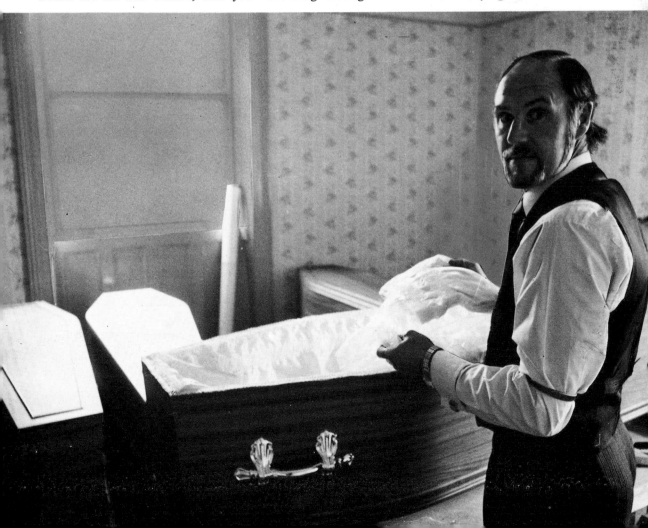

Golcar Socialists...the reserve side!

'I just loved playing. In fact I'd still play now, but I've had three operations on the knee. And it's still not sorted out. The talk with the specialists has been of having another operation, either stiffening it or putting in one of these artificial joints. But I think they felt that the joints at present wouldn't stand up to the pressures of someone as young as me. They'd be alright if I was 65. I have a lot of trouble with it, but it's something I've learned to live with.'

The injury also deprived him of the pleasure of turning out when benefit committees have gathered together the 1966 side for occasional testimonial appearances.

His reaction to the inability is another indication of the sensitive side of Ray Wilson. 'I used to love every minute of it, but with being the eldest I was always going to be the one who would be missing first—though in fact it was George as far as League football was concerned.'

There's no doubt, however, that Ray Wilson does not live in the past; the demands of his occupation ensure that. Yet the recollections that come tumbling out when he is pressed on the old days suggest a hint of regret that it's all behind him.

The privacy of his life also indicates some relief. 'I always found the public side of football embarrassing. I find it difficult to idolise people myself, so I find it hard to understand when people make a fuss of me. It would be difficult for me to go into Huddersfield to watch Frank Sinatra. Alright, so you have your gift.

'So I had a good left foot, but take the lad Malcolm who works in our joinery business next door. He can do anything intricate with furniture. So when you put his gift alongside of mine, it just seems a shame that the balance is wrong with the public.'

I wondered whether he felt that there had been less ballyhoo about his playing days than some of the other boys of '66 because he had been cast in the unglamorous role of full-back. 'I don't think the full-back thing has anything to do with that. I think life has to do with it.

'You'll get your Bobby Charltons and you'll get your Bobby Moores. And then you'll get people like myself and Roger Hunt. I think you get people who don't get publicity and you get those who do. In all walks of life. I don't feel any envy. It's something that you come to terms with. I used to feel it, but I was that sort of person. It would've been hard work for me to go on television, or work in public relations, or write articles. Having to push myself. It wouldn't have been me.

'I must just have one of those faces that people tend to forget. Many a time when I went back to Everton, the fans used to get me mixed up with Dennis Stevens. "Sign here, Dennis", they used to say. Dearie me, I used to think, 63 times for England and within a year or so people are getting you mixed up with another bloody guy.'

Wilson's World Cup winners medal is hidden away in a drawer, where it often takes half an hour to find when visitors to his home ask for a peek at it. Also stored, and not on display, are his international caps.

But all his England number three shirts have been given away for charitable causes. 'I've kept a couple of shirts that I exchanged, and I've got a German shirt from 1966. I was a silly bugger changing instead of keeping my own shirt. It didn't seem that important at the time. And of all things, I finished up getting a guy's shirt who didn't even play. That's the story of my life really...

'When I see lads on television going on to the field at Wembley now for internationals and Cup finals, I don't think how I'd love to be there. I can feel the tension for the lads. In many ways I can think "By Christ I'm glad that I'm sat here." Like looking back at the World Cup final. If I had to do it now, I don't know whether I could face it. But then we'd been attuned to it over a long period.

'When I finished playing soccer, and had to work with different people, then I started to realise that soccer wasn't everything. I used to think football was the most important thing in the world. But now when I hear guys on the television, saying things like it's a tragedy that we lost today, I think is it bloody hell. It's more of a tragedy, for example, that there are kids about who aren't being looked after properly.

'That's why I'm glad in many ways that I've detached myself from it...'

# NOBBY STILES

**Born Collyhurst, Manchester, 18 May 1942; St Patrick's School, Collyhurst and Lancashire Schoolboys; 5 schoolboy caps 1957; joined Manchester United Sep. 1957 and turned pro June 1959; 6 youth caps 1959; League debut 1 Oct. 1960 v Bolton (away, 1-1), but not a regular for several seasons; missed 1963 FA Cup final despite 31 League games that season, and replaced by brother-in-law Johnny Giles; 3 Under-23 caps 1964; full debut v Scotland at Wembley 10 April 1965 (2-2), following a season helping United to Championship; scored for England v W. Germany at Wembley Feb. 1966 wearing No 9 shirt, and won more than half his England caps during extended World Cup season...**

The passing of 15 years had left little mark on the player who most typified England's success in 1966. The false teeth were firmly in place. The thick-rimmed glasses that once won their owner the accolade of the country's 'most distinctively bespectacled man' replaced the contact lenses. Yet it was very much the same Nobby Stiles who danced his way into the hearts of millions up and down the country on the World Cup lap of honour.

Those 15 years have been spent inside the game that gave him his identity. Early in 1981, keeping Preston North End alive in a difficult economic climate, his football life held less glamour than in a playing career that apart from 28 England caps also included a European Cup winners medal as the highest peak in a glittering era with Manchester United.

Nobby Stiles still lives in his beloved Manchester. He also retains all the passion for football that turned him as a young player from what

*Vindication as well as celebration for Ramsey and Stiles. The manager had refused to bow to pressure to drop Nobby after the France game.*

Alan Ball once described as the oldest-looking Under-23 international he'd ever seen into a fearsome competitor whose reputation spread worldwide with nicknames like 'The Assassin' and 'El Bandito'.

He clearly relished the opportunity to discuss the past, more than once thanking me for my interest, and is still vexed by those in the media who subsequently have been disparaging about the nature of England's victory.

But he was also in the mood to dispel some myths. No, he hadn't lost his teeth diving bravely into a ruck of flying boots for a rescuing header. As a boy he had fled in terror from every appointment with the school dentist. His front teeth, so prominent in his days at Manchester's St Patrick's School, had simply rotted from lack of care. 'My children now go to a private dentist, which is one of the many benefits that football has brought me.'

Nor was his famed short-sightedness, as was attributed in his heyday as a player, the product of a childhood accident. Sure, he had been sent flying by a trolley-bus—what happened to the vehicle is not recorded—but the call to the opticians was prompted by straightforward myopia, natural shortness of sight.

As for his nickname in the England squad of Happy, that too was not what it seemed. 'It got in the papers that my nickname was Happy because I was such an nice, easy-going type of fellah. It was in fact the complete opposite—you know, like short people are often called Lofty. Shay Brennan gave me the nickname at United because I was a nark on the pitch. I was *bad-tempered*.

'If you see the World Cup final, you'll see me shouting and ranting in the wall at that free-kick that the Germans scored from. I used to have goes at everyone, even Bobby Charlton. Sometimes he wouldn't talk to me for days afterwards.'

That distinctive Stiles aggression, both verbal and physical, almost cost him a place in the final. There were those among the England officials who would have been delighted for the quieter life they would have enjoyed had Alf Ramsey bowed to outside pressures.

Ramsey's loyalty to Stiles is clearly reciprocated to this day. Much of it stems from the England manager's reaction to the incident in the team's third match of the tournament, against France, when Stiles launched into a fearsome challenge that threatened to break Jacques Simon in two. Even some England players blanched. Foreign observers called for the offender to be thrown out of the competition.

Nobby Stiles did not duck the responsibility, even at the time. Now the recollections are still sharp in the memory—and depicted in an accent that continued to surprise throughout our discussions: 17 years of marriage to an Irish girl have left a legacy in his vocabulary, emphasised no doubt by the time spent with his brother-in-law and best pal, Johnny Giles. At first hearing you could be forgiven for thinking that the symbol of England's one World Cup success is Irish himself—or at the very least from Liverpool.

'It was a bad tackle. I'll be honest, I felt I had to nail Simon. And when I say nail him, I don't mean kick him. I felt he was a very good player, and I was looking for a chance to hit him fifty-fifty, to come out with the ball but just to shake him a little as well, within the laws of the game.

'So I timed my approach. But it was a bit skiddy, and he turned too sharp for me. I couldn't get out of it. I wish I'd been able to. He went down, and for the last twenty minutes of that game I never took part. I was absolutely sick. It was a bad, bad tackle. I got stick and I deserved to get stick.

'Alf didn't say anything that night. But two days later we were playing five-a-side in training and I was still going through the motions. People were saying I should be out of the side, and that I couldn't play anyway. Well, I didn't doubt my ability. You don't represent Manchester United and England if you can't play.

'Alf came to me that morning, and asked me if I'd meant the tackle the way it turned out. I told him that of course I hadn't meant to kick Simon but if I'd frightened him he would start laying balls off when he's no need to. Everybody was saying that there's no way I should play against Argentina, but Alf told me that I would play as long as I performed like I did against France for the first seventy minutes, not like the last twenty minutes.

'There was a lot of extra pressure on me then, and I remember dear old Les Cocker and Harold Shepherdson taking me into the big bathroom at the dressing-rooms at Wembley before the game. And they said you owe this fellah something, keep your head no matter what. And I did, even though there was a lot of provocation.'

England's victory and the subsequent part played by Nobby Stiles in quelling the threat of Eusebio in the semi-final against Portugal ensured that the side's most controversial player had overcome a personal crisis. Yet he could have been forgiven another flutter of uncertainty when the superstitions before the final took an unlucky turn.

'On the Friday night a number of us went to the pictures. It was *Those Magnificent Men In Their Flying Machines* in Hendon, and I had a lucky cardigan that I always wore. And funnily enough I left it in the picture house after, so that wasn't a good start for me at all. I phoned up the next day but it had gone.

'And on the morning of the match, I got up early, round about seven o'clock, and went to church. I was rooming with Ballie at the time and he wondered where I'd gone. I came back to bed again, but I didn't sleep. And there was no way that I'd slept during the night anyway.

'I'm not very religious. I suppose I'm a bit hypocritical at times. I do go to church every Sunday. It's the way I was brought up in a heavy Irish-Catholic district of Manchester. It's just I suppose that if I want something, I go to church and ask for it. You can't always get it, but you go and ask...'

On the afternoon of 30 July 1966, those particular prayers were answered, and he recalls with amazement the turnabout in the public's attitude towards him. Banners proclaiming 'Nobby for Prime Minister' were a reminder of the English love for the underdog which he had suddenly become in the face of the witch-hunt caused by the Simon episode. Their hero arrived at the ground —minus the lucky cardigan but in the same suit, shirt and even underpants that formed a ritual attire on match days.

His memories, too, focus on the key incidents in the match. 'I can remember in injury time when they got their equaliser feeling sick and probably swearing a bit. But I'll never forget Ballie running into the back of the net to pick the ball out and get back to the middle to try to win the game. Really positive, when I was thinking what a complete disaster.

'The next thing was extra time and we were drained. But Alf said, "Have a look at the Germans". We were on our feet but they were flat out on their backs, and getting massages. And he got us all up off the ground and told us to keep doing the simple things. To stop giving the ball away.

'And then with about ten minutes to go, I went to go and cross a ball into the box, and everything just went

*Stiles and his great rival Billy Bremner after England's 4-3 win over Scotland at Hampden in April 1966. Bremner later sent him a telegram before the quarter-final against Argentina: 'All the best. Don't let it get you down. Chalkie.'*

*World Cup star Stiles pictured at his modest club-owned house in Stretford three months after the final. The eldest of his three sons, John is now on the verge of League football.*

out of me. I hit the ball just straight behind for a goal-kick. I was absolutely gone. There was nothing left, and I remember Ballie and I think it was Ray Wilson shouting at me "Come on, get back". And it was a complete physical effort to do it.'

But it was the events after the final whistle that endeared Nobby Stiles to the nation; a totally spontaneous show of joy that manifested the feelings of every England supporter who saw the match live or on television. John Bull himself could have conjured no more appealing national trademark than this small, balding figure with a gap-toothed smile who danced like a court jester brandishing the Jules Rimet Trophy above his head.

'I can't remember doing the famous dance, which is what everybody

remembers me for. But what I do remember is when the final whistle went, I dived on George Cohen. And George was a great fellah, but he could be a bit sombre. And I think he wondered what the hell was going on for a while.

'But what my wife hasn't forgiven me for is going up to meet the Queen without my teeth in. She had said before the game that I should have my teeth there so I could slip them in, but I told her that if we won there was no way I was going to do that. And I didn't.'

In the final, as throughout the competition, the teeth in Stiles' tackling technique, in his defensive mid-field role in front of the back four, built a platform for those who played in advance of him. Those who decry his skills as purely destructive would do well to recall his extra-time pass behind Schnellinger. Ball had read his room-mate's intentions and his low cross reached Hurst for the moment that settled the destiny of the World Cup.

For Nobby Stiles, the day's only spell of discord came when the organising committee called for a formal conclusion to the competition. 'We hadn't seen our wives for something like seven and a half weeks, and while I was away at Lilleshall my youngster Peter was born. I still haven't lived it down at home that I wouldn't ask Alf to release me for a couple of days, because I wanted to play for England so much.

'After the banquet on the evening of the final I went to the Playboy Club with my wife, John Connelly and his wife and Alan Ball and Lesley, his girlfriend then. I think we were the first to arrive there, and we were asked to stand behind a rope. They wanted us to get all the team together for a photo. But we got tired of waiting for the others so we moved on to Danny La Rue's club.

'Geoff Hurst and his wife were there already, and we all had a fabulous, fabulous night. Ballie got up on the stage and sang San Francisco and sang it very well. They'd provided a big cake with World Cup Winners on it. But I never saw Danny La Rue —only his head waiter, who came up when we went to pay what was by then a pretty large bill. And the waiter said that the bill was on Danny La Rue. Seemingly all the other lads had gone to the Playboy, where it had cost them a fortune!'

For Nobby Stiles the celebrations were the start of one very short week off before the new domestic season. During that week he vowed to keep away from trouble on the field, even striking a bet with Shay Brennan, his United mate, that he wouldn't be cautioned before Christmas. The money was lost inside days.

On a club tour of Europe, he was sent off for the first of only two times in his career, in a friendly against FK Austria in Vienna. Later he would defend the case successfully, avoiding suspension but not a fine. 'I took my shirt off and threw it at the referee, which was *ridiculous*. I fine my players now, here at Preston, for dissent. Yet

I was the worst one for getting booked for dissent. I was always opening my mouth and having a go.'

Stiles ended 1966 with a 13th caution of a three-year spell—not excessive by the standards of the 1980s but more than extravagant at the time. After the latest indiscretion, at Villa Park, he commented: 'Today I feel sick with myself. This should have been a great year for me. I don't want to be remembered as the footballer who couldn't keep out of trouble.'

His second sending-off became an international cause célèbre. United's somewhat dubious right as European champions was a two-legged fixture with the champions of South America for the World Club Championship. It had already become a competition

*Looking more schoolteacher than 'assassin', Stiles leaves for the notorious encounter with Estudiantes in 1968. The Argentinians, convinced of a European conspiracy in 1966, built up a massive pre-match campaign against him, and he was eventually sent off—for dissent.*

tainted with violence, and United's meeting with the Argentine club Estudiantes was to take a similarly bitter course.

Stiles' reputation had reached Buenos Aires ahead of the team. 'The things that went on in that match were unbelievable. I remember it as plain as anything. I was playing against a fellah called Doctor Bilardi. Bill Foulkes cleared a ball, and I was following it out of the penalty area when this Bilardi stuck the nut on me. Then a couple of minutes later he did it again. I went for him this time but before I touched him he

*Stiles lays down the law as captain of Middlesbrough. He had two Second Division seasons at Ayresome Park before moving across to join Bobby Charlton at Preston.*

fell on the ground writhing in agony. The referee came over to send me off, but luckily he'd cut my eye and I could point to the blood.

'They were playing offside all the time, so we said at half-time if Pat Crerand got a ball on the right, I would make a run from my own half on the left...which I did and I was straight through. But the linesman flagged. I didn't give the V-sign, but I threw my arm straight up in the air in protest—and was sent off. Looking back now that might have been the same gesture in South America as a V-sign here. I went to the dressing-room and cried my eyes out.

'I was also in tears on the plane home when I found out that I'd been misquoted in a British paper, supposedly saying that "these bastards were after me even before I got off the plane." Reading that back home they would have thought I always use bad language. I don't.

'I was sorry for the reporter, whom I got on with very well, but they did publish an apology a couple of days later in the paper.'

Two cartilage operations threatened Stiles' place in England's bid to retain the World Cup in Mexico. He had played so little first-team football that Ramsey was accused of sentimentality when his ball-winner of 1966 was included in the 28 provisionally selected in 1970. Ken Aston, the deputy chairman of FIFA's Referees Committee, made a more accurate interpretation of the decision: 'Stiles is Ramsey's symbol of his determination to win; his independence and his refusal to bow to whispered pressure behind the scenes. Stiles' inclusion will worry a lot of countries.'

In the home internationals he returned to give a typically combative performance against Scotland at Hampden Park, but in the event the solidity of Alan Mullery restricted Stiles to a role as a frustrated non-playing substitute in Mexico. The loss of pounds in weight while sat watching England's opening match against Rumania perhaps indicated the intensity of his commitment as much as the fearsome nature of the Mexican heat.

Within six months of returning he made a break that reflected his determination to play on despite the increasing wear and tear from top-class

football: he ended his love affair with Manchester United. 'My mind is made up,' he said at the time. 'It's no rush decision. I've been considering this move all season. Even thinking of leaving Old Trafford after 14 years is like cutting off my right arm. But I know I have four or five top-flight seasons in me and I think a move now would be better for me, and for the club.' Five months later he joined Second Division Middlesbrough for £30,000, still only 28.

'If I'd stayed at Manchester United I would have got a testimonial and I'd now be financially secure. I got a pension out of it, but in no way does that compare with a big testimonial. But I wouldn't change going to Middlesbrough, even though it was a bad experience family-wise. We just didn't settle. I'm a Manchester lad. A townie. A city person. We lived in a beautiful place called Yarm but all the quietness was wrong for us.'

The latter stages of Nobby Stiles' playing career and his first steps into management became closely entangled with two of his colleagues of 1966,

the brothers Charlton. In Jack's first deal as a League manager he sold Stiles to Bobby, who had just taken over at Preston.

'It wasn't personal with Jack that made me leave Middlesbrough. It was a family decision. I took a drop in wages to get back to Manchester.'

In his first season as manager Preston won promotion to Division 2, where life for the manager became more about survival and making sure the books balanced. When we spoke Preston had not won for nine games, but one of the most awkward decisions he was facing was whether to offer an apprenticeship to his eldest son, John.

'My kids are not Manchester United supporters. They're Preston supporters. They love Preston North End, because they were too young to remember my days at United. John's got ability but I have so many youngsters who come to the club who seem good enough at sixteen and who don't make it as a professional.

'A midfield player, but he doesn't play like me. Someone said to me recently when I was watching him

*Just nine months after his transfer—'leaving United is like cutting off my right arm'—the FA Cup drew Middlesbrough away at Old Trafford; and Nobby, always a folk hero with the fans there, got a great reception as he led out his side. He also took them to a gritty goalless draw before losing the replay 3-0.*

63

# Preston North End

that he's more like his Uncle John [Giles]. Well, if he's any way like his Uncle John that'll do for me. But I don't put pressure on him.

'Peter, my middle boy, he likes running. He's a promising athlete. The biggest pleasure for me last year was that he ran for Sale Harriers at Crystal Palace in the 'B' race but against good-class opposition. He's a hurdler.'

His third son was named Robert Francis, after Bobby Charlton and Francis Burns. 'He loves football and he's a big Preston supporter. And he's the type of lad who can give you all the details. All the facts and figures.'

The new generation of soccer-loving Stiles has been accepted with a sigh of inevitability by the long-suffering Kay. 'My wife hates football. Her father was a footballer, and her brother of course. She gets sick of football what with the kids as well, but her lack of interest in it means she can always knock me down a peg or two, which is important.

'But I'm a private sort of person really. I don't go out for dinner much.

I never really went out with other players when I was at United. I'm a bit selfish, I suppose. I'm not a great socialiser.

The Stiles household is not littered with the souvenirs of 1966. All his football memorabilia rests with his mother, who also still lives in Manchester. 'My mother has my medals and my caps. They give her a great deal of satisfaction. And I've got Ballie's shirt from the final. We swopped after the game. We were big mates then.

'But I go back to places now and they remember me, and for me that's great. Some take a look and ask how on earth I could have been the hard man. Some people talk about my contact lenses and tell me that was why I mistimed some tackles. I tell them that the only two times I was sent off were abroad. In Austria, where I got off, and Estudiantes. I was never sent off playing in England.

'And I'm proud that I am one of those remembered from the World Cup...even though its because I was The Assassin!'

64

*What it was all about: a gold statuette only a foot high and weighing less than 9 lb, bearing the name of the former president of the French Football Federation, who began it all in 1930. Jack Charlton gently supports it...as though after all that effort it might crack in his hands; Geoff Hurst is curious, almost overawed; Alan Ball can't wait to get a closer look, like a new father; Bobby Moore, for whom picking up trophies at Wembley was becoming an annual event, seems quite relaxed as a photographer's hand sets it up like a still life. While the foreign press talked about the side's luck—being the hosts, Rattin sent off in the quarter-final, the controversial third goal in the final—England set about celebrating in style the biggest day in her football history. The record since then*

*puts the win in perspective: a quarter-final defeat when qualifying as hosts in 1970 and failure to qualify at all for 1974 and 1978. Not that much had been achieved before 1966, either: Alf Ramsey played in England's effective elimination by the USA in 1950, while in 1954 and 1962 more skilful South American sides (Uruguay and Brazil) proved too strong in the quarter-finals, and in 1958 the side lost to the USSR in a group play-off. Before 1966, in fact, England had won just three of 14 matches in the final stages—so five wins and a draw in 1966 was no mean feat. 'It was lovely...a fantastic moment,' says Bobby Charlton, pictured here in the background after his 74th full international. 'And when it was all over I thought "whatever happens nobody can take that away".'*

*The England squad pictured during the last training session at Lilleshall before the warm-up tour of Scandinavia in late June. Standing: Jimmy Greaves, George Eastham, Ian Callaghan, Geoff Hurst, Norman Hunter, Peter Thompson, Gerry Byrne, Roger Hunt, Bobby Charlton, John Connelly, Gordon Milne, Ron Springett, Jimmy Armfield and Bobby Moore. Kneeling: Gordon Banks, Peter Bonetti, Ron Flowers, George Cohen, Jack Charlton, Martin Peters, Johnny Byrne, Keith Newton, Terry Paine, Alan Ball and Nobby Stiles. Missing from the 27 are Ray Wilson—and Bobby Tambling, who with Thompson, Milne, Johnny Byrne and Newton would be quietly told by Alf Ramsey on the walk back to the hall that they wouldn't be in the final squad. 'We all knew it was happening,' says Hurst. 'Waiting for him to turn and beckon "Got a minute, Geoff?" was pure hell.' Hurst at least got the nod, and again in 1970; Peter Thompson was left out of the last 22 on both occasions. Five of the players would finish their England careers on the subsequent tour—Eastham, Springett, Armfield, Flowers and Gerry Byrne—while Connelly and Paine would win their last cap during the World Cup. The squad of 27 included five players from League Champions Liverpool, four from West Ham, three from Manchester United and two from Blackpool, Chelsea and Leeds.*

*RIGHT:* **The superbly worked goal that put England into the last four. Hurst finds space in a depleted Argentina defence to glance Peters' curling cross past Roma and inside the far post. 'That goal was super—one that Martin and I had practised a million times,' says Hurst of the moment that celebrated his return to the England side. 'So to pull it off in a game like that, to win one we damn near lost... well, that took me right to the top. There didn't seem any higher place for me to go. That's the way I came to the final...satisfied.'**

LEFT: *Alan Ball, Gordon Banks and George Cohen in happy mood at the Hendon Hall Hotel during the finals.* 'I got on better with the boys from the north,' says George, hamming it up just a little here. 'Don't get me wrong. I didn't have any problems with the other Londoners. It's just that the northern lads had a down-to-earth style that really appealed to me.' Gordon reckons that though there were differences in temperament the way people mixed was vital. 'One of our biggest assets was that we were really a team—like a League club.'

BELOW: *Jimmy Greaves and Roger Hunt the day after England's 2-1 win over Portugal had put them in the final.* Hunt certainly had to look over his shoulder; Greaves was fit again and the press were already clamouring for his return. 'I expected to play because I'd played in all the other five games,' says Hunt, 'but a lot of people still say it was me who took Greaves' place. But it was Geoff Hurst.' Hunt, too, for all the criticism levelled at him during England's games, had still scored three of their seven goals—including the pair against France that saw them safely through to the last eight.

*RIGHT: It was something of a goldfish existence for the England players as they entered the seventh week virtually away from home. Jack Charlton was at least sure of his place: he had appeared in 21 of the 22 games since his debut (he was rested against Norway) and there was no real rival in the squad.*

*BELOW: The West Ham trio around whom the final glory would be centred. The group image later led to a real identity crisis for Peters: 'It was always "Moore, Hurst and Peters". Always three names. Always in that order... "and Peters". I wasn't jealous...I just wanted to be my own man...and I wanted to be with a successful club team.' In 1970 he went looking for that success with Spurs.*

**ABOVE:** *Portugal's Pereira can only parry Hunt's shot and the ball runs to the edge of the area—for Bobby Charlton, who had pushed Wilson's fine long ball on to Hunt, to sweep it home and put England 1-0 up in the semi-final. This proved the best 'footballing' game of the tournament, full of fine moves and almost free of fouls. Charlton's performance, including both goals, persuaded Helmut Schoen to shadow him with Beckenbauer in the final.*

**LEFT:** *A moment of relief for Gordon Banks, protected by his two full-backs, during the final. In this game, his sixth of the tournament, he conceded his first goal from open play. While he admits to part of the blame for Haller's goal, he had no chance with Eusebio's penalty in the semi-final and little with Weber's equaliser—and was understandably surprised when Lev Yashin was named best keeper of the competition.*

**RIGHT:** *Not a German in sight as Hunt, Hurst and Peters celebrate the latter's goal. The men on scoreboard duty will change the England number to 2 when their delight has subsided; Stiles kisses the ground; and Banks, dutiful as ever, hesitates before running to congratulate the scorer.*

It's all over. The final whistle is buried in the tumult following Hurst's goal. Sheer delight breaks out in the England camp as Gerry Byrne, Ian Callaghan, Ron Flowers, Harold Shepherdson and Peter Bonetti rejoice in victory. And in the middle of it all sits the man who said it would happen, 'admiring

*the commitment of Overath's run'. He could be the losing manager—though that was the fate of Helmut Schoen (far left). Jimmy Armfield offers congratulations, team doctor Alan Bass seems to offer a bag. And Jimmy Greaves, understandably, just can't believe it's happening.*

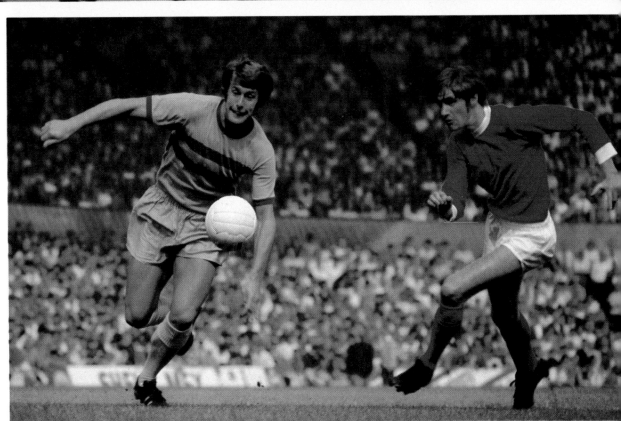

LEFT: *Juventus' world record buy Pietro Anastasi drops back to mark Jack Charlton during the second leg of the 1971 Fairs Cup final at Elland Road—when Anastasi's goal wasn't enough to prevent Leeds, and Charlton, taking the trophy for the second time. Jack's record of 102 goals in competitive matches would please many a midfield player, though the vast majority came from set-pieces, where Charlton pioneered the controversial ploy of standing on the goal-line.*

BELOW LEFT: *Geoff Hurst causes problems for Paul Edwards at Old Trafford. In the seasons after the World Cup—he scored 41 goals for West Ham in 1966-67—Hurst developed a more penetrative game, allying attacking skills on the ball to his formidable talents as a target man. 'I couldn't go anywhere that easily. I lost count of the times I heard defenders shouting for help against me. Can you imagine what that sort of thing did for my confidence?' It also meant he was a target man in more senses than one...*

BELOW: *A youthful Frank Lampard and Alan Stephenson wisely turn their backs on a Bobby Charlton special in the same game. Endless afternoons of patient practice as a teenager behind the United stand had given him the confidence as well as the sure touch to try his famous shots. 'When I used to shoot from twenty or thirty yards, it was what the crowds loved to see,' he says—and his power and accuracy brought three of England's goals in the finals.*

LEFT: *Bobby Moore, every inch the schoolboy image of the commanding captain. But it wasn't all plain sailing for Moore at Ron Greenwood's West Ham: on 30 June 1966 he refused to sign a new contract following a transfer request, and Ramsey helped paper over the cracks for the duration of the World Cup. Like Hurst, and more especially Peters, he found the club's lack of concrete success frustrating after the heady days of 1964 and 1965. In the end he stayed at Upton Park longer than either, eventually moving to Fulham early in 1974. The following year he faced West Ham in his second FA Cup final—and his first club defeat at Wembley.*

ABOVE: *Roger Hunt fires a shot past Manchester United's Alex Stepney at Old Trafford. He was a prolific scorer for Liverpool, and his 18 goals in 34 games for England is no mean record— particularly as Ramsey so often demanded a harrying, chasing role of him. Hunt now runs the family haulage business. 'We've got eleven vehicles and a staff of sixteen, including the family.' His contact with football is limited to membership of the PPA's pools panel, and he rarely sees a game. 'It must be a couple of years ago now. I don't enjoy watching...I feel an outsider. I thought that I couldn't live without football, but I don't miss the game itself.'*

ABOVE: *Ray Wilson with his family outside their home shortly after his retirement from the game. He now runs a funeral business near Huddersfield, where he began his career. 'The memory of the World Cup is now like a warm glow. Because I'm not in the game the recollections are not so much of the matches but the people...and those special times. You miss the comradeship. I certainly haven't missed the game itself.'*

LEFT: *Alan Ball's talents tempted two managers—Harry Catterick and Bertie Mee—to break the British record for his services, the first just days after the 1966 final. 'I wish it could happen to me now. I want something like that again in my life. Then it didn't mean that much to me. Only now do I appreciate it.'*

RIGHT: *Wednesday's Kevin Taylor chases hard during Martin Peters' first game as player-coach for Sheffield United in the derby League Cup tie on 9 August 1980. After a great start at Bramall Lane results fell away in the autumn—and in January Peters packed up playing to become manager.*

Ray Green catches Nobby Stiles in clowning mood at Old Trafford. After United's dramatic European Cup success against Benfica at Wembley in 1968—when as in the World Cup semi-final he blotted out the menace of Eusebio —his career was a disappointment, triggered by 10 months of niggling knee injuries. Ramsey then named him in the England squad for Mexico after only a handful of games because 'he's a good player. He's good for the party and he's good for England.' World Cup and United team-mate Bobby Charlton remains convinced that Stiles was a better player than he was ever given credit for: 'People tended to overlook the more subtle side of Nobby's game because of his aggression and tenacity. He seemed to have a sixth sense of knowing where the action was going to be and made sure he was in the best position to deal with it. And he always did.' Stiles moved from Jack Charlton's Middlesbrough to Bobby's Preston in 1973 and became chief coach shortly before the latter's resignation in 1975. Two years later he took over from Harry Catterick as manager, winning promotion in his first season in charge but returning to the Third Division (on goal difference) in 1981.

# JACK CHARLTON

**Born Ashington, Northumberland, 8 May 1936; Hirst Park Modern School, East Northumberland Schoolboys, Ashington YMCA, Ashington Welfare; joined Leeds (where Uncle Jimmy was a full-back) 1950 and turned pro May 1952; League debut v Doncaster 25 April 1953 (home, 1-1) but then did national service; regular first-teamer 1955; after early differences with Don Revie became pillar of Leeds revival; England debut v Scotland at Wembley 10 April 1965 (2-2) as Div. 2 player; subsequently unchallenged as his country's No 5, playing in 26 of the next 27 internationals...**

Though I had an appointment, I was relieved to find Jack Charlton in when I called. His office at Hillsborough, the home of Sheffield Wednesday—on the surface an obvious meeting point —is not always the surest place to locate the club manager.

They originally called him 'Big Jack' because of his raw physical size —a gawky 6 ft 4 ins, long in neck and stride, a footballing giraffe. But England's centre-half in the World Cup campaign of 1966 is now big in a wider sense, an extrovert whose charisma transcends the boundaries of the game which made him famous— and continues to do so. Unlike so many of his more intense colleagues in management, he keeps his football business in perspective.

In the middle of the week you are more likely to find him on the moors, letting fly at grouse with his shotgun. His priorities were illustrated no better than in the signing of one new player for Sheffield Wednesday, when Ian Mellor was driven deep into the country to complete the deal; Jack was not shifting from the river bank and his fishing rod.

Hence my relief at catching him for once stretching back behind his desk, pleased with the efforts of the two loyal ladies in his life, wife Pat and secretary Norma, to co-ordinate his bewildering shifts in emphasis and environment. He had just arrived back from a speaking engagement in Norwich. Norma reminded him of a similar appointment in Salford, a rugby function. Pat, long past anticipating his movements, wanted to know the details of a shooting expedition to Scotland, which seemed to coincide happily with a match at

Newcastle. Or was it the other way round?

Outside the office, a pair of Swedish journalists, sternly Scandinavian, were waiting to translate comments in the Northumberland dialect for a magazine in Malmö. And there was still that night's Second Division home match to consider...

At 29 Jack Charlton was the second oldest of England's World Cup winners. A long-time rebel on the field, he was long in the tooth in the professional game before making the necessary adaptations. After an initial battle of egos, he had responded to the encouragement of Don Revie so well that just over a year before the World Cup Ramsey had capped him for the first time against Scotland.

After England's triumphs he continued playing for another seven seasons: Ramsey took him to Mexico in 1970, but only as a cover for Brian Labone. To Charlton's own consternation he was played only once, against Czechoslovakia.

Even while he was finishing his playing days, on the way to a club record 629 League appearances for Leeds, he was negotiating with Middlesbrough to become their manager. In his first season he inspired the Teesside club to push aside their feeling of inferiority to their North-East rivals, Newcastle United and Sunderland, and make headlines of their own; Boro ran away with the Second Division Championship by a Football League record margin of 15 points.

Three years later he quit—even though, or perhaps because, Middlesbrough had settled into a competent First Division outfit. Jack left while

*The end of extra time...'I suddenly realised that I was knackered. Really knackered. I sank on my knees and put my head in my hands. A sort of "Thank God that's over". People reckon I said a little prayer, but I don't think I actually said a conscious prayer. It was just relief at the end of two hours of football.'*

he was ahead, a philosophy that he freely admits he will follow as long as he remains in football.

The challenge of Sheffield Wednesday tempted him to his second managerial appointment. Wednesday were a fallen giant of a club, drowning at the bottom of the Third Division. On the morning that I arrived to trigger his World Cup memories, a refurbished side stood fourth in Division 2 after gaining promotion.

Jack Charlton's managerial style reveals much about his character. His penny-conscious background is reflected in the pride with which he tells you that he has bettered both the clubs he has managed without falling into the pitfall of contemporary football, a large overdraft at the bank.

His teams play in the practical manner that typifies his temperament, a defence organised in the way that he learned his trade as a professional defender; plenty of physical power and aggression and a dash of flair in attack, always providing that commodity is not too expensive. The purists on the coaching floor of Lancaster Gate might cringe, but on a Football League ground thick with mud in the depths of a Yorkshire winter it is usually effective.

So much has happened to Jack Charlton since 1966 that I wondered if the pressures of the present ever gave him time to reflect. 'I'm always reminded of it because everyone else hasn't forgotten it. Whenever I go to dinners or whenever I get introduced to somebody, it's as Jack Charlton, who used to play with Leeds and was a member of England's World Cup winning team. I'd have thought that people's memories would have been dulled about it, but it doesn't appear to be the case.

'It does get shown on television from time to time. But I've never seen it. The only thing I saw was the film *Goal!* I saw that once, but I've never seen the whole game. I'd love to see it, particularly to see what I looked like!'

Jack's recollections took on the same shape that has made him a regular choice as a television pundit, a mixture of colourfully-worded clarity and staggering gaps of memory, all topped off with his idiosyncratic pronunciation.

As an ITV panelist in the 1974 World Cup, his expert analysis of the Dutch occasionally laboured under the handicap of Jack's version of Johan Cruyff's name, uttered like a well-known dog show. Ray Wilkins became Wilkinson, one of a number of leading players whose skills still shone through Jack's precise comments, even if their names were distorted.

'What's 'is name' played a regular part in the post-match discussions, to the glee of his fellow panelists. And I can well recall asking Jack for his team changes before one television commentary, when he replied with all seriousness: 'The centre-half is the fella I signed last week. What's 'is name?'

'People ask me what I remember about the World Cup final. I remember it was hot. I remember we worked bloody hard. I remember incidents in the game without remembering anything about the pattern of the game. One in particular when a fella went past me on his left-hand side and hit the ball. It hit George Cohen in the balls, but it was a good stop by George because it was a good chance. The fella had just run past me as though I wasn't there. I felt I had to watch him going down that side of me because he was a bit quick. I forget now just which one it was. Left-sided? Left-winger?' We assumed it must be Lothar Emmerich.

'After that I ran him a couple of times to the touchline and won the ball off him. And then I knew that he wasn't gonna beat me down that side any more. And I remember Martin Peters' goal particularly because I'd gone up, and the ball was crossed and knocked out, and then somebody had a shot. It came across the goals, and it was coming straight to me. Then all of a sudden Martin popped up in front of me and whacked the ball in the net.

'No, I didn't feel cheated. I was delighted, in fact, because I'm glad the bugger never come to me because I'd have kicked it over the bar or something would have gone wrong.'

Like every other member of the side Jack is adamant that Peters' goal should have won the game. 'The equalising German goal should never have been allowed because he hand-balled it, you know. The free-kick was given against me. The boy [Emmerich again] hit the ball. It

*RIGHT: Charlton takes the award from Sam Leitch to succeed brother Bobby as Footballer of the Year in 1967. The honour has been won by four of the World Cup final side.*

*BELOW: A less pleasant meeting with Scotland's John Gordon later that year against Wales. Charlton's outspoken nature has meant inevitable confrontations with authority.*

ricochetted back across the face of the goals, and as it came across it hit him [Schnellinger] on the arm and dropped for them. Bobby Moore put his arm up in the air. I put my arm up in the air, but the referee gave the goal. But nobody made any song and dance about that one.'

As a defender Jack didn't have the best view of the moment that altered the course of the match back into England's favour—the contentious third goal. His patriotism, so fierce that he registers in hotels as English rather than British, held no doubts. 'Roger Hunt said it was well over, and he had no reason to lie. I think the Germans probably had a photograph or two showing the ball over the line but kept them to themselves.

'I remember getting my medal because when I got it I thought, "Hell's bells it's in a cardboard box." It was in a red and black cardboard box. A World Cup winners medal in a black and red cardboard box. The box has long since disintegrated. And then we were all sort of pushed around for photographers, before we went round on our lap of honour...

'I was at the front, and I remember looking back and seeing Nobby doing his dance. He looked so funny, and I got a bit emotional then. It was like wanting to cry and laugh at the same time. You get a sort of hic in your throat, just for a split second. I was so full of everything, and just to watch Nobby dancing like that made me feel emotional...very emotional.

'Things affect me very quickly. Anger affects me very quickly. I rise to the bait easily. Frustrations affect me very quickly. But I get over them just as quick. I get what you call a lip twitch. When I'm very angry or I'm gonna hit somebody my lip starts to go. And the same thing when I get emotional, when I come near to tears. And that's happened a few times to me. New Year's Eves, for example, when I was away from home.'

Jack in 1966 might have had a double celebration about which to feel emotional. Pat Charlton was confined to Leeds, expecting their third child, who was due on the Sunday after the match. Pat watched the final on television, flanked by reporters all secretly hoping that the excitement would precipitate the happy event.

But the stubbornness of the family extends beyond Jack: Pat was a week late in giving birth to Peter, dubbed World Cup Willie by the media— following an older son John, who now plays football in Australia, and daughter Deborah. Having checked on the maternity situation, Jack was left alone to celebrate after the victory banquet at the Royal Garden Hotel.

'Everybody else was all with their wives, but I didn't have anybody in London. My mother and father were there, but you don't go out with your mother and father after winning the World Cup. For the first time in the day I found myself pretty much on my own, but I bumped into Jimmy Mossop, who now writes for the *Sunday Express*, who was just leaving the banquet and going back to Manchester. I said "You're not. You're coming out with me." I had a couple of hundred quid in my pocket, and I said to Jim, "Let's go out and spend the bugger".

'The crowds were so big that we had to go out a side window to slip away without being seen. And just when I thought we were free of them, I got spotted out on the road. So we jumped into a taxi which was getting held up by all the people. The fella in it, I never did find out his name, he told us he was a professional violinist and he'd just finished playing in a concert.

'We were dropped at the club which used to be the home of all the footballers, the Astor Club, and we got

involved in a party of all the East End of London. They'd been to the match, and the whole place was one big party. I got so drunk I don't remember much about it after that, but I can remember Jimmy and I slept in some house in Leytonstone on the floor and on the settee.

'The house belonged to a lad called Lennie and his wife. In the morning I went down into the garden and there's a woman popped her head up over the wall, and she says, "Hello Jackie"; incredibly it was a Mrs Mather who lived right opposite us in Beatrice Street in Ashington. She was on holiday down in London with her son. Amazing!

'My mother of course gave me a right telling off. Where had I been all night? Geordie people don't understand you spending the whole night out. They want to know where you've been. Specially with Pat expecting and that. So I told them where I had been and all about it, and I think it was the one time where I didn't have to make excuses as to where I'd spent my night.'

Jack Charlton's World Cup medal is now on show in a bureau in his home on the outskirts of Barnsley, a recent innovation after many years of keeping all his football souvenirs in a plastic bag.

'I offered the medal to Leeds United. I thought it would be nice if they put it in a cabinet so that everyone who wanted to could come

*Jack and Bobby wait at Heathrow before the trip to Mexico— where both would soon end their international careers. 'As an ambassador for the game he's second to none,' says Jack. 'When you go abroad with him you realise how warmly he's thought of. He should have been given some special post to promote British sport abroad. Given a knighthood. To me he was wasted taking over a football club. I told him I thought he was making a mistake taking the Preston job. I always thought it was a mistake for him to go into management at all.'*

*Goodbye Leeds ...
Big Jack waves to
the 34,000 at his
testimonial against
Celtic on 7 May 1973
—after 22 years at
Elland Road. He
played 629 League
and made 770
competitive
appearances for
Leeds, both club
records. He also
scored 96 goals, a
remarkable total
for a centre-half.*

and see it. But Don Revie advised me to take it home with me. Some newspapers reported that I offered it to him. But that was wrong. I thanked him for all the help he'd given me in achieving it, but I never offered it to him.'

Eight years later Revie would succeed to Ramsey's throne as England's team manager, but the man who transformed Leeds United from a tumbling Second Division club to one of the world's most competitive never established his influence in the manner in which Jack Charlton described Ramsey's role in 1966.

'Alf's major contribution to us winning the World Cup was his making of international players. You knew who was the team, with the possible exception of the forward players. All of us knew who the goal-keeper would be and who the back four would be for at least a year, maybe eighteen months before the World Cup. We knew Nobby would play. We knew Bobby would play. We thought Ballie would play, but we didn't know how he would balance out midfield. In fact he brought in Martin Peters. He didn't have a clue who he would play up front. There were quite a few front people in-

volved in the whole thing at that time.

'I asked Alf once, leaning on a bar at Lilleshall, why did he pick me? After all I was 28 when I got involved with England. He said it was because I had attributes that he needed to fit in with what ideas he had about the team. He said I was good in the air and very mobile—and at that time to be fair I was very mobile. I'm sure he picked George Cohen for the same basic reason.

'I think he needed someone like me to get around Bobby Moore. Someone who could get around the back of him, and didn't leave him to compete for everything in the air cos that wasn't his strength. And Bob and I quickly sorted out our responsibilities on situations.

'The relationships that I formed was only really with those who played close to me—the back four and Nobby and Our Kid. They were always consistently in the side and we could build up an understanding. You can't keep changing international sides. Take George Cohen as an example. You knew with George that no-one was going to run him down the outside, but you knew that if anyone took him on the inside he struggled. But over a year you learned how to cover for that sort of thing.

'You knew that if Our Kid was confronted with someone on the edge of the eighteen-yard box then not to stand off in the box. You had to go in behind Bob because there was no way he would win the ball. The fella was going to come past him with the ball. But if it was Nobby, there was no way the fella would come past. The ball might, but no way would the fella!

'Bobby Moore would always accept responsibility. He would always take the ball off the goalkeeper and start attacks. I *never* would. If he gave it to me I'd give it back to him, and say kick the bloody thing. These are little examples of the relationships that made us into a winning team.

'Alf always said he didn't pick the players on form. He picked people whom he knew would perform in a certain way at that level.'

Ramsey continued to pick Jack Charlton after 1966, including the 34-year-old defender in the squad which set out to retain the trophy in Mexico. His only appearance in the competition, however, came against Czechoslovakia when a number of key players were rested.

'I felt that Alf made a mistake. I felt he should have played me all the time in Mexico, because I had more success with Leeds that year. We went for the League, the Cup and the European Cup. Didn't get anything in the end, but I'd had a terrific season, I thought.

'But it was a very, very hard season, and I'd missed a lot of international matches that I was picked to play in, and had to pull out of, either because we were playing in Europe or I had a bit of a knock to get over. But I'd never been fitter in my life than when we went to Mexico, and I was amazed when Alf didn't play me. He preferred Brian Labone, and in fact Brian Labone was even more amazed than me he was picked instead of me.

'I never lost a World Cup match, you know. That's what I used to say to them. I would like to have been given the opportunity to lose a game before I got kicked out. I never lost one. It was disappointing.'

While England were losing to West Germany in that agonising quarter-final in León, their reserve centre-half sat in a café close to the stadium.

As a spectator he had feared the worst when the Germans had started to make inroads into England's two-goal lead. He took the defeat worse than many of those who actually took part; it offended the professionalism that lies at the very roots of his thinking.

His realism brought him into trouble with the Football Association a few months after he returned from Mexico. In an interview with Fred Dinenage on Tyne-Tees Television, he admitted that there were the names of two fellow professionals in 'a little black book'; if he got the opportunity he 'would do 'em'. The remarks were widely quoted in a press field day without capturing the mischievous spirit in which they were uttered.

Even brother Bobby was moved to criticise him in print, implying that the remarks would destroy the image of the professional footballer. The FA formally rebuked him. Later he would name the players as Johnny Morrissey of Everton and Bertie Auld of Celtic.

Whatever the consequences, Jack Charlton has always been one to let you know what's on his mind. The first time I met him, as a raw editorial assistant on the television coverage of an important match, I was deputed to

*Hello Middlesbrough. Jubiliation as Boro score on their way a runaway Second Division title by a 15-point margin in Charlton's first season—an achievement that brought him the Manager of the Year award. He consolidated the club's position in the First Division before leaving, and later dropping to the Third to take over at Sheffield Wednesday.*

pick out a number of highlights for him to analyse. My choice and his didn't coincide, and he lost no time in telling me so. Others might have been more diplomatic, but I later realised that it was no personal attack. Jack is a straightforward, uncomplicated person who will say exactly what he thinks. Usually instantly.

It's a characteristic that's kept football authorities regularly on his track. In 1968, he became the first player to contest a booking, administered by a young Clive Thomas for 'persistent infringement' in a European tie against Hibernian. Jack's appeal was upheld, and he now firmly believes that the right of appeal which has been taken away from the player has hit at the democracy of the game.

Inevitably his background led to talk of following in the footsteps of his two mentors, Ramsey and Revie, as England's team manager. But in 1977, when the job became vacant, Jack Charlton's pride took a considerable dent.

'I got a phone call that said that two of the members of the FA selection committee wanted me to apply for the job. So I said yeh of course I'll apply, and I did, in writing. But I never heard a thing. I was very disappointed not to even get an interview. Because to this day I feel that my qualifications were better than

anyone else who applied for the job, except perhaps people like Bobby Robson, who'd been in management longer than me. But my international experience was vastly superior to theirs, that's all.

'I suppose when you think about it no-one who was in any way associated with Revie would get anywhere near the job. I'll admit that a lot of the managerial things that I do are directly attributed to what I learned under Revie. Plus the fact that they wanted what in fact they got, which was an establishment man. And in Ron Greenwood they got an establishment man who settled the job down.'

Did he now covet an opportunity to succeed Ron Greenwood and have the task of putting England back into the World Cup limelight that he relished so much as a player? 'I think I'm too outspoken, and I disagree with too much in football at the moment. I disagree with the way managers are treated. I disagree with the way their clubs are treated. The way that referees are protected. The way the public are abused in the cause of crowd control. I think I've got too many strong views to become England manager. I would apply again, but in the way that you normally apply for jobs. Not in writing. I'd let it be known that I was available if I was wanted . . .'

*An incident-packed start to the 1980-81 season for Charlton culminated at Oldham on 6 September, when Wednesday fans rioted after Terry Curran was sent off. They ignored the dramatic and angry appeals of their manager and Charlton was forced to back off to safety. 'There were kids lying on the deck everywhere. People behaving like animals. I thought, "What the bloody hell do you do now".'*

# BOBBY MOORE

**Born Barking, Essex, 12 April 1941; Tom Hood School, Leyton, Barking & Leyton Schools, Barking Youth Club; joined West Ham early 1958 and turned pro (as centre-half) June 1958; League debut v Manchester U. 8 Sep. 1958 (home, 3-2); won record 18 England youth caps 1958-59, 8 Under-23 caps 1960-62; full debut as cover for Bobby Robson v Peru 20 May 1962 (4-0) on pre-World Cup tour, but stayed in; switched to centre-back next year, when captained England for first time, v Czechoslovakia; led West Ham at Wembley 1964 for FA Cup (also voted Footballer of the Year) and 1965 for European Cup Winners Cup; already successful in promotions and business ventures well before World Cup...**

You couldn't blame Bobby Moore if he recorded his recollections of the World Cup final like some talking timetable. Next to requests about his health, the time and the weather, the topic of England's greatest hour is never far away from the man who somehow symbolised the nation's most revered football occasion.

Bobby Moore graciously agreed to another stroll over familiar terrain. We met up at the South Bank studios of London Weekend Television, where the passing of the years had led to no lessening of his impact. A car-parking space for his maroon Jaguar was made available where normally there are none. Hard-bitten security men stepped into his path not to check his identity but to brandish scraps of paper for autographs. Technicians who work with the stars still gawped with recognition and admiration.

If hindsight now shows the World Cup victory as a golden age of English football, Bobby Moore became very much the golden boy. His credentials were impeccable. His authority as a defender gave him genuine world stature as a player; his hunger for winning was always masked by an unemotional attitude on the field that easily satisfied those who still saw the British as upholders of fair play.

Moore was also well cast off the field. Blond, with rugged good looks, he stepped straight from the pages of schoolboy fiction, the ideal concept of an England captain. The companionship of Tina, his glamorous wife, added to the image.

Just a few weeks before his 40th birthday there was little sign of any tarnishing on the gilt. A pound or two over the playing weight, perhaps, but still the smoothness of the man whose sense of style was perfectly, if coincidentally, reflected in his last League match. It just happened to be his 1,000th senior game: a perfectly rounded end to a perfectly rounded career that few could better.

Yet after that last League appearance—in 1977 for Fulham at Blackburn—the expected step into management or coaching did not materialise. Great players do not necessarily make great managers. The unhappy Highbury experience of Billy Wright, Moore's most renowned predecessor, is ample testimony to the possibilities of failure. But most do try; like Wright, like Nat Lofthouse, like Bobby Charlton.

In December 1979, Moore did take a step back into football—but in a most unexpected quarter. He accepted an offer to manage Oxford City, struggling at the bottom of the Premier Division of the Berger Isthmian League. Built into his contract was promotional work for the club's sponsors, Free Newspapers Ltd, but nevertheless the sense of incongruity was unavoidable—the great Thespian organising the local repertory company.

Largely through the misfortune of one bad investment in a country club at Chigwell, Bobby Moore was in no position to reject the financial advantages of the lucrative deal. Yet he explained that he was drawn back into the game by a genuine sense of absence in his life. 'I didn't feel I'd missed the game at all from a playing

point of view. What did come home to me was that I'd missed the camaraderie of the dressing-room...the footballer's sense of humour.'

The realisation came earlier that season when he accepted an offer from Terry Venables to coach Crystal Palace's young players for two mornings a week. 'When I retired from playing, I had no immediate thoughts about my future. I've always had a few business commitments outside the game. For the first fifteen to eighteen months I spent about a third of that time travelling to accept various footballing invitations around the world. I went to America, to Canada, out to Hong Kong, to South Africa.

'It was the first time in my life I'd been in a situation where I could do what I wanted, where I wanted and how I wanted, without having to ask anyone's permission. And it was so enjoyable that it helped me through that spell when I might have missed playing at the top level very badly.'

The globe-trotting also prevented the full consideration of a number of offers from within the League to return full time to the game. In Jeff Powell's authorised and comprehensive biography, published in 1976, Moore says: 'I never thought much about running my own team but now that prospect excites me as well. It would have to be right. I wouldn't want to start at the bottom all over again, scuffling about in the lower divisions. But the right challenge at a good club, great!'

By 1981, 15 months' experience at Oxford City had changed the perspective. 'When you're a player at the highest level, you only have to take care of yourself, and you're not quite aware of all the other factors in the game. Maybe you say one or two immature things. But I've found out that it's like when you leave school and start a job...you start at ground level. Really as manager your playing experience is immaterial at that point. Only in the long run will what you've achieved as a player stand you in good stead.

'You're starting at scratch because there are certain decisions, certain aspects of the job that you've never been faced with before. By going to Oxford City I've had a training ground that as a player I probably felt that I didn't really need. But because

of it I'm much better equipped to be a League manager than I would have been had I gone straight in.'

These days England internationals are about the only matches from the top drawer that Moore sees. 'I haven't been to a League game this year. Instead of now looking at the big print, I start at the bottom of the page to check how the teams in the Isthmian League are doing. And my midweek visits are all to non-League grounds now, scouting for players and checking out the opposition.'

For all his obvious enthusiasm for his new role, the contrast still remains with the majestic figure who epitomised England's triumph 15 years earlier. The memory of his contribution in the final is crystal clear—the inspiring defending, the two impeccable passes that provided Geoff Hurst with England's first and fourth goals, the receiving of the World Cup from the Queen.

What is not so well remembered is that Moore was very nearly not eligible for the tournament. His career at West Ham was to be regularly blighted by his dissatisfaction that the club was rarely in the forefront of the hunt for honours. In 1966 Moore particularly feared that Norman Hunter's outstanding form for the emerging Leeds United might ease him out of the England set-up. The result was a transfer request that manager Ron Greenwood would not grant—a club's right in the days before freedom of contract. However, the incident snowballed when Greenwood released the story of Moore's discontent to the national papers.

With the World Cup only weeks away Moore was so furious that he refused to sign a new contract with the club. His old deal expired on 30 June, leaving him officially without the qualification to be selected for his country in the finals. A compromise was urgently arranged, with Ramsey prompting the details. A one-month contract was brought hurriedly to the Hendon Hall Hotel: Moore pledged his allegiance to West Ham—but only for the duration of the competition.

'At the moment I was signing that one-month contract I felt convinced that Ron Greenwood was so sick of the whole business that he would let me go. If England had done badly I would have been on my way to

*OPPOSITE: Intense concentration from Moore as he goes forward against Wales in the 1-1 draw at Cardiff in 1970, with Bobby Charlton looking on. While Charlton won his 100th cap in the next game and went on to pass Billy Wright's England record later in the year, Moore overhauled both before playing his last match for his country—his 108th appearance coming in the 1-0 defeat by Italy at Wembley in November 1973. He played 100 of those games under the direction of Alf Ramsey, all but a handful as captain.*

Tottenham the minute the World Cup was over.'

His club difficulties were not the only problem Bobby Moore had during the World Cup. He was billeted with his good friend Jimmy Greaves, and saw at close quarters Greaves' agony—first at being injured, then at not being recalled when he was fit for the final. Greaves made it clear on the morning of the match that he would not be taking his place at the evening festivities, whatever the afternoon produced; it would be Moore's lot to explain his friend's absence to Ramsey while the celebrations were at their highest.

Moore's own singularity of purpose and ambition had already been summed up by one of the remarks most often quoted about him. Ron Greenwood had gone on the record at West Ham's training headquarters: 'We're going to win the World Cup, and that man's the reason why. He can already see in his mind's eye a picture of himself holding up the World Cup, and he's calculated down to the last detail just what that will mean to him and to his career.'

Today Moore talks about 'having no control over the way other people see you' but he clearly possessed the mental strength to divorce himself from these difficulties off the pitch—as he was to show again four years later in the notorious Bogota bracelet episode. In 1966 his concentration focused wholly on the job of winning the Jules Rimet Trophy.

Bobby's initial recollection of the final is of the chaos that disturbed his own high standards of preparation as the kick-off drew near. 'I was always very calculated in what I did prior to a game. I was always there an hour before the start. And I remember saying to Jack Charlton half an hour before the kick-off that this was the most important game of my life and yet the place was still packed with television cameras, photographers and film crews. Jack replied, 'It's the World Cup final...and you've never played in one of these before.'

'He was right I suppose. But it was still so different for me. If I'd had my way, I would have co-operated up until two o'clock, but then cleared the decks because the job still had to be done.'

If the temperature of the Moore sang-froid rose, it was only temporary. Six aching minutes after Haller had struck for West Germany, England's captain spread relief with his vision at a free-kick. Hurst's fine header completed the scoring move that had its roots deep in East London.

'But basically the game for me is all about that minute in injury time. Martin has put us in front, and though we are all brought up to play right until the final whistle, you sense that it's getting nearer and nearer.

'When you look back at it now, I'm always amazed at what an innocuous incident the free-kick was given for. But what catastrophies stemmed from it.'

Bobby Moore is among the many who still believe that Schnellinger's

*Pelé, always a great admirer of Moore's play, sought him out for an exchange of shirts after the game against Brazil in 1970. The England captain had given yet another text-book display, highlighted by a superb tackle on Jairzinho, but the result (as for five other boys of '66 in the side) brought the first taste of World Cup defeat.*

hand-ball was intentional and that England should not have been forced to endure extra time. Nevertheless it gave him one more platform to show off his pedigree. He still laughingly refers to England owing their victory to 'the best appeal of all time'. But his class ensured that any debate over the third goal could be easily settled by reference to England's fourth.

If any one moment in his glittering career encapsulated Moore's philosophy it came in the creating of the moment that led to Geoff Hurst's hat-trick. Jack Charlton would have had the ball in the stands, but a different kind of upbringing took over.

'It's always been in my manner to try and play, whereas others with another type of make-up might have tried just to hit a corner-flag ball in that type of situation. The space was there, and they had thrown caution to the wind, and it gave us the opportunity to get in behind them. It was the best way of finishing the game as it turned out.'

A modest description underselling a superb pass that again was a feature of West Ham's play. The satisfaction of the goal blended into the joy of the final whistle.

'I was elated but then who wouldn't be in that sort of situation. I looked around and saw Jack Charlton on his knees...Some lads were crying... Others just running around in ecstasy. The one thing you obviously got, when you sit back and think about it, is the tremendous satisfaction of

*A rare moment of relaxation against Liverpool at Upton Park. Moore's quick humour and sense of fun has usually been kept under wraps in public; the image, in fact, was always one of great self-control, both on and off the pitch.*

*Consolation from West Ham team-mates Billy Bonds and Graham Paddon after Fulham's 2-0 defeat in the 1975 FA Cup final. It was his first failure in four finals at Wembley.*

achieving what you set out to do... and of reaching the highest pinnacle in the career you have chosen. But at the time events happen so quick. Everything is arranged and pre-planned by the organisers. You're shuffled from one place to the next... and before you know where you are it's all over.'

The World Cup final was Bobby Moore's 47th cap. By the time he played his last international, his 108th, against Italy at Wembley in November 1973, he had set records that will stand the test of time. More than half of his England days were spent trying to emulate the achievement of 1966, and it was the failure to qualify for the 1974 finals that effectively ended his appearances for his country—only a matter of months before Ramsey (Moore's manager in

100 matches) was also discarded.

In 1970, as both men strived to repeat England's success, fate again cast a shadow over Moore's appearance in the competition. Ramsey's acclimatisation period in South America included a warm-up game in Colombia. There, an innocent search for a present for Bobby Charlton's wife Norma ended in the notorious episode that whisked the Mexico World Cup from the back to the front pages of Fleet Street.

What has passed into history as the 'Bogota affair' took place in the shopping area of the Hotel Tequendama. The central figure was Clara Padilla, who claimed that Moore had pilfered a trinket worth in excess of £600. Alan Mullery, another member of the squad, put the fiasco in perspective: 'Steal a bracelet? With Bob's money he could have bought the shop. It's ridiculous.'

Nevertheless the Colombians' attempts at seeking 'justice' tested even the considerable nerve of England's captain. Ironically Moore was detained only because of Ramsey's own thoroughness. With Moore, England had left Bogota for Quito, where another pre-World Cup international was played. To fly from Ecuador to Mexico City the England party had to change planes in Bogota, and to kill time Ramsey had arranged the showing of the feature film *Shenendoah*. To provide a comfortable break, the party then returned to the Hotel Tequendama.

It was there that Moore was arrested, taken to a jail—and then, at the 11th hour, allowed the 'courtesy' of house arrest. The England party kept to their schedule, with Ramsey.

On Monday 27 May, Bobby Moore played one of the coolest 90 minutes of his life. In a reconstruction in front of a Colombian judge his own innate sense of advocacy broke down the shopgirl's false accusations. It was a further two days, though, before he was allowed to leave the country, and it was another five years before the Colombian authorities finally put an official closure to their inquiries. It remains the one subject about which Bobby Moore can still lose his famous composure; he has often felt that his innocence has never been acknowledged as fully as it should have been.

The saga perhaps sharpened his competitive instincts for the 1970 World Cup, when he again produced a succession of peerless performances, notably against Brazil.

This time, however, a contest with West Germany, the quarter-final in León, had an outcome totally opposite to the joy of 1966. After the 3-2 extra-time defeat the desolation of the moment remains firmly in the Moore memory. 'Alf was trying to console the players. Some were in tears. Everywhere he was looking at blank faces with sunken eyes, and he must have been thinking "What can I say to them?"

'Really the silence said it all. Everyone in their own mind was trying to work out what had happened. Though I've had some bad personal moments this was by far the worst in a team situation. Nobody could believe that we'd lost. We'd played brilliantly against Brazil and against West Germany, by far our two best performances in the competition. Yet

*The man who so often captained England leads out 'Team America' for the bicentennial game against Don Revie's side at Philadelphia in May 1976. Though Alan Ball was the last of the 1966 line-up to play for England— his final game was against Scotland a year before—Moore can claim to the player who appeared most recently in an international. He was then with San Antonio Thunder.*

*A parting wave as Moore says farewell to League football at Ewood Park on 14 May 1977, when Blackburn beat Fulham 2-0 in what was his 804th competitive club game. Always in good trim, he missed just two matches in his last season. The following year, aged 37, he played seven times for Seattle Sounders in the NASL to round off his 20-year career.*

we'd lost both of those games.'

The following domestic season also had more than its share of problems. There were threats to Tina and to his two children, Dean and Roberta, which brought a police guard to the Moore household. Another distressing episode centred on an anonymous Saturday lunch-time call to Tina that Bobby would be shot during that afternoon's match. At the final whistle, to his own surprise, he was encircled by police but safely bundled down the Upton Park tunnel. But he was shot down, metaphorically, for staying out with Jimmy Greaves, Brian Dear and Clyde Best at a Blackpool night-club until one o'clock on the eve of a third round FA Cup tie against Second Division Blackpool. West Ham, dreadfully brittle at times against lower division opposition, succumbed 4-0 on an ice-rink of a pitch. Moore, Greaves and Dear

were suspended for two weeks and fined a week's wages. Ironically the announcement of Ron Greenwood's sentence was withheld until Bobby had been featured on *This Is Your Life*. The suspension cost him his place in England's European Championship match in Malta.

The final chapter of Moore's playing days was written in West London, in the friendly surroundings of Alec Stock's Fulham—not quite the perfect setting for the family-named Robert Frederick *Chelsea* Moore. But the transfer, in March 1974, was a prelude to one more romantic journey to Wembley. Fulham cavorted happily through a succession of potentially fatal Cup ties until an extra-time goal by John Mitchell at Maine Road took them into the final itself. The opposition could have been hand-picked by their most senior player: First Division West Ham United.

The Cup run itself had its omens, notably the night after Fulham had upset Everton at Goodison Park in the fifth round. The burglar who picked his way into Bobby Moore's home possessed a sufficient combination of football knowledge and sentiment to leave behind, stacked on the lawn, his collection of souvenirs from the game.

When asked now where he keeps his World Cup medal, the answer is 'a safe place...they're things that people love to see and things that you love to show people. But they're irreplaceable.' Those locked-away mementoes include the red shirt he wore on Saturday 30 July 1966.

Moore's role at the tiller steered Fulham through a number of storms along the voyage to the Cup final. I was one of a number of fortunate reporters who were welcomed into the Craven Cottage family as their remarkable season took shape. Those Second Division players who had never savoured such experiences constantly looked to Moore and Alan Mullery for guidance. Less than 24 hours before the Wembley kick-off I watched Moore's considerable sense of humour—often kept under wraps on more public occasions—defuse a situation which could have disturbed the players.

Fulham were involved in a wrangle over which boots they were contracted to wear at Wembley. The calm of

Friday afternoon's tea at the West Lodge Park Hotel in Hadley Wood was shattered by the arrival of a bailiff brandishing a writ issued by an aggrieved manufacturer. Tension threatened to sweep over the relaxed atmosphere until Moore cracked the joke that put the younger Fulham players' back at ease: 'Now we've got an outside-writ, an inside-writ and a writ-half!'

Fulham's fairy-tale, however, held no happy ending. Bobby Moore's last big occasion ended in a 2-0 defeat. At the end he strode head high from the ground he had graced so many times. Again a public front hid his bitter disappointment at leaving a loser for the first time in a final.

Retirement came two years later, and with it a greater reliance on the business interests that were initially fostered by his central role in the winning of the World Cup. But like many top-class sportsmen he has found star athletic success has not been a guarantee of commercial boom. Bobby Moore is not the millionaire that seemed so likely when he was the most fashionable footballer at a time when the business world was intent on exploiting his name.

'Lots of business associations I've had throughout my career have been in name only. From my own point of view there has been only one really costly exercise, which was the country club affair. You can't stop people forming opinions about the worth or cost of other involvements.

'Sure, if it had all gone well the financial aspect of it might have been absolutely tremendous. Some deals did go wrong...but they haven't been particularly costly to me. I don't have any regrets about what's happened. The main thing, which I've said all along...and which is the greatest reason why all the commercial aspects haven't been as sound as they might have been in the past...is that football has always been a full-time commitment, and you're always relying on other people.'

The country club, at Woolston Hall, right in the heart of an affluent part of Essex, was envisaged in 1971. Sean Connery was another of the partners in a venture that appeared to be totally sound. The club began trading in 1972, but after two years of escalating losses the consortium sold out. Moore found that his position as a guarantor took an even greater toll, and the final reckoning ran into a hefty five-figure loss.

As a player Moore acted under the business guidance of Jack Turner, who for a long time was employed by West Ham. The two developed a much closer relationship than the usual player-agent arrangement. Newspaper columns, public appearances and a successful sports goods shop opposite Upton Park were just some of the profitable enterprises. Turner, also, felt a genuine responsibility towards the good name of his client: Moore would not advertise any product he did not believe in, and refused to accept a fee for taking part in a national anti-smoking campaign.

In 1981 Moore is still very much the businessman. A public house company which began, in the latter stages of his playing career, with the opening of *Mooro's* in Stratford, has swollen to four tied houses with Watney Mann and a freehold establishment on the border of Essex and Hertfordshire.

At the same time he was embarking on the second year of Bobby Moore Soccer Schools, an enterprise instituted by Corals Leisure Group. When that organisation withdrew its support Moore had been so stimulated by the reaction of the youngsters that he took over the project himself.

'You get to a stage when you do appreciate that your life and your main business has always been around

*Tony Rosser, chairman of Free Newspapers, welcomes Moore to Oxford City as manager on 12 December 1979, just 10 days after his company, a group comprising 11 weeklies, had taken over the Isthmian League Premier Division club. Despite rumours of links with various clubs over the years, both big and small, this was his first managerial post. Promotion work for Rosser's firm is built into his contract, and he still retains a number of successful business interests, mainly through his pubs.*

*'Former England captain Bobby Moore and his wife Tina with Margaret Thatcher at a Central Council for Physical Recreation reception on Tuesday night... (16.12.75)...' Moore was perfectly cast for the part he played, though many accused him of image-building. 'As England's captain I just dealt with things as they came along,' he says. 'The only thing I worked at was my job... learning the game. And I worked hard at that.'*

football. This is why I've now become involved in the other sides of it... the managerial work with Oxford City, and taking on the soccer schools. It's not only a business with a fair amount of potential...it's also a terrific way of passing on knowledge and information to those youngsters who love the game.'

Bobby Moore was made to measure for his role as England's leader, but denies that there was any premeditation involved in coping with the demands of the job. 'It's like now starting to become a football manager. You don't know what the next test is going to be. As England's captain I just dealt with situations as they came along. And I did it in a manner which was myself. The natural me!'

The natural Bobby Moore is in fact very approachable. He has always possessed the footballers in-bred sense of fun. His sociability would surprise those who have viewed him only from afar. Jeff Powell's sensitive portrait includes one example of the difficulties Moore's image has sometimes unwittingly caused:

'Alan Ball highlighted to me how people had trouble getting close to me. The first time he got picked for England he went back to Blackpool, his club at the time, and all the players asked him what Bobby Moore was like. He told them: "Just like the rest of you". They said: "Don't believe you". Once you're put on a pedestal where no-one thinks you're touchable, you can't convince them that you're the same as them.'

By returning to football at the humble level of the Isthmian League, Bobby Moore has surely proved that he does not believe he is 'above' the ordinary person, though he is aware of cynical remarks about his motives. Those cynics should look closely at his comments when I asked him finally to place the World Cup in the context of his life:

'Obviously it's the pinnacle. You can't get any higher. But I can also remember the satisfaction, which still stands out in my mind, from when we beat Manchester United 3-1 in the FA Cup semi-final in 1964.

'And recently I was thrilled when Oxford City beat Slough, the Premier Division leaders of the Isthmian League, in a friendly. It was an indication of the progress we'd made and I came into the dressing-room with the old fists raised in triumph...'

# ALAN BALL

**Born Farnworth, near Bolton, 12 May 1945; Farnworth Grammar School; joined Bolton 1960 but rejected 1961 as 'too small'; joined Blackpool Sep. 1961 and turned pro May 1962; League debut 20 Aug. 1962 v Ipswich (home, 1-0); after 7 of 8 Under-23 caps made full England debut v Yugoslavia (as No 10) in Belgrade 9 May 1965 (1-1)...**

My telephone rang. 'Ballie here,' said the voice at the other end of the line, still distinctively high-pitched enough not to require the identification. 'Yes, come down if you want a chat. Be delighted...as long as I'm not racing.'

'Come down' meant to Southampton, where he had just bounced back into First Division football as a player two months short of his 36th birthday. When we met Southampton had won the first two games of his return to the club he had left in March 1980 for a tilt at football management.

A year in charge at Blackpool had ended with the sack. I had been pencilling in my intended visit to talk about the World Cup since November 1980, but I kept putting it off until Blackpool won a game. Their next victory did not come until 21 February; nine days later Alan Ball was out of a job. Five days after that he turned out for Southampton against Manchester United.

The saga was totally in character with the most passionate, most overtly competitive of the boys of '66. Ball was born just a few days after VE-Day, and victory has always been his prime motivator. He cultivated the habit of signing autographs with the postscript WIN, like others might put OBE, or BBC Television. An outstanding career that included 72 England caps has been scarred with brushes with authority and shows of petulance, but his bursts of temper have usually been a product of his caring, of his wanting to be the best at his job.

Alan Ball arrived at Wembley in 1966 on course towards becoming a great player, a life plan mapped out by his father Alan Ball senior, a former professional with Birmingham, Oldham and Southport, and later a manager with a list of clubs almost as long and varied as a railway timetable. Once, when his father scored a goal in a Cup tie at Accrington, Ball junior ran onto the pitch and had to be carried off by the referee. Referees would later escort him from the playing area in more sensational circumstances, but clearly Alan Ball, as much as is possible, was shaped to be a footballer.

His precocious talent took him to Blackpool, where Sir Stanley Matthews once had him hauled out of a practice match because he insisted on playing passes to make the elderly 'wizard of dribble' run rather than deliver the ball to the famous feet. By 1966 Everton, Leeds and Stoke were disputing over purchasing Ball's gifts; indeed two weeks after the World Cup had been won Blackpool sold him to Everton for £110,000—a fee so massive at the time that Brian James asked in the *Daily Mail*: 'Can soccer afford so much for one man?'

From the start Ball revealed a combative nature which threatened his international career. In 1965 he was sent off in an Under-23 match against Austria. Ramsey issued a stern warning, but Ball still lined up, a raw 21-year-old, as England opened the World Cup with the frustrating goalless draw against Uruguay. He was then omitted from the next two group games, but while England's team against Argentina in the quarter-final is often recalled for Geoff Hurst stepping in for the injured Jimmy Greaves, there was one other change which helped Ramsey achieve the balance he craved: Ian Callaghan gave way to Alan Ball.

Today Ball's memories of the 1966 World Cup final are sketchy...a fact which frustrates him. 'I wish it could happen to me now. I want something like winning the World Cup again in my life. But then it didn't mean all that much to me. It was just a matter-of-fact job for me. Winning a Cup final. I was just a kid.

*Everton manager Harry Catterick welcomes the 21-year-old Ball to his first training session at Goodison after his British record £110,000 transfer—just 16 days after the World Cup final. Ball's fine performance at Wembley had sharpened the interest in him, and Stoke and Leeds also matched the figure. Ball chose the Cup holders, the nearest club to home—a decision that thwarted Don Revie's determined attempts to create the 'greatest midfield ever' of Ball, Bremner and Giles.*

Only now do I really appreciate it.

'Alf didn't tell me until quite late whether I was playing or not. I think he was worried about me being nervous. But I was too young to have any nerves.'

On the morning of the match Ball lazed alone in his room, high in the attic of the Hendon Hall Hotel, while his room-mate Nobby Stiles had gone to church. At the stadium the message of his father's telegram echoed in his ears as he got changed: 'You're there. Don't miss a minute of it. Be magic, little man.'

The little man was just that. His wholehearted commitment harrassed West Germany through normal time, and in the next 30 minutes gave England a precious extra gear. 'It was the most instinctive game I've ever played in my life. I just played. I didn't play to any orders. I just worked and ran and played football. And thoroughly enjoyed it. It's difficult to recollect the match except that I gave everything I had.

'There was no set pattern really. It was a one-off game that we just had to win. And we did it by everyone giving everything that they had...in a team performance. I had young legs which kept me running, and I just kept saying to myself in extra time: "We just can't get beat. Keep going. Work...work. It'll come right." And thank God it did.'

Ball acknowledges, like so many of the squad, that thanks were also due to Bakhramov, the Russian linesman. 'I remember Nobby Stiles hitting a long ball down the line, and I thought "Oh, no!" But I had to go for it and I got it. I crossed it...and ran off the pitch as Geoff Hurst rattled the bar. I was probably in the best position, apart from Roger Hunt, to see whether it was in or not. I was right on the line...but to be honest with you I couldn't tell whether it was a goal or not.

'I was very close to the linesman and I saw the referee come across. The linesman just said one word: "Goal". But I don't think he could have seen it because I was in a better position than him.'

Ball might have joined the list of scorers when England broke away in the dying moments of extra time. He sprinted forward, in that characteristic pumping style, alongside Hurst:

'I was shouting at Geoff because really he should have given the ball to me. We broke when Bobby Moore hit this great ball. I can always remember running square with Geoff, and we're two against one. Everybody else was dead. I was screaming to him to square it to me and I could've walked it in. I was just about to curse him for being greedy, and then I had to change my tune. The curses stuck in my throat and then I was yelling.

'Then at the final whistle I saw the older players...like Jackie Charlton...Bobby Charlton...they all broke up in tears. And I wondered what it was all about. I would be like that if it happened to me now. But then I just wanted to get my medal, give it to my mum or my dad, and take my girlfriend out. And I can remember Alf being tremendous to me. As we walked off the pitch, he said to me. "Well done. You'll never play better in your life again".'

Ball and Stiles swapped their shirts after the game, and later Ball chose his mother as the recipient of his medal—a decision that kept it safe when his own house in Worsley was burgled six years later.

So at 21 Alan Ball had achieved the greatest reward in the game, and justified the lifestyle according to the sternest of rules set up by his father. He once admitted that he never squeezed the spots on his face because

he wanted to 'be repulsive and keep the girls away.' Lesley Newton, however, was the exception. On Alan's 21st birthday they became engaged, and Lesley shared the post-World Cup celebrations, courtesy of Danny La Rue, with the Stiles and the Hursts. They were married in May 1967.

His greying memories of the World Cup details have not disturbed his view of the reasons for England's success. 'Good players, complementing each other. Alf saw the blend, and he knew what he wanted. He pulled us all together and tidied everything up. A very honest man...a very emotional man...a different class fella, really.

'He knew when and where to play each player. He brought me back for the Argentina game, when he knew it would be hard, and he knew I was the right type of player for that game. Then it was up to me to stay in the side. There were so many good players there, but he knew what he wanted. And most important the players knew that he knew what he wanted.

'But the only thing the World Cup did for me was to give me something to tell my kids about. I'm a professional and I played in a final for my country, which any person my age would have died to do. It was a job of work to me. I can't say it was any more. I wish I could. But the older I got, the more it meant to me, the more pride I got in playing for my country. I wish I could play for my country in the next international. It would mean far more to me than playing in the World Cup final. Because I'm at an age now when I would appreciate it all.'

Certainly that sample early in his career did not mar Alan Ball's taste for success. In fact it sharpened it. His transfer to Everton opened the way

*ABOVE: Ball and Howard Kendall, who with Colin Harvey formed the midfield trio on whose work and creative skills the Everton League title team of 1970 was built.*

*BELOW: A congratulatory pat from full-back Keith Newton after the 1970 Charity Shield win over Chelsea.*

to further honours. In 1968 there were two near misses—runner-up in the FA Cup to West Bromwich Albion and third with England in the European Championship. In 1970 Everton won the League Championship, their platform built by the midfield of Ball, Colin Harvey and Howard Kendall.

Eighteen months later, however, Everton were prepared to create a new team without him. He was sold to Arsenal for another British record of £220,000, a switch that led to another FA Cup disappointment—the defeat by Leeds United in the centenary final of 1972. Ball revelled in the style of Arsenal, a club rightly renowned throughout the game for providing the very best for their playing staff. That chapter, however, would have an acrimonious ending, as would his England playing days.

Ball went to Mexico with Ramsey for the 1970 World Cup finals, playing in all four of England's games, including an appearance as substitute for Bobby Charlton against Czechoslovakia. His shot against the Brazilian bar might have turned that defeat into a draw, but he too was sucked into the whirlpool of disaster as the Jules Rimet Trophy slithered from England's grip in León. No England player felt the loss to West Germany more painfully.

He remained in Ramsey's plans until a double failure to beat Poland effectively ended an era. Ball very nearly perished with his manager. On 6 June 1973 in Katowice, England lost their World Cup qualifying game—and Ball was sent off for grabbing Cmiekiewicz by the throat and pushing the Polish defender to the ground after the Pole had kicked Martin Peters in the face.

It was his fourth dismissal, following the Under-23 episode, and transgressions for Everton against Newcastle in 1968 and for Arsenal at Sheffield United in October 1972. The international punishment, suspension for two World Cup games, included the return with Poland; when he left the Katowice pitch Ball was walking away from World Cup football for the last time.

Ramsey took a sympathetic view. 'When I'd been in trouble playing for Alf before he'd really told me off. But this time he sympathised with me...sat up half the night with me. He realised how distraught I was. He just knocked on the door and he was there. If I'd been in the wrong he'd have told me so. He knew how I felt and he did something to ease it. A marvellous man.'

Ramsey would have only six matches left, and Alan Ball played in only a handful of minutes of the very last, in Portugal, where he was not an original selection. But when injuries disrupted Ramsey's planning, Ball happily rushed to the airport to make up the numbers. A month later he broke his left leg playing against Queen's Park Rangers. It was the same week the FA sacked Ramsey, and Ball remembers with deep emotion that Ramsey still found time to write a consoling letter about his injury.

In the early weeks of the following season Ball broke a bone in his left ankle and was kept restlessly on the sidelines for another seven weeks. Overcoming that—and a fifth sending-off, at Derby in February 1975—he clawed his way back into the England set-up, now under the aegis of Don Revie. That, too, would end with a letter...but one which was received with distinctly less respect.

The relationship between Revie and Ball went back a long way. Revie had tried to sign him for Leeds United when he was a raw recruit at Blackpool. If Ball held misgivings about his style of management they were all dispelled when Revie not only recalled him to the England team but, in his 67th international, chose him for the first time as captain. The fact that the opposition was West Germany—including Beckenbauer from '66—added extra cream to the treat. At the time Ball declared: 'This must be the highest point of my career. Even better than winning the World Cup in 1966. I'll take some shaking off. I don't need two hands to grasp the chance. Just one's enough to hold on.'

England overcame the world champions 2-0, then crushed Cyprus with all five goals from Malcolm Macdonald. Kevin Keegan was the only scorer in the return in Limassol, with Ball continuing his spell of leadership into the home internationals. England drew in Belfast and against Wales at Wembley before winning the British Championship

with a thumping 5-1 win over Scotland, again at Wembley.

Ball shared Ramsey's passion for beating the Scots, and I was one of a number of reporters who were happily embraced by England's captain in the immediate joy of the occasion. Revie had never hidden his initial belief that the appointment had been short-term, but he had also made it clear that if Ball continued to measure up to the role as a player the captaincy would remain his property. Against Scotland he had been at his most inspiring and creative.

But on 19 August Don Revie dictated a letter, thanking Ball for his contribution but dropping him from the captaincy and the squad of players. Various theories have been put forward as to why the England manager pulled the trigger. There was a much-publicised incident at Ascot racecourse during that summer in which the behaviour of Ball and Alan Hudson was called into question. Ball also

admits to breaking a curfew during a voluntary get-together for Revie's England players.

Today Alan Ball is unrepentant. 'I'll always thank Don Revie for making me captain. That first time against West Germany was such a proud moment. But I got 72 caps for my country, and he cut me well short. I would have got a hundred. I was good enough at that time. I've never discussed it with him since, and I'll never forgive him.' The deep disappointment was aggravated by the lack of Revie's personal signature on the letter, which was 'dictated and signed during his absence.'

The following year Ball left Arsenal after falling out with new manager Terry Neill. To the annoyance of his father he dropped down into the Second Division. Southampton paid £60,000 for his influence—one which, within 18 months, provided a strong base for their promotion. Ball, who freely admits that he needs to be

*Ball has never been a player to hide his feelings—this time in the World Cup against the Czechs in Guadalajara, when he came on as sub for Bobby Charlton. His desperate desire to be a winner, instilled from the pram by his footballing father, has led to a career peppered with confrontation and blighted by six sendings-off.*

*Balance and control for Arsenal. Ball broke the transfer record for a second time when the Gunners signed him from Everton for £220,000 in December 1971, but success eluded him at Highbury. He was in fact a loser in all three of his Wembley club finals; once with Everton, once with Arsenal and once with Southampton.*

appreciated, to be 'loved', found that type of relationship with manager Lawrie McMenemy. After that successful 1977–78 season he declared: 'My life has changed since I came to Southampton. Lawrie McMenemy has given me stability and the kind of affection in football that I haven't had since Sir Alf Ramsey was in charge of England. I don't think I've ever been happier. I love the big fella.'

In December 1978 Ball and Revie were bracketed together for one last time, an unhappy episode in which the FA fined Ball £3,000 for admitting in his book—*It's All About A Ball*, that he received questionable payments from Don Revie in 1966. At the same hearing Revie received his ban from British football for his defection from the England manager's position to the Middle East.

The severity of Ball's fine was eased when McMenemy allowed him to fix a lucrative deal with Vancouver Whitecaps of the North American

Soccer League for the summer of 1979. He had spent the previous summer in Philadelphia, where another controversial episode included the sixth sending-off of his career, for fighting with another Englishman, Len Cantello of Dallas Tornado.

Vancouver offered a far happier experience. In September 1979 I was in New York to watch him lead the Canadian club to the League championship, the winning of the Soccer Bowl against Tampa Bay Rowdies. In the style of the Americans, Alan Ball was named the game's Most Valuable Player. Most important to him though was that he had become a winner again—six months after reaching the League Cup final with Southampton but leaving Wembley, seemingly for the last time, a loser to Nottingham Forest.

Ball's life has rarely been less than complicated, typified by the announcement on 18 February 1980 that he had accepted an offer from his first club,

Blackpool, to become their player-manager. The complications involved the month of his playing commitment to Southampton that he still had to fulfil, *and* a contract to return to Vancouver for the summer. To compound the problem Blackpool were teetering on the brink of dropping into the Fourth Division for the first time in their history.

Amid this chaos of conflicting responsibilities, Ball travelled north to take charge of Blackpool for the first time—a Friday night home fixture against Colchester, themselves worried but about the more palatable problem of whether they would win promotion. I was despatched to cover the game for ITV's *On the Ball*.

The script was pure Hollywood. Ball took a pre-match bow in the glare of the television lights in front of a crowd that had almost doubled because of his presence. Blackpool had lost their previous four games, but in front of their new boss won 1-0 with a goal from Tony Kellow. Ball answered my post-match questions with the aplomb of a practised manager. Despite his subsequent return to Canada, Blackpool avoided relegation with a good late run.

The sweet honeymoon was followed by a short, unhappy marriage. A year later Blackpool terminated his contract, with the club again staring Fourth Division football in the face. Within the game the Ball style had been criticised for being too demanding for lower division players. Certainly his lucrative contract seemed beyond Blackpool, who were reported to be losing £5,000 a week at the time.

By returning quickly to the First Division as a player some of the hurt evaporated...but not all. 'I made mistakes, but they were that I was too strong. I flew in people's faces. People told me that I shouldn't do things but I find it hard to go against my own beliefs. And if I've got to learn a lesson, it's that . . . to say Yes, sir, No, sir, I'm sorry, sir. I'll find it hard but I'll have to do it I suppose.

'I'm a good coach, and I've never taken a badge. I know the game...it's as simple as that. And people will have to put up with my shortcomings if they want somebody who knows the game. The shortcomings? My strength. I'm a strong person, and I just don't suffer people who don't

feel the same as me. They've got to love me. The more they love me the more they get from me.

'When they told me I was sacked I felt hard...I felt cold...I felt empty. And I battled them for my compensation, which I hated because I hate talking about money. As I walked out I said to myself: "Ballie, you've go to go get yourself a job, son." Within the week I played in the First Division.

'I phoned Lawrie McMenemy to ask him the best way to go about my compensation. He gave me the advice I wanted, and then he said that he might have a little proposition for me and to stay in the house. And he came up with the offer to play for Southampton for the rest of the season. That suited me, because it was down to me to convince him that I should have a contract for next season. That's the way I like it.'

For Alan Ball it represented another gamble, an instinct that's the key to

*Pictured with wife Lesley in 1978. As a Blackpool hairdresser, she was his girlfriend during the 1966 World Cup, and they married the following year. Ball says the loyalty and love of his family—he now has two daughters and a son—have provided him with the support he has needed to survive in football.*

understanding his maverick nature. Though he no longer owns horses himself, the flavour of the racetrack is addictive to him. 'I love the sport. It relaxes me. I love the people in it. The characters...the gamblers. I love people who are down to their last pound who come up with a thousand pounds. Those are my sort of people because they'll always have a go in life.'

If football has enabled Alan Ball to pay for such an expensive hobby, the love and loyalty of his family have provided him with the support to survive in football. Alan talks of the 'strength' that Amanda, the eldest of his three children, has had to show at school as the daughter of a famous father. Keely, a second daughter, was born at the time of his transfer to Arsenal. Son Jimmy is the youngest of the three, born when dad was on the Arsenal transfer list in 1975.

But when one thinks of the Ball family, the Svengali influence of his father—whose presence alongside his career continued in a consultative role at Blackpool—always remains near the surface. So how much of Alan junior's positive attitude is a product of his upbringing? 'You never know, do you? I didn't know where thank you came from, or I'm sorry. I didn't know where my manners came from, my habits. They were just there. I'd like to think that my dad has given me good habits both as a professional footballer and in life. We've stayed

together all the way through. Of course we row from time to time. But if you're too nice all the time then you're false.'

In 1981 Alan Ball continued to make the headlines, wearing his emotions on his shirt. His obsession with winning—he once deceived an opponent, Sean Haslegrave of Stoke City, by changing the pitch of his voice in calling for the ball before scoring a First Division goal—makes it easy to assess his importance to England and Alf Ramsey in 1966. Even though he was the junior member of the side, his approach to the occasion needed little shaping.

The World Cup is rarely now in his thoughts. 'The only time I think about it is when people mention it to me. It's not something I need in my life to tell people about. And I hope I never have to capitalise on it. When I'm with the other lads who played I do get a feeling that it was something that we shared together.

'The future now is how I want my life. It's all down to me. Backs against the wall. It's up to me to graft. That's the only way to play your football...that's the only way to be in life.

'And when I come to the end, I want to go racing every day...'

*BELOW RIGHT: Player-manager Ball shows Paul Gardner how it should be done at a Blackpool training session. In March 1981, after a year in charge but with the side one from bottom of the Third Division and sinking, his old club gave him the sack.*

*BELOW: Within days he had rejoined Mike Channon at Southampton as a player, despite overtures from Bolton, Derby and Geoff Hurst's Chelsea; 15 years after the World Cup final, Alan Ball was still playing football—and in the First Division.*

# BOBBY CHARLTON

Born Ashington, Northumberland, 11 Oct. 1937; Bealington Grammar School; 4 schoolboy caps 1953; chose Manchester U. from 18 clubs June 1953 and turned pro Oct. 1954; 1 youth cap 1954; League debut 6 Oct. 1956 v Charlton (home, 4-2) scoring twice; FA Cup final 1957; survived Munich crash Feb. 1958 and became focus of rebuilt United; full England debut at Hampden 19 April 1958 (4-0), scoring with spectacular volley; dropped after 3 games and despite press campaign missed World Cup matches; returned next season; also 6 Under-23 caps 1958–60; helped United to FA Cup win 1963, League title 1965; converted by Matt Busby to midfield general 1964, Ramsey following suit 1965; Britain's best-known player before and after 1966 series...

One warm afternoon in June 1980 I was killing time at the Sao Paulo Stadium in Naples, where that evening Italy would play Czechoslovakia for third place in the European Championship. With the kick-off still some three hours away, two ageing Italian gatemen on duty represented my only company.

A few poorly pronounced words soon exhausted our knowledge of each other's native tongue, and the conversation was in sharp danger of closing until one of the two Italians uttered the two words of English he knew best. 'Ah, Bobby Charlton!' He could not have spoken the name with more reverence.

The object of their worship was attending the match in his capacity as a television pundit, and Bobby Charlton duly arrived. He happily dispensed autographs and BBC badges to my companions, who greeted him as breathlessly and as wide-eyed as any teenager faced by a favourite pop-star.

It was a scene that is regularly repeated all over the world. In England Bobby Charlton ranks high on the short-list of sportsmen who are genuinely loved as well as respected. The type that if they were buildings a preservation order would be issued on them. Abroad he is no less appreciated, both as a great player and as a gentleman of the game. The passing of time has done nothing to diminish his reputation.

Today Bobby Charlton sees plenty of that world. As a partner in a travel agency with three retail outlets in the Manchester area, he still gets about. When we met in the traditional rain of the north-west his all-year tan shone through, this time the legacy of a trip to Kenya. Japan and Hong Kong were on his forthcoming schedule, the centre of such journeys often an appearance in a match for charity.

Jack Charlton still jokes that 'our kid will go anywhere for a game of football.' Bobby remembered a week in Australia where business was way down the list of priorities and one match was by far the main reason for such a long trip. On his office desk lay a file containing the details of an intended match between the England and West German squads of 1966. So even in 1981 the World Cup was not far from his mind.

'Ray Wilson and I were in the same room and we used to travel everywhere together, and we never believed for a moment that we weren't going to win. And we were beating them. But when they equalised in the last minute, I thought that there was at least ten minutes to quarter of an hour to go. I'd lost all sense of time.'

Bobby Charlton's recollections also throw new light on the dispute involving the legality of England's third goal. Charlton's high quality as a player has always been married to integrity, and his testimony on the issue of Hurst's second goal bears the stamp of an expert witness. 'The ball definitely crossed the line. I was right there and I saw it with my own eyes. I was positive, and at the time I was really frustrated because I thought the linesman was flagging to disallow the goal.

'When Geoff Hurst got it, I've moved forward in case he pulled one square. So I was right in position to see. They've used these telescopic devices and sometimes it looks now as though the ball didn't cross the line. But it was over. It *was* over.'

Charlton asked particularly about

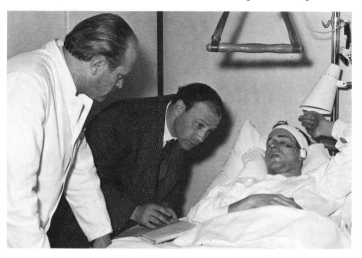

my visit to Ray Wilson, his firm friend from 1966. 'He never wants to come out of the hills now, does he?' The pair shared much of their international experience, including the build-up to the World Cup final. Bobby easily recalled the Saturday morning shopping trip that had also stuck in the memory of his old room-mate.

'We went down to Golders Green. I'm not sure what we went for... maybe to change a shirt or something like that. Really it was just to get out...to get the time passed so that we could get on with the game.

'Little Ray was superstitious. Our Jack was the same. One or two others as well. And they tried to do the same things before every game. I'm not superstitious at all. But I went along with most of it. Ray would carry the bag which had both our sets of boots in. He would throw the boots to me one at a time. Another part of the

*ABOVE: Flashback to 1958: 20-year-old Charlton gives a bed-side interview the day after the Munich air crash, in which eight team-mates died. Only two months later he scored on his international debut at Hampden.*

*RIGHT: Ten years on —and Manchester United have attained the dream shattered at Munich with a 4-1 win over Benfica. Charlton shares the joy with Nobby Stiles and Bill Foulkes, the other survivor from 1958 playing that night. Charlton finds it impossible to say which of the two Wembley wins means most to him. 'I've got to put them together because they were different types of successes.'*

ritual was that I had to sniff at a smelling-salt capsule. It was a formula that we always seemed to fit into. And on that particular day we were meticulous about it.

'I'll never forget the journey to Wembley, because you've got to remember that we'd been sheltered from the public. It had been a routine of stadium, training ground, hotel all through the competition. Not until that day did it really get through to us how important it all was. We drove past Hendon fire station, and they'd brought all the fire engines out. When we actually won and we were going back through London to the Royal Garden Hotel there was no one on that route who wasn't hanging out of the window. And I thought "Hell, what if we'd have lost today!"'

Most of those supporters would have put Charlton top of the list of players likely to be England's match-winner against West Germany. His superbly struck 30-yard shot had got England off the mark against Mexico. He, too, had settled the more poetic semi-final against Portugal, with both the goals that took England into the final.

Yet his role against West Germany was more restricted. Franz Beckenbauer, less experienced then than Bobby Charlton but on the verge of becoming no less a world-class player, locked into a midfield duel that had a cancelling affect on both players.

'I didn't really contribute much from a forward point of view. I had a couple of cracks at goal, one of which glanced against the post. But I had to keep to the pattern of play, the system which didn't allow for any passengers. My job was to watch Beckenbauer, and he was always looking to get forward. I knew that if I ran with him I'd be able to stop him playing. And he was never without me during the whole match.

'That probably stopped me doing a few things, but weighing up the percentages I thought that was the best way of doing it. Midfield suited me a treat, because it gave me freedom to run all over the place. Some people used to say, in fact, that it was a fault of mine that I used to waste energy going everywhere. But I loved coming from midfield because I could go and get the ball off the full-backs or the goalkeeper. When I played on the wing for England I used to hate it because I depended so much on other people giving me the ball.

'I wasn't a strong tackler. But what I did do, whether I had defensive qualities or not, was to get the right side of the player. And that was all Alf Ramsey ever asked me for. But I felt more like a forward, more that it was my job to avoid players rather than to get in to contact with them. So I tried to get as many goals as I could, but also to have enough defensive attributes as well.'

Bobby Charlton's contribution to the final was couched in unselfish terms. His feared shooting only surfaced genuinely in extra time when one left-foot effort rebounded off Tilkowski's post to strike the goalkeeper in the face before the German defence cleared the danger. The most vivid picture of Bobby at the final remains of his tearful reaction to the victory.

'I'd never cried before over a football match. But I suppose we'd been working together for weeks and weeks and weeks. And we'd achieved the ultimate. The sound of the emotion of the public just got to me. I've never ever been tearful when we've lost, but it was a very emotional thing, because I'm very patriotic.

'Afterwards I thought I was a wee bit unprofessional crying, but now when I look back I don't see any other way that I could have handled myself. It was lovely...a fantastic moment. And when it was all over I thought whatever happens nobody can take that away. You were the best. Not personally, but the best team in the world at one particular time.

'Even now I choke up a bit when I see any sort of success that's patriotic. When I see Sebastian Coe or Steve Ovett win, or some particular effort that you think is extraordinary.'

It was those tears that contributed again to the nation's affection for a footballer who had already attracted much mass loyalty. As a survivor of the Munich tragedy which wiped out the core of Manchester United at a time when they were on the verge of becoming the game's outstanding club side, Bobby Charlton became a symbol of the public's sympathy.

Years later that bond grew even stronger as Charlton climbed the

Wembley steps to become the first Englishman to receive the European Cup. This time his own impact was heightened by his two goals as Manchester United beat Benfica 4-1. The success represented the final product of 10 years of effort to provide a fitting epitaph to those who had perished in Munich.

'Everybody asks me what was the bigger of the two occasions. I've got to put the two together because they were different types of successes. I always say "Don't push me" because I really wouldn't like to give a priority to either one.

'From a country point of view winning the World Cup is something totally special. After all the competition only happens once every four years. To win it at home when everyone can join in and be a part of it is exceptional. From the professional point of view winning the European Cup requires a different approach. It's a much longer competition— becoming champions of the League and then taking on the champions from all the other countries. It's obviously very satisfying winning with your team-mates who you work with every day. Especially in our case when you've failed so many times and had so many trials and tribulations along the way.

'Both matches were played in front of crowds where the atmosphere was unbelievable. I never thought we'd lose either of them. I thought we were destined to beat Benfica just like we were destined to beat West Germany. With England we were a terrific Wembley team. A lot of sides got caught out when they came to Wembley because it was a bit heavier, and you need to play a certain way. So I fancied us right from the end of the 1962 World Cup in Chile, where we did quite well.

'When we got into the European Cup final after beating Real Madrid in Spain, we had such a good record against Portuguese players that I never worried about the game. It just seemed predestined.

'I personally felt that it was a tribute to those who died at Munich. I wouldn't say that all the other players did because they didn't all play with them. I really had felt that at the time of the accident the team was good enough to be champions of Europe.

We might have won in 1958 instead of 1968. But they never got the chance . . . through no fault of their own. So the feeling was to try to put that right.'

The souvenirs of his success have been stored caringly, a reflection of the sensitive and sentimental nature of Bobby Charlton. I kept my shirts from both those finals. The World Cup medal is locked away though occasionally I'll bring it out to show visitors to the house. I value every memento, and I've got all my caps in plastic bags so that they don't lose their colour.

'Only once have I given a shirt for auction and that was for Jimmy Murphy, who was the person I learned more from than anyone else at Old Trafford. I keep all my stuff. They all mean so much.' However, he gave his support to the Year of the Disabled by lending an England shirt and his precious European Cup winners medal to be shown for fundraising activities around the country.

In all Bobby Charlton won 106 caps, a record Bobby Moore surpassed in 1973. His last international was a sorrowful occasion, pulled off by Ramsey in León to save his 32-year-old legs for a semi-final that never materialised. In 1973 he played his 606th and final League game for Manchester United, oddly on the same day that that brother Jack turned out for the last time for Leeds United. Both games were, sadly, away.

Later that summer he accepted an offer to manage Preston North End, to the surprise of brother Jack. 'I don't really think that I'd accepted at the point Jack and I spent that weekend at the Cup final. We hadn't talked about a contract, so I thought that I would keep it close to my chest, in case it all fell through. Maybe I should've told him that Preston were interested in me.' And with a big smile, he added, 'But I don't remember Jack ever phoning me up to ask for advice!'

For a year he hung up his boots, but that first season Preston dropped into the Third Division. Nobby Stiles, bought from Jack at Middlesbrough, was assisting him with the coaching at the club, and on 17 August 1974 Bobby played again, hoping to guide his players at closer quarters back into the Second Division. In February 1975 they stood second in the table and

the manager had played in every game, but a poor March ended their chances and on the 29th a crowd of under 7,000 saw Bobby Charlton leave the pitch for the last time as a Football League player.

In that summer relationships behind the scenes grew strained, culminating in his resignation on 21 August 1975. In keeping with his character the final issue was over a a point of principle. The Preston board had authorised the transfer of centre-half John Bird to Newcastle without the manager's consent.

Bobby Charlton made this statement: 'The directors insisted that for economic reasons they could not refuse the money offered by Newcastle plus one player for John Bird, but I think the deal is totally unrealistic and I'm not prepared to back it. The directors' assessment of the value of Bird simply does not agree with mine, and I will not have players at the club I do not want. So far as I'm concerned neither Alex Bruce [who did return to Preston when the deal went through after Charlton's resignation] nor Micky Burns, the players offered, could get a place in my team. If the directors are going to make the decisions and just want someone to carry them out, they can get anybody to do that.'

Nobby Stiles offered Charlton his support, though he subsequently remained on the coaching staff. The

players also made clear their feelings that he should stay, stating that 'the directors should concentrate on raising money and leave football to the professionals.'

Today, though, there is little evidence of any scars from his experience with Preston. 'I really enjoyed the job. I was prepared to suffer a few body-blows if I didn't find myself as good at management as I thought I would be. That proved to be true . . . and I did take a few blows. But at the same time I really enjoyed it . . . and I would've succeeded there if I'd stayed.'

At the time of his resignation it seemed unthinkable that Bobby Charlton would be out of football for very long. Yet to date that resignation ended his paid association with any one League club. A month later his close friend Freddie Pye, then chairman of Stockport County, invited him to become a director of Halba Travel, a venture into which he threw himself with more effort than many ex-footballers have applied to their entry into business. Six years on he looked very much at home amid the brochures, airline timetables and telex machines of his trade.

'It's a very going concern, and it suits me nicely because our business is really about meeting people. We sell the same holidays as other

agencies, but I suppose being Bobby Charlton helps me get introductions to customers. It also gives me the chance to travel. We put on special football trips, taking groups to World Cups and other top matches.

'And it doesn't tie me down totally. It gives me time to do other things. Freddie Pye and myself bought some shares at Wigan Athletic, so I'm on the board there. I'm an honorary member of the Football Association, and I'm involved with the Manchester County Football Association. Last year I tried for the first time to run some soccer schools, and it was such a success that we're doing the same again this year. In Manchester . . . a residential week . . . for six weeks round August . . . and at Easter as well. Things are very busy with me at the moment, which is nice.'

But is this hectic formula just a substitute for a lack of full-time involvement in football? 'It's not a substitute. I never have felt that football would be part of my life for ever . . . although in many ways it still is. I still go to two matches a week. I'm always writing articles for foreign magazines—and giving interviews.

'Much as I want Wigan to do particularly well, I'm not really working for one club. But now I'm just on the outside of football—if that's the best way of putting it—I think

I'm able to contribute more on a wider scale. I feel that what I've got to offer is general rather than specific.

'I was very grateful to Preston because they took a big chance on me in giving me an opportunity in management. I appreciated that, and I learned a lot that stood me in good stead. I was disappointed that it ended in politics, but there was no way it could be resolved.

'So when I finished there I had a look at my life. I'd never been without football since I could remember. I was playing with my uncles as soon as I could walk. So I decided to sit on things for six months to see what life is like without football. Then I came into the travel business on the proviso that I could go back into the game if I wanted to. But it's just taken over.

'It's got to the stage now when I couldn't have the time to take up the game full-time again. And I don't think I'd want to. I think I can contribute more maybe on the administration side. I really do enjoy my association with the FA, because its a worldwide body.

'I also get a lot of pleasure from my work with the BBC. They're marvellous. They never put me under any pressure...just tell me to give my feelings and opinions. To go to World Cups and to be actually paid for doing it makes me a very lucky lad.'

Jack Charlton's involvement with ITV often means that football's biggest events are still graced by the game's most famous brothers, an association highlighted of course by their sharing in the experiences of 1966. 'When we played against one another we never really played as though we were brothers. And for England we regarded ourselves as professionals, and we didn't allow the fact that were brothers interfere with that. He was the centre-half, and if he made a clanger at the back I would have a go at him. And vice versa. During the game it was player-player, not brother-brother. But then when it was all over, of course, it was extraordinary really. Something we're both very proud of. At the final whistle we had a special hug for one another.'

The contrast in temperament between the two remains as vivid as their differences in size, and maybe the thickness of Jack's hide always made him the more likely to withstand football's slings and arrows in a management role. Bobby is conscious of the individuality of their own make-up. 'Our Jack is very positive and says what he thinks. Occasionally I've seen people hurt when that sort of thing has happened...whereas I've always told myself to be careful, to have another think before I say anything. I'm sure all brothers are different really. I've two other brothers, Tommy and Gordon, and I'm just as proud of them. Everyone talks about the two Charlton brothers, but there are four—and every one is different.

'Jack is his own man. He is what he is. And we let him get on with it. We don't have any problems...we get on pretty well. But we have our own ways of doing things. Maybe I'm a little bit more sensitive about hurting people. I'm not saying that he does that deliberately...but sometimes that's the result. He's an extrovert,

*Charlton became a manager in August 1973, but after a season watching his side fight in vain against relegation he decided to play again 'while there was a chance of promotion'. Preston were on course until March—they were leading the Third Division when this hair-raising picture was taken—but a bad run ended their hopes. Charlton resigned on 'a matter of principle' in August 1975.*

*Charlton's main interest is now as a partner of Halba Travel, an agency with three outlets in the Manchester area. But he's still very involved with the game, not only through the business—which organises football trips—but also through the board of Wigan, the FA, BBC television and other contacts. He still spends a fair amount of time away from wife Norma and his three horse-mad daughters, going all over the world to play in exhibition and charity games.*

but I'm not. I tend to think that I'm a little bit careful...that's the difference, really.'

These days Bobby Charlton takes his performances in charity matches as seriously as if a World Cup winners medal still depended on him. I well recall his outshining a host of the game's former stars in Buenos Aires in 1978, a galaxy of talent that included di Stefano, Kopa, Wright, St John and most of the 1966 Argentina side.

'I love playing...I really do. The only thing that's hard to swallow is that I haven't the time to train now. I always was very fit, and though I'm in good shape now I'm not as fit as I would like to be.

'But I can't play any match without wanting to win. Like when the '66 side got together to play Norwich for Martin Peters. We only lost in the last few minutes, and that was against their first team!'

Today Charlton is well aware of the esteem in which he is held, but also of the responsibility that such a heralded position creates.

'I know how warmly people feel towards me. But I was well taught. The old man used to tell me to take it easy when things were going right and everyone was saying good things about me. He taught me to keep my feet on the floor. That stood me in good stead, and at Old Trafford Jimmy Murphy preached the same gospel. And I've always tried to take praise—much as I appreciated it—with a pinch of salt.

'But some things happen that I still find unbelievable. When I go to London, for instance, two out every three taxi rides I get free if I want. I'm very well received when I go abroad, and though I enjoy it I hope I don't play on it. I don't know why I generate this affection. Perhaps it's because I come from a mining background. No great shakes, but I'm proud of that. An ordinary working lad that people can identify with.

'Perhaps it's because I always seemed to do what people wanted me to do. We got reasonable results for England and for Manchester United. And when I used to shoot from twenty or thirty yards, it was what they loved to see...'

# GEOFF HURST

Born Ashton-under-Lyne, Lancashire, 8 Dec. 1941; Chelmsford Schools, Essex Schools (family moved to Essex); joined West Ham 1958 and turned pro April 1959; 6 youth caps 1958–59; League debut 27 Feb. 1960 v Nottingham F. (away, 1-3); two seasons as wing-half before converted by Ron Greenwood to new type of centre-forward 1962; 4 Under-23 caps 1963–64; starred in West Ham's Wembley wins 1964 and 1965; full England debut 23 Feb. 1966 v W. Germany at Wembley (1-0) and scored v Scotland in next game...

'The rewards for my part in the 1966 World Cup are still coming in' said Geoff Hurst. 'Only last week, there was this toasted teacake.' While you wait for him to explain this cryptic remark, there's time to take in the man sitting almost insolently at ease in the office five paces from the audible bedlam of the dressing-room he then ran. The hair is longer, the waist is now a little nearer matching that always-noticeable square chest, but the easy, jagged-toothed grin etched into our memories as he turned after scoring that fourth England goal is still there...making him instantly recognisable.

The teacake...? 'Ah yes, last week, going north to scout a match, my coach Bobby Gould and I went for the British Rail tea. Usual thing, few little sandwiches, bit of toast, then a toasted teacake. I'd scoffed the lot, then I felt this nudge on my arm. The BR steward. He slid a second teacake on to my plate, all furtive like. And whispered..."them three goals...smashing that was." Can you imagine! After 15 years, this lovely chap felt I deserved this special favour. Bobby Gould was killing himself. "You, you're still bloody living on them goals, aren't you?"

'Had it been anybody else saying that I'd have got the needle. Because I have tried *never* to lean on what happened that day. In fact, it's brought me nothing that I can see. Not this job? No way! I got this job because I went out and learned my trade as a manager and coach, not because someone at Stamford Bridge decided to hand it to me because of 1966...like another teacake.'

Pressed on the 'brought me nothing' remark, Hurst ticks off the players of that team one by one and proves, to his own satisfaction anyway, that none of them owe their current fortune (or lack of it) or status (or its absence) to that day in 1966.

'Those who have a good business were going to be good businessmen, anyway, because that's the way they were made. Those who are coaching or managing were heading that way even before 1966, because that's the sort of thinking players they were. Take the most famous blokes in the side—Moore, Bobby Charlton...did their World Cup "names" help *them* get top jobs, or keep them? Not bloody likely.'

When pressed Hurst's memories are more of the summer of 1966 than of that one special afternoon. He remembers the longest walk of his life from the training pitches back to the hall at Lilleshall at the end of England's last get-together before departing on the pre-Cup tour of Scandinavia and Poland. There were 27 players trudging tiredly along that forest path: one by one Alf Ramsey pulled five of them to one side and broke the news that they would be missing when the final squad of 22 was announced.

'We all knew it was happening. Waiting for him to turn and beckon "Got a minute, Geoff" was pure hell.' But it was Bobby Tambling, Peter Thompson, Keith Newton, Gordon Milne and Hurst's clubmate 'Budgie' Byrne who finished that longest walk in unconsolable silence.

Hurst remembers that tour, when his delight at making the party vanished in an hour in Denmark as he played 'probably the worst match of my life, certainly the worst of my international career.' Here I was,

115

supposed to be making my mark for the coming World Cup, and I don't think I did a thing right all afternoon. Not a shot, not a pass, not a tackle...it was an absolute nightmare. I didn't want to talk to anyone for days. I was sure, I *knew* I'd blown it.'

He remembers the minutae of waiting, like the illicit walks to Golders Green High Street that he and Peters used to take in the afternoon instead of resting as Ramsey had ordered. 'No point. No way we were going to sleep...we used to sneak out the back door and go shopping. Take two hours choosing a tube of toothpaste to pass the time.'

But the fewest fragments seem to be about *the* game. He is as puzzled as you over this, and loyally casts about for answers.

'Look, what you have to remember is that I was already made up, just by being there. In the first place, I'd been picked for England the year before to partner Budgie Byrne. That was how it all started...Alf was looking for someone to do the job in his team that I did at West Ham. He tried half a dozen before he got around to me. So, in that sense, I'd sort of sneaked into the reckoning; and still hadn't quite got over how lucky I was. The fact I had been knocking in about 40 goals a year hadn't sunk in with me. Or with half the critics. If ever I started to think I had "arrived" there'd soon be a bit in the papers making it clear that wasn't everyone's point of view.

'Then there was the thing about making the cut from the first squad of 40, then from the 27, now the 22. After that debacle in Denmark, I just wanted to train hard in case I was needed...but sure I wouldn't be.

'So when Jimmy Greaves got hurt, and I got a game against Argentina, I thought I'd had cracked it. That goal was super—one that Martin and I had practised about a million times. So to pull it off in a game like that, to win one we damn near lost, well, that took me right up to the top. There didn't seem any higher place for me to go. Even though I got in the next one, too, had a good game against Portugal, laid on the goal for Bobby...well, that was a bonus. I'd had my World Cup—the rest was going to be up to the others. I was never first choice, see?

'That's the way I came to the final...satisfied. Like someone at Sandown who's had his money back ten times over on the first races and is now backing with the bookies' money ...can't lose. Lovely relaxed feeling it is too.'

But what did the game leave with Goeff Hurst? 'Sorry, I know what you want, but I can't give it to you. I've tried to tell people a million times, and never get it right. I remember the goals, sure. I remember what I did, what other people did. But the mental pictures are not all touched with rays of gold-dust or shafts of fire, as people seem to expect. I was well-trained and ready ...razor sharp...and I did what I was paid to do...and what I did was enough...and I was deeply satisfied ...and delighted that it meant so much to so many people. But this other...well *magic*, thing...it simply isn't there. Not for me.'

Hurst watched the tape reeling for a minute. Then... 'That's it, I'm afraid. Great revelations aren't coming. I think I understand how odd this seems. I remember watching Liverpool play Bruges at Wembley. And watched Kenny Dalglish score a beauty of a goal that gave Liverpool the Cup. I was leaping about like a loony, delighted for the man, saying to myself, "Christ how must he *feel*... getting a goal like that to win the Cup for his club?"

'Then I looked at him. He was pleased, sure...but *calm*. He'd done his job. He had a look of "What's all the fuss?" Suddenly my mind went back to July 1966...and I sort of remembered. That's how it was that afternoon. Outside, its bedlam. Inside, just a sort of funny, peaceful calm.'

Hurst watches the tape a bit more, and there's a silence. 'I'm afraid this is getting a bit deep. Perhaps the truth is even simpler. I simply wasn't knowing enough to get the most out of that hour. I was only 24...a real baby in so many ways. If I'd have done the same thing four years later, I might have been readier to look around take more in, draw more from all that was going on.'

We leave the office and go up to the Chelsea restaurant for coffee. The place looks familiar: suddenly you remember that it was there, in that corner, that TV cameras filmed much of a dramatic programme about Jimmy Greaves, and his climb back from alcoholism. Hurst remembers the programme with bitter clarity.

'I watched it, yeah. And I could feel the hairs on the back of my neck crawling. You have to remember that Jimmy was a mate...and here he was telling the world about how he'd been crawling in gutters, boozed out of his mind. And tracing it all back to that day when I got in the team for the final—wearing his shirt. Well, ask yourself, how *would* you feel?

'Of course we knew he was sick being left out. Couldn't be otherwise, could it? He was a genius...no other word. The greatest goalscorer England has ever had. And this was the greatest match ever staged in this country...and he was left out. But the thing about Jim is that grin never left him...never...and you swallowed it...took him at his word... that it was 'just another game'...and "no ill-feelings, that's football"...all the things players say to each other.

*Geoff lets one go at Coventry in 1972, during the first of his three seasons with Stoke. 'I enjoyed playing for Tony Waddington, and we had a fair run while I was there. But after 15 years at one club anywhere would have been strange. And I found that World Cup thing a bit of a burden... one or two of my new team-mates seemed to resent the fact I'd come with a bit of a reputation. Not the good 'uns...but those who'd never quite make it.'*

*Hurst is congratulated after scoring for Telford in their 3-0 win over Tividale in the second qualifying round of the FA Cup in October 1976 —his first season as manager. 'As a player you never begin thinking about the manager's problems—until they concern you. Those problems, and how to solve them, was what I had to learn. That's why Telford, and not trying to grab at the first deep-in-trouble League club that would have been glad to sign up a name to take the pressure off.'*

'I remembered how I had been embarrassed at the time, waiting for Alf to announce who was in. I thought it would be Jimmy. I hoped it would be me. Every time we passed on the stairs that last day it was a bit hard to look him in the eye. I mean if he was laughing all over his face it could only mean one thing...he was in. When the news came, he was one of the first to bang on the door. Wished me luck.

'Christ, if only I had known how he had been gutted when Alf told him. Still, even if I had known, what could I have said that would have helped? Not a word. Even so, it haunts me a bit, that it was the start of the slide for Greavesie...one of the real greats. To be involved, even in my innocent sort of way, in a thing like that. The only way it helps, is to remember that he *did* come back. Not quite as a player. But as a bloke...he's got it behind him, and he's using what happened to help other people.

'And it even helps a bit that having taken his place I didn't waste it. I wouldn't want to get into all that stuff about would he have got the same three goals if he got the chance ...you'll drive yourself mad thinking along those lines.

'But it would have made the Greaves thing even more horrible if I had taken his place and had a total stummer. Can you imagine what would have been said then? Almost the nicest thing that has ever happened to me was hearing Jim on that TV programme gently slagging off the pressman who were slagging off Alf... "Listen," he told them, "in Alf's position I'd have done the same. Picked Geoff." To be able to say that, after what that decision meant to his whole life...well, as I say, the little bloke's definitely a one-off. You have to remember not too many people agreed with Alf on the morning of the match. I had to astonish half of Britain that afternoon, just to stop them wanting to string Alf up for leaving Jimmy on the bench.'

If Hurst had astonished half of Britain with his performances during the World Cup match, then he dumbfounded the rest by the way he played afterwards. Here was a man whom success changed absolutely.

A forward whose greatest— apparent—skills had been the ability to run endlessly, to position himself intelligently to receive long-hit passes, and play them instantly down to a team-mate before racing off to take a

*The Cup trail ended two rounds later with a 5-2 home defeat by Matlock, though Hurst didn't play. 'Because I stay calm it doesn't mean I take defeat lightly...I don't,' he said. 'I've got my pubs as outside interest. But this is my life, not my hobby.' After a three-season 'apprenticeship' he moved to Chelsea as assistant to the new boss Danny Blanchflower.*

fresh position, was now doing all that and a great deal more. Now he was taking passes, turning and attacking defenders with purposeful dribbles, and beating them in ones, twos and even threes. Not with any fantastic Latin subtleties, but with a basic body-swerve—taken from about Chapter Two of any How To Play Football manual—that was effective only because it was carried through with speed, strength and seemingly undentable confidence. His reputation grew, and so did his value.

Even today Hurst does not like giving details of the number of times he was illegally 'tapped': fellow internationals would shuffle up embarrassedly at England matches and murmur: 'Look...I've been asked to have a word...they fancy you at our place...if you were interested, there'd be quite a few bob in it.' But the most famous approach was rather more straightforward. Manchester United's Matt Busby sent West Ham a telegram offering an astounding £200,000—thus almost doubling at a stroke the record transfer fees of £110,000 paid for Alan Ball by Everton and Denis Law by United.

West Ham manager Ron Greenwood, probably angered by yet another attempt to woo away his hand-built star, replied in another telegram now famous for its curt brevity: 'No. Greenwood'.

Hurst did not, at the time, even know of United's offer. Nor did he explode when the news was finally leaked. At that time he was convinced that West Ham's World Cup trio were to be the basis of enormous club success—and he had an amazingly sound rapport with Greenwood.

One story nicely illustrates that regard: Hurst had gone into the World Cup earning not much more than average First Division pay, say £60 a week. That hat-trick had made him worth, clearly, rather more salary, and in an attempt to make him happy and secure West Ham had offered him a contract—four years initially, plus a four-year option—that would virtually make him their player for the rest of his career.

The snag came on the day Hurst was due to sign. Because of a misunderstanding over dates, the club's board had not yet met and agreed the wages. When the news was broken, Hurst was temporarily non-plussed. Then 'Never mind, boss' he told Greenwood. 'I'll sign anyway. I'll trust you to fill in the figures later...

*'This lad knows a thing or two.' England manager Ron Greenwood is flanked by Kevin Keegan and Hurst at a training session in September 1977, five days after he had asked his old player to join his staff. 'I feel like I've won my 50th cap,' he said at the time. 'Ron hand-built me to his own design and I've rung him many times for advice while I've been at Telford.'*

you know what I'm worth.' Hurst later reported himself 'well-pleased' with the salary scale inserted. His relationship with Greenwood has remained close—he is now one of the England manager's coaches on the international set-up.

It was only the lack of that promised success of the team that eventually persuaded Hurst he would be better to leave West Ham. And once again his regard for Greenwood tripped him up. Having made up his mind he would ask for a transfer, and spent three days carefully compiling a press statement that would explain exactly what had forced the decision, he waited outside Greenwood's office one Thursday morning to deliver the request for a move.

He barely noticed the man who eventually passed him on the way out, as he walked in to find Greenwood sitting behind his desk looking grey. Before Hurst could explain his mission Greenwood began: 'That was Martin Peters who just left...he's asked for a move. I can't believe it. Like you, he's part of the heart of this club... impossible to replace in the team...

says he's unhappy here now...I'm really shattered.'

Greenwood fell into silence, then looked up. 'Sorry for all that Geoff... what was it *you* wanted?' 'Nothing, boss,' said Hurst. 'Nothing that won't keep.' Then he went outside and tore up his press statement. 'I thought Ron was near to tears about Martin. There was no way, just no way, I could make it two in a day.'

So Hurst stayed on at West Ham— and for a long time remained a fixture in the England side. Of the rest of his internationals the two he remembers most vividly were also against West Germany. The first, in León in 1970, was the 3-2 defeat in the World Cup quarter-final.

'It's ludicrous we lost that from two up. We'd have got to the final, no doubt whatsoever. And there...who knows? Brazil had been a bit lucky to beat us 1-0 earlier in the competition. I tell you, no way they wanted to play us again.' Alan Ball, incidentally, often claims that Hurst played better in this World Cup defeat than he had in his hat-trick match: 'We only had two up front...Hurstie and Frannie Lee. They were magic, kept the whole German defence at full stretch. No matter how much pressure you were under, you'd glance up and sure enough there'd be Hurstie steaming into view, always making himself available.'

Hurst's other memory of Germany is dated 29 April 1972. Playing at Wembley in a side trailing 1-3 he was pulled off the pitch to be replaced by Rodney Marsh. 'I knew then that was the end. The press had been clamouring for changes...get rid of the "old guard." I'd had 49 caps...not bad for a bloke who'd supposed to have got in as a makeweight. But that didn't make it any easier seeing the end. My only regret is that Alf didn't tell me himself that I wouldn't be in the next team...I heard it on the car radio, and that did hurt.'

Only the clear hints that West Ham were beginning to step up the search for his eventual replacement finally persuaded Hurst to leave the club in 1972 and join Stoke. 'It seemed the right thing to do at the time. It probably was. I enjoyed playing for Tony Waddington, and we had a fair run in the three years I was there. But after 15 years at one club anywhere would have been strange. And I found that World Cup thing a bit of a burden...one or two of my new team-mates seemed to resent the fact I'd come with a bit of a reputation. Not the good 'uns...but those who'd never quite make it.'

So did some of their wives—a factor that instantly soured Judith Hurst, a down-to-earth lady whose admirers included Alf Ramsey. 'If every player had a wife with her feet as much on the ground as her, the job of all managers would be a bloody sight easier,' he once said. Tony Waddington obviously agreed; it was to the Hurst home he sent, as a lodger, the wilful, wayward Alan Hudson after the gifted young forward had strayed yet again off the road.

But Judith found the transition from Upton Park to the Victoria Ground more difficult than her husband. 'It's bad enough up in the section of the stand where the wives all sit together at any time. The bitchiness, you wouldn't believe. All that "Pity your Fred missed that goal, darling,"..."Yes dear, but when he gets passes like your Bill gives, well what *can* he do, dear?" Honestly!'

From Stoke Hurst went to West Bromwich...for a fairly wasted six months. 'I had about a dozen or so games. Didn't do too well. Saw I wasn't going to stay in the team as a regular and thought it over. My career as a player was coming to its end. Not going to get any better now. I've got ambitions to be a manager...so why waste time hanging on? These weeks when I could be running my own side will never come around again...time to go.'

He went to play in America for a season, with Seattle Sounders, and then got an offer from Telford of the Southern League. But why start at Telford, when with his name he could have gone almost anywhere...'But that was the point. Ask yourself, when are most managers appointed? When the vacancy occurs because they've just sacked the bloke who had been doing the job, that's why. And why did they sack him? Because the club's in trouble, usually...either about to be relegated, or at best about to miss promotion that everyone had been banking on.

'So what does all that add up to? That most managers get the jobs because someone reckons they can get the club out of a fix. It's a pretty bloody awful way to start a new job, isn't it? And a bloody silly thing to let yourself in for, until you've had a bit of experience.

'I'd always said I wanted to be a manager when I packed up playing. But when the time came close, I realised I hadn't a clue what I really meant. What was a manager...what did he actually *do*?

'All I had ever been was a footballer ...and as a player it's a bit like living in a box. Someone takes you out to train and for the games, and makes all the decisions for you. I've seen players—famous players, all internationals—in an airport lounge all get up and follow one bloke into the lav. Six of them, maybe, standing there not wanting to piss, but following the bloke who does. Like sheep... because that's the way they have been trained. Start training when someone says, stop when he blows his whistle. Run, or kick, or shoot, according to orders.

'Then at the end of the week, get into this coach...catch this train...

*Geoff Hurst, Second Division manager. Chelsea were struggling when he moved up from assistant to manager in September 1979, and by December they were top. But a bad run in the spring cost them promotion—as it would do the following season. The diabolical run in 1981—ironically with an amazing inability to score goals the cause— also cost Geoff his job. He was sacked before the end of the League programme.*

sit down and eat this meal...go to bed in this room...get up at this time...it's the system. So you live all your life in blinkers, thinking only about yourself. You never even begin thinking about the manager's problems—unless they concern you. But those problems, and solving them, was what I had to learn...at Telford.'

Soon after he took over the job, Hurst persuaded most of the World Cup team to play a benefit for him. The tiny ground at the New Town has never had a football night quite like it... The Telford player whose benefit night it was profitted mightily: Hurst, too, found himself vastly rewarded, as he was to tell another writer shortly afterwards:

'That time we got together at Telford, it was all there again. After what, a dozen years? Together Moore and Ballie, the Charltons and Martin. We played again as though '66 had been only yesterday. It was beautiful. The looks on all their faces, they all felt it, too. But that night, sitting around having a drink. We didn't talk about the old days. Funny? I suppose so. What we talked about was the current England team. Comparisons...yes...of course. Actually it is *only* with people of your own football age, people who had been part of that outfit, that we can say what we think of things now.

'Why? Because we're part of the past...when they fired Alf Ramsey they fired us, too. If we said anything about the way the game went after Alf, we'd have been slaughtered... made to sound like old men trying to turn back the clock. Alf, and the lads in the team, and blokes from the press who were with us all through that...we are all wrapped up together in a way that doesn't need reunion dinners. We had some great times... great tours. In the end we did the bit that made it all worth the effort. So we leave it at that. Good memories, and a place in the books. It's enough.'

I reminded him of those words. 'Those who were around at the time who saw the match have their memories...and perhaps they are fading a bit. But now there's a new crowd coming up, people who were too young and who now want to know about what is to them a legend.

'So that's my problem, really. People recognising me and steaming over, friendly as anything, wanting to talk about something in my past. I want to end up being remembered as a manager who won the lot, not a player. Getting people to understand this, that I'm as ambitious as hell to succeed and not be just another good ex-player, is still a problem. It's the old image thing.'

We talked for a bit about 'the image' and how surprised some of us were at the way he had begun his reign as Chelsea's manager—by dropping, then sacking, his old England team-mate Peter Osgood, the very man who had led the players' public appeal that Hurst be promoted from coach to replace Danny Blanchflower.

'Right, that's it,' said Hurst. 'I'm a very much misunderstood bloke. Because I've always enjoyed a joke, smile a lot, doesn't mean I'm soft. This "nice guy" thing started when I was getting whacked in every match after 1966. Just because I didn't blow my top and start booting people ...didn't mean I was a patsy. Go back and ask them I played against. They'll tell you I was a big, heavy guy...and I tackled my full weight. They all knew they'd had a battle.

'I have no idea if Ossie thought I'd be a soft touch. But though he'd been a great player, and is a good enough bloke off the park, he wasn't what I needed to get that club right. Chelsea should be in the First Division—and promotion was my priority. Then everything had to be geared up to that. It was expected by everybody at the club. In the first 18 months I was in the job we were only out of the top three once: that was the last week of the '79–80 season and it stopped us going up. May not seem a bad record. But anyone at Chelsea knew that it wouldn't do...look at the place, that great stand, those huge terraces ...anything less than a First Division place is failure.'

'Failure' it was then for Hurst and assistant Bobby Gould, sacked after a long goal drought saw Chelsea tumble from promotion pushers to mid-table also-rans in the late stages of the 1980–81 season. It makes it even harder for Geoff Hurst to shake off his past and keep his word about the future: 'That hat-trick gave me a great start in life, but it is not...it is *not*...going to be the one thing I'm remembered for.'

# MARTIN PETERS

**Born Plaistow, East London, 8 Nov. 1943; Fanshawe School, Dagenham, Essex and London Schools; 6 schoolboy caps, captaining England v W. Germany in last game before joining West Ham May 1959; turned pro Nov. 1960 and won 12 youth caps over next 3 years; League debut 20 April 1962 v Cardiff (home, 4-1); a regular next season, but left out of 1964 FA Cup final side; starred in Cup Winners Cup success v Munich 1965; like Moore and Hurst, played both legs of 1966 League Cup final; 5 Under-23 caps 1962–65; full England debut v Yugoslavia at Wembley 4 May 1966 (2-0) in No 4 shirt...**

Performance on the football field is about skill but can also be a true indication of character. Certainly so in the case of Martin Peters, whose unruffled style and sense of timing on the pitch is totally reflected in his personality.

Still playing at 37, he had outlived the active days of all his World Cup colleagues with the exception of Alan Ball. By a strange coincidence I arrived to disturb his memories of 1966 the morning after the two had met once more on the field—Peters in his capacity as Sheffield United's new player-coach, Ball as Blackpool's

player-manager. Even the score had a nostalgic ring: 4-2, in Peters' favour.

To stretch the irony even further Geoff Hurst had been in the directors' box, in his role as Chelsea chief, and Peters now operated in a city where his club vied for the limelight with Jack Charlton's Sheffield Wednesday.

At the Bramall Lane offices they told me that Martin would be on time for our appointment—a belief in punctuality in keeping with the sense of precision on which he built his career. For Peters, who had only short spells as an out-and-out attacker, approaching 200 League goals from

*'Mr Versatile', as seen by the 'Daily Express' in a feature in December 1966. While his all-round talent and subtle play were constantly praised by coaches and managers— most notably by Ramsey—ball- watching fans did not always see him as a great player.*

*Double-header...
Martin helps out
Bobby Moore and
Alan Stephenson at
Upton Park in one
of his last League
games for West
Ham and (opposite)
in a classic Peters
picture, he steals
in for a near-post
header against
Forest shortly after
joining Spurs in a
record £200,000
transfer deal in
March 1971. 'I've
always worked on
my technique, and
my heading is good.'*

midfield is ample testimony to a talent for timing.

Of the boys of the summer of '66, Martin Peters is among the more complex. Another reflection of his playing style, perhaps, which was often misunderstood and unappreciated on the terraces by supporters who could not fathom the praise in the label pinned on him by Alf Ramsey.

That tag, which at times Peters was forced to wear as a millstone, was delivered in 1968. He had been England's scorer in a 1-1 draw with Scotland at Hampden Park, and Peters recalls that he might have had a hat-trick. Ramsey responded: 'Martin Peters is a player ten years ahead of his time.' More than 12 years later, along the highways of the Third Division, the jibes that his time was past could still be heard.

'Alf was trying to get across that ten years on there would be a more fluid style of football. As indeed there has been with teams like the Dutch. I would have been useful in that style because I'd played in every position for West Ham.'

Ramsey was also praising Peters' high degree of individual technique— and an awareness beyond even a competent international player. He blossomed into a footballer with a rare combination of talents. His critics pointed to a lack of genuine pace, to a tall man's lack of incision in the tackle. Yet time and time again he would appear, as though some magician had uttered the appropriate phrase, in the most dangerous of positions, unmarked and with the skill and composure to finish the job. 'The ghost' became his nickname; blind-side running was the term the coaches groped for to explain the phenomenon of Martin Peters.

But if the skill came instinctively, the ability to live with a lack of appreciation in his audience did not. Not really until his England days were over, and the absence of a replacement emphasised his worth. Campaigns were instigated in the press, calling for his return to the side, even in his mid-thirties.

Peters discounts them. 'It was never going to happen, though I would dearly have loved to have played one more game at Wembley. Like Alan Ball did in the 1979 League Cup final. He knew it was his last, so he could relax and go out and play.'

Ron Greenwood was England's manager at the time when the media were last calling for the recall of Peters' experience. With Greenwood, however, his star had never shone as brightly since he asked to leave West Ham in 1969. 'Ron promised me that if we didn't win anything that year I could go. But he took it personally, perhaps because it broke up the trio of Bobby Moore, Geoff Hurst and myself. Only recently have we really started to get on with each other once again.'

That linking with Moore and Hurst provides a clue to Martin Peters' life since 1966. For him it was so often Moore, Hurst...and Peters. The third man behind the golden boy and captain of England, behind the only man to score a hat-trick in a World Cup final. Yet if West Germany had not been granted that contentious equaliser in the last minute of normal time, Peters would have worn a different label, that of the man whose goal won the competition for his country.

*Martin pictured with wife Kathy and and children Lee-Ann and Grant in 1979, just before the fourth anniversary of their move to Norfolk. 'It took a good two years for Kathy to settle to it all after London. It was another difficult time for the family. But it was the right move.'*

It was only human to wonder what difference it would have made to his life. Only partially for the financial benefits; more so for the recognition it would have brought. But he only really wondered in the years following the event—immature years, as he now admits: 'I only really grew up after my move to Tottenham.'

These days Martin Peters looks back on his involvement in the World Cup with almost genuine surprise that it happened at all. 'I'd played four games for the England Under-23s, but they were back in 1962 and 1963. And I hadn't been involved with them for a long time. Then I was suddenly called up for a game at Blackburn. I played quite well and we won 2-0.

'From that I got picked for the initial squad of 40, and I was still there when they cut the squad down to 28. But I remember phoning Kathy, my wife, and saying that there was no way I would be in the final 22. I really was the new boy.'

That crucial match at Ewood Park, against Turkey on 20 April, a mere 12 weeks before the finals were scheduled, turned a corner for Peters. A fortnight later he won his first full cap against Yugoslavia at Wembley and, after a fine game, selection for the four-country tour, the last opportunity for Ramsey to shape his first-choice side.

'I was picked for the first game, against Finland in Helsinki. I did quite well and got one of our goals in a 3-0 win. I was just starting to feel that I might make some sort of contribution, but I was still staggered that I was there at all, since it was well into the year of the finals before I was considered.

'But then I was left out of the next two games, and when Alf started to read out the names for the final game against Poland in Katowice, I thought I was out again. In those days he used to give the team in the old-style ordering. When he got past number six without me, I thought "that's that". Then he said "Number 11 ... Peters". Afterwards he explained what my new role would be, on the left-hand side of midfield. Having got so far it came as something of a disappointment when I was left out of the opening match of the finals against Uruguay.'

The fumbling confusion of that

goalless draw earned him a recall five days later for the match against Mexico, and like an emerging actor his lines grew more significant as the plot thickened. In the 77th minute of the quarter-final, his delicate work on the left touchline answered those critics who called for more orthodox wing performers. His cross also had the great virtue that Hurst, his club colleague, could anticipate its flight.

Such was Ramsey's technique of leadership that no player knew he was in the team for the final until he was directly approached by the manager. Peters' recollections are not certain, but they retain the flavour of the moment. 'The night before we played West Germany some of us went off to the pictures. I think Alf had a quiet word with me there to tell me I was in the side. I was rooming with Hurstie and when I got back we compared notes like two kids letting out a secret.

'He'd been taken aside by Alf as well, and he was picked. If you remember that was big news then because Jimmy Greaves was fit for selection again.'

Peters almost marked his appearance in the final with the opening goal—a raking shot from 25 yards that Tilkowski, with some uncertainty, pushed round the post. After both sides had scored, a shirt-pulling incident brought him a caution from Herr Dienst.

The episode that almost made Martin Peters the match-winner came just 12 minutes from time. Ball's irrepressible energy forced Tilkowski into conceding a corner. Ball took it himself, and the Germans bundled their clearance only as far as Hurst, whose first-time shot arched off a defender and looped invitingly into the goal area.

But it was an invitation that only a player with Peters' excellent technique could accept with confidence. In replay the moment appears sheer simplicity; in fact Peters, even at this early stage of his career, was exhibiting his facility for a reaction that would be difficult for those blessed with a lesser touch.

'When I look back now,' he replied after a pause for thought, 'the memory is not the dissatisfaction that it didn't

*Dennis Tueart, one of many successors in England's No. 11 shirt, beats Peters at Maine Road in March 1980. His contribution and example in five years with Norwich proved major factors in their maintaining a solid position in the First Division: Peters helped them to promotion in his first season—and in his five full seasons at Carrow Road he missed just 13 League games.*

turn out to be the winner. It's more real annoyance that we let West Germany equalise. Professionally my goal should have been the winner because with such little time remaining we should have held out.'

The consequences of that incident were not seen for three years but Weber's equaliser, and Hurst's response in extra time, cost West Ham United a player. The attention heaped on Moore and Hurst, coupled with Peters' own versatility, which meant that his niche in the team continued to vary, left him with a genuine identity crisis.

In the 1968–69 season he scored 24 goals for West Ham, but a poor start to the following year culminated in his being dropped. 'I've been playing badly,' he admitted at the time. 'Ron Greenwood is right to drop me. I can't pin it down. My heart is no longer with the club. I've got to be playing well to go to Mexico, and I don't really think I can do it with West Ham.'

Greenwood countered by suggesting he take a holiday. 'I've heard he's going to ask for a transfer. But he just ain't going—it's as simple as that. He's got to start again, maybe in the 'A' team or the reserves, until his attitude changes. No other club has ever inquired whether Martin is for sale. All football knows it's unthinkable we'd sell him. Such players as this are very, very rare.'

West Ham eventually bowed to Peters' insistence, but only after the most painful six months of his life. His own considerable composure was disturbed by the goldfish bowl existence as the saga continued with the constant daily requests from the media for news of how the conflict with his club was developing. And for his wife Kathy, a more volatile character than Martin, the pressures at times were unbearable.

When his transfer request was first made public, Kathy was in the last stages of pregnancy. Their son, Grant, was born early in November 1969 when Martin was in Holland representing England. By that time the cracks at West Ham had been papered over. Words like 'compromise' and 'understanding' were side by side with the report that he had withdrawn his request. But Fleet Street remained aware that it was an uneasy peace, one

that might only stabilise if West Ham could co-ordinate all their talent in a chase for honours.

The Peters household continued to live under the bombardment of journalists. For Kathy coping became harder and harder, and her nerves were stretched to breaking point. With her husband so often on the road she suffered great stress, not helped by an illness for their new-born son which once had Martin flying dramatically back home from Liverpool.

The worst of the ordeal ended on 17 March 1970, when Greenwood finally relented. With 39 minutes remaining before the transfer deadline Peters became a Tottenham Hotspur player, his 1966 colleague Jimmy Greaves moving in the opposite direction as part of the move. The deal was valued at £200,000, a new British record. Peters' own reward from the transfer was £10,000.

The move smacked of the frying pan and the fire. Terry Venables, himself harshly treated by the followers at White Hart Lane, once commented cryptically: 'I wouldn't say the Spurs crowd are hard to please. They don't start moaning until the third week.' Peters at least marked his debut with a goal, though Tottenham lost 2-1 to Coventry. The settling-in would be difficult, but the struggle and the consequent responsibility of captaincy would be maturing experiences.

So it was as a Tottenham player that Peters was re-united with Moore and Hurst in Mexico as England attempted to retain the World Cup. Despite some callous sniping from afar, his contribution was again recognised by Ramsey. Malcolm Allison, from the soft chair of a London television studio 7,000 miles away, was only one of his critics: 'Martin Peters? He's the one who's ten years ahead of his time, so we've got to wait for him to come good.'

Ramsey remained loyal, and when Peters' goal put England 2-0 ahead against West Germany in the quarter-final at León, it was Peters and Bobby Charlton who were substituted. Ramsey wanted to rest two important talents for the semi-final place that seemed secure.

The loyalty flowed in both directions. 'Alf was like a father with his family. He kept a certain distance, and he commended great respect and affection. He was a players' man first and foremost, which was why he upset the press and television so often. He always felt he was doing his best for us.'

At Tottenham, Peters achieved his ambition of picking up some of the game's trinkets for his trophy cabinet. Spurs won the League Cup in 1971 and 1973, with the UEFA Cup sandwiched between. In 1974 they could not quite keep up the sequence, and despite eight goals in 12 games from Peters they lost the 1974 UEFA Cup final to Feyenoord. But the equilibrium was badly disturbed in the September of that year when Terry Neill succeeded Bill Nicholson as manager at White Hart Lane.

A personality clash reached crisis point on 9 February 1975, when Peters refused to watch events after being substituted in the 67th minute of a 2-0 defeat by Stoke. The two had strongly disagreed about a change of tactics at half-time.

Again the solution came on the last day before the transfer deadline, a cut-price £50,000 sale to Norwich City. It was a drop to the Second Division, though only for a few weeks with John Bond's side poised for promotion. The five years in North London that had given him his identity were over.

Peters' response to the new challenge of Norwich City was nothing less than immaculate, as Bond will testify. 'I played with Martin at West Ham and thought he was a damn good player. But nothing more. I watched him and I felt the same. It was only when I signed him and had to examine him in a more analytical way that I came to realise what a *great* footballer he is.'

Bond would often refer to Peters as his 'little pot of gold', and his skills, unbowed by the passing of time, did more than most to keep First Division football in Norfolk. Yet what an illuminating comment that a top manager like Bond had to see Peters playing in his own sides to truly appreciate his gifts. Small wonder that the troops on the terraces were often perplexed as to his real worth.

There's little doubt that he would

*Coaching the youngsters while with Norwich— before he moved on to handling the bigger lads at Sheffield United. 'I was always prepared to take a chance with a run, and now as a coach I'm trying to get my players to do the same, to look at the flight of the ball and time their arrival.'*

*Player-coach meets player-manager: Peters and Alan Ball were the only two members of the 1966 side still playing in the League when their sides met at Blackpool in October 1980. United completed the double with a 4-2 win. Peters finished playing the following January when he became team manager — and saw the club slide into Division 4 for the first time ever four months later.*

have been playing in the First Division in his 38th year but for the persistence of one of football's most persuasive and colourful characters. Harry Haslam, who swaps funny stories as cleverly as he wheels and deals on the transfer market, desperately needed an injection of a major force into Sheffield United; under Haslam United's first season in the Third Division in their 91-year history had fallen away in ruins when promotion looked a certainty. He wanted skilled help to survive and he cajoled Peters to begin his managerial apprenticeship by moving to Sheffield as player-coach.

Sheffield United responded immediately to his example, winning four of their first five League matches, with Peters himself scoring in three of the games. But it didn't last. When the first round of the Cup arrived in November he stood down as a player,

and began to concentrate on coaching. He wasn't helped by a troublesome achilles injury with which he had started the season, and an X-ray revealed an arthritic hip. Finally the bones of 'the ghost' were feeling the passing of time.

The game was about to lose a player of a rare type. It's a common analysis of England's World Cup win to refer to the three 'great' players that ran as a solid core through the centre of the side: Banks, Moore and Bobby Charlton. At 22 the young Martin Peters was still short of that superior quality, but in patches his genius touched the 1966 team. Later it would flourish, but in the manner of the artist whose paintings only become collectors' items after his demise.

I asked Martin if he could describe his own talents. 'I was called a ghost, and no-one used to notice what I did. At Tottenham I might make 15 runs, and I'd get the ball only once. The crowd would never spot those other 14 runs I'd make. So when I got the one, and it worked, they'd think I'd never done it before. At Norwich in the later years my role changed. I played more centrally in midfield, and I caught the eye more on the ball.'

And on those occasional quiet evenings at home, do the thoughts still stray back to 1966? 'Well, I was very lucky that in 1978 I was given a testimonial at Norwich and most of the team from '66 came down to play for me against the Norwich first team. It was a great night. We only lost in the last few minutes, and people like Bobby Charlton and Roger Hunt, who hadn't played for ages, they were brilliant. Alf was there as well, and all the old feelings came flooding back.

'But generally I don't think too much about it now. Winning the World Cup came very early in my career, and I was very lucky to have some success with my other clubs. I don't dwell on it very often.'

The present beckoned in the shape of another reporter who wanted to talk about Sheffield United. But Martin Peters left me with an explanation as as to why at 37 he was still deeply involved in the game on which, for all his self-doubt, he has left an indelible mark of quality.

'I show it differently. I'm not volatile. But just like Alan Ball I have a very strong will to win...'

# ROGER HUNT

**Born Golborne, Lancashire, 20 July 1938; Culcheth Sec. Mod. School, Leigh Grammar School, Croft Youth Club, Stockton Heath; joined Liverpool May 1958 and turned pro July 1959; League debut 9 Sep. 1959 v Scunthorpe (home, 2-0); England debut 4 April 1962 v Austria at Wembley (3-1) during season when his 41 goals took Liverpool into Div. 1; scored but was dropped—a fate suffered in first 6 matches, despite 7 goals; in 5 cases was replaced by Greaves, though both started World Cup campaign; 31 goals in 1963–64 and 30 in 1965–66 helped Liverpool to 2 League titles; had faced three of the German side in Cup Winners Cup final only weeks before the World Cup...**

You can find Roger Hunt in the Yellow Pages: *Hunt Bros. (Culcheth) Haulage*. An appropriate occupation for a man who travelled long distances in England's cause and who carried a heavy load, both physical and mental, throughout the summer of 1966.

At 43 only an extra line or two around the eyes revealed any ageing from the days when Hunt set a record of 245 League goals for Liverpool. But his fitness is no longer a product of the training ground and the weight-room. Nowadays his activities are those of the company director—the squash court and the golf course.

His life revolves around Hunt Bros. which, as the name implies, is very much a family concern. Roger's father, Richard, started the business and at 68 still loves nothing more than climbing into a lorry and driving. Uncle Harry is even older and still takes on a role in the offices midway between Manchester and Liverpool, though Roger and his younger brother Peter have bought out his partnership. The third generation is already learning the trade through David, Roger's son; and a sixth Hunt, Peter's boy, is also earmarked to keep the wagons rolling in the future.

It's a business that has enabled Roger Hunt to make a smooth adjustment to the world that most of us know, away from the glory of 11 years of automatic selection for Liverpool and of 34 appearances for England in an international career which stretched over two years beyond the World Cup. Yet away from the recognition of the team headquarters, he was all too often the least appreciated

and revered of the boys of '66.

Though he totalled 18 goals for his country—three of which came in the World Cup finals, two on his 28th birthday against France—Hunt rarely enjoyed national acclaim, continually suffering in comparison to a Jimmy Greaves whose sleek style was easy on the eye of the fan.

At times Hunt's strength and aggression did lack a sureness of touch, but he was central to Ramsey's pattern of play. In internationals he harried and chased the composure out of defenders. The label of unselfishness was rightly pinned on his work, but often as a back-handed compliment for implied short-comings...

What was unselfish, though, was his willingness to submerge in the team cause the undoubted talent that made him a First Division goalscorer just as feared as Greaves. For England he acted out instructions from Ramsey with which he personally disagreed— and which led to a half-time row in the final itself.

'I didn't really enjoy playing the system that England played, because it was completely foreign to the way I played at Liverpool. It was mainly a running, chasing role. Always more defenders than forwards.

'Once we got to Wembley for the final and I got on the pitch I was in another world for twenty minutes of play. It was such a big occasion. It seemed a bit unreal in a way because of the importance of it, and I couldn't take it in for a while, until I got really involved and then it was just another game to me.

'For this particular game Germany were playing with a sweeper, and Alf

*Frustration for Hunt as he goes close against Newcastle at Anfield in October 1968 while searching for a goal to equal the Liverpool League record of 233, set by Gordon Hodgson. He eventually passed the record the following January.*

asked me to try to get as close to that player as possible. I know the longer the game went on Alan Ball attacked more, but really it was a 4-4-2 system. And I wasn't getting in the game. So after going beyond the first quarter of an hour without getting a kick, I started roaming around and coming back a bit to try to get hold of the ball to get a bit of confidence. Just staying on the sweeper meant I was marked all the time, with no room.

'So I remember coming in at half-time and Alf wanted to know what

was going on and why I was not doing as I was told, pushing up on the sweeper. I didn't actually blow up but I replied that I wasn't in the game, I wasn't getting involved. Then Bobby Moore stepped in and said to leave it as it was. We'd equalised of course by then.'

Hunt had taken his place in the team despite a barrage of publicity—one that he became hardened against but never totally impervious to—calling for the return of a now-fit Greaves in the final.

'I remember the night before the

final we went to the cinema, and as we were getting off the coach Alf Ramsey pulled me to one side and told me that I was playing. With all the speculation about Jimmy Greaves he was putting my mind at rest. I did expect to play because I'd played in all the other five games, but a lot of people still say it was me who took Greaves' place. But it was Geoff Hurst.

'Before we went on tour prior to the World Cup I'd been a regular in the England side for quite a few games, but when we got the numbers we would wear in competition I was given number 21. I was really sick about that. I think the first eleven players was his original team, but during the tour he had a change of mind. I forced my way into the team. So when we beat Portugal I couldn't really see how he could change the side. But it was still nice when he told me I was in and I couldn't wait to phone home and give them the news.'

Despite the half-time altercation with Ramsey Hunt's commitment retained its unrelenting quality, and though his efforts earned him few headlines he looks back on his performance in the final with more satisfaction than in the preliminary games, when his name featured on the list of scorers.

'The longer the final went on the more room I seemed to get. I don't know whether they tired a bit perhaps. I enjoyed that game more than any of the others, because I thought I played better. I didn't get any rave write-ups, but I wasn't expecting any because nobody seemed to give me any write-ups at all. But I thought I did particularly well with regard to getting hold of the ball and using it.

'I would have loved to have scored in that game. I really would. And we won it twice didn't we? I can always remember thinking when they equalised how near can you get to winning a World Cup winners medal and not win it?'

The sureness of Hunt's play in the final has been largely forgotten in the face of the more spectacular memories created by Geoff Hurst. When his part is recalled it's often only as the chief witness to the moment of controversy on which the destiny of the Jules Rimet Trophy finally hung. Hunt was taking up his usual pre-

datory position as Hurst pivoted and shot against the underside of the bar in extra time.

'Geoff turned brilliantly on the edge of the goal area, and I was about on the six-yard line. And when the ball came down off the bar it looked to me to be at least a foot over the line. Now I'd scored lots of goals on rebounds, and my normal reaction would be to go in. But I was so certain that it was over that I turned away.

'People still say to me why didn't I follow up and put it in. But I wouldn't have got to the ball. Weber,

*Hunt with his final League total for Liverpool, set in 403 games. His overall total for the club was 285 goals in 488 competitive matches. In three closing seasons at Bolton he scored 25 goals in 88 games.*

*A stroll with his daughter the day after he broke the Liverpool scoring record. Six weeks later he was pulled off against Leicester in the Cup; eight weeks later he told Ramsey he did not wish to be considered for future England teams because he felt he had come to the end of his usefulness.*

who was man-to-man marking me, in fact headed it behind for what would have been a corner. I know I turned away, but I don't think even if I had followed in I would have got there before him.

'Immediately I looked over and the linesman was still on his way forward. There's no way he could see whether it was over the line or not because he wasn't even in line with it. So when he gave the decision I don't know how he came to it because I'm sure he didn't know!'

Hunt's recollections of the rest of the day have become hazy over the passage of time, but they include following a tearful Bobby Charlton up to receive his medal, swapping his shirt with Weber, his shadow through the match, who would later praise the industry of the England forward, and of spending the evening in the team

hotel with squad member Gerry Byrne and their wives.

'I wouldn't say I felt any more excited about winning than I did the previous year when I won the FA Cup with Liverpool. I still don't.

'I used to get that much stick from the Wembley crowd for one thing. Plus the fact that the press were always against me, because it was always Jimmy Greaves versus me. Before the World Cup it was either Jimmy or me, and afterwards it was just the same because I was the first one to get dropped after the World Cup. And it was Jimmy who replaced me, against Scotland.

'I suppose all that gave me a bit of an inferiority complex. And also playing that system in which I was doing a job which the ordinary person did not understand.'

But Hunt retained his place in Ramsey's plans through the European Championship in which England finished third in 1968. The following season he chose his own moment to step down after public criticism mounted again when at Wembley, against Rumania, he missed a straight-forward scoring chance. England's next opponents were France, and as the squad gathered prior to the game Hunt sought out Ramsey.

'As I've said all along I wasn't happy playing in that system. I enjoyed international football more before they started playing 4-4-2. I'd been going through a bad spell at Liverpool, and I was coming up 31. Also I never really wanted to play in the next World Cup, because after '66 I had felt the whole experience had been a tremendous strain. I felt I didn't want to go through it again.

'So I'd made up my mind after I'd had what I felt was a particularly bad game against Rumania that I wanted to finish with international football. I had a word with Alf, and he said that if that's what I wanted than fair enough. He did say: "Aren't you coming to Mexico with me", even though it was almost eighteen months before the finals there. And when the Mexico squad was announced I did feel a bit rotten then. I would like to have been involved but I wouldn't have relished playing that same type of role again.'

If Hunt bowed out of England's squad at his own request, the break with Liverpool was far from voluntary and clearly much more painful. Only days after what turned out to be his last cap he broke the club scoring record, but six weeks later Bill Shankly called for a substitute for him when Liverpool were struggling against Leicester in a fifth round FA Cup tie. If the Anfield fans were astonished—there was talk at the time of a boycott of home games—Hunt was staggered, at first refusing to leave the field and then ripping off his shirt and throwing it at the bench.

'I'd been in the team for eleven seasons and we never used the substitute rule for regular players. I just couldn't believe that I was being pulled off.

'That was probably the start of my career coming to an end at Liverpool. If Shanks thought he could pull me off, he must have thought that I wasn't doing the stuff like I used to. He decided to break the team up anyway, and about six more as well as me got dropped or sold when we could have all expected two or three more years with any other club.'

In December 1969 he finally made the break; after initially rejecting the overtures of Bolton Wanderers he accepted the move at a fee of £32,000.

'It was terrible. I badly wanted to finish at Liverpool, to play until I was about 34 and retire there. But I didn't want to finish up in the reserves. I was still, I thought, playing well, still top scorer, but Shankly made it plain I wouldn't be in the team.

'It took me a long time to get over leaving Liverpool. Bolton were not having a very successful season. They were in the bottom half of the Second Division. It was such a change. I didn't realise the gap. Being with Liverpool all my career I thought everywhere was like that.

'And I love Bolton Wanderers. I used to support them. They're the nearest ground to where I live, and I used to love watching Nat Lofthouse, and Nat was the manager who signed me. Everything looked as though it would be okay, but unfortunately it didn't work out very well.

'I'll always remember one of the very first games I played there. We played Blackpool on a shocking day. And we came out and there was no spectators behind one of the goals on

that big embankment at Burnden Park. They were all huddled under cover. Such emptiness when I was used to 45,000 every week at Liverpool. It took me a long time to adjust to that.'

Four managers in two and a half years while Roger Hunt was there emphasised the uncertainty of Bolton's performances. His own game also began to wind down as Wanderers dropped into the Third Division, and talk of being farmed out on loan to places like Workington and Tranmere Rovers hastened his decision to retire before his 34th birthday.

He didn't pass into the ranks of former players without one remarkable tribute from the Liverpool supporters who idolised 'Sir Roger'. In an unprecedented manner the Anfield gates were locked half an hour before the kick-off for his testimonial night

*Roger Hunt of 'Hunt Brothers'. He began by 'helping his father and uncle a couple of afternoons a week' while with Bolton, but now he runs it full time with his younger brother Peter. 'We're not going to be millionaires, but we should be set up now. It was a hard slog for four or five years.'*

135

on 11 April 1972. Thousands were left outside as 56,214 saw Liverpool's 1965 FA Cup winning side play an England side that included many from the 1966 final team.

Hunt took into his new life some £25,000 from the gate receipts to help secure a future outside the game. While at Bolton he had been helping out his father and uncle 'a couple of afternoons a week'. And gradually he gravitated towards the family haulage business.

'I started by doing a bit of driving, so I had to take out a Heavy Goods Vehicle License Class One, so I went on a course for that. Then I went on a management course for a week in Staffordshire, and worked my way in. I didn't really enjoy it at first, but I gradually got more interested. I was just a worker to start with to see how I was going to find it. If I hadn't grown to like the business I wouldn't have stayed. But when my uncle wanted to lessen his load, my brother and I bought him out and we were made directors.

'For the last four or five years it's been a slog paying all that off. But we've been expanding the business by getting new vehicles. And it's become more and more interesting for me. Now even though business isn't good we've got a solid firm.

'These days it's very rare that I go out driving. My typical day would be to get in the office about nine, and my job is sorting all the work out. Loads here, loads there. Return loads. Pricing loads. Going out visiting customers. And I'm usually still in the office at half-past six at night.'

He confesses to missing the fellowship that goes with life in the dressing-room, but not the so-called glamour that went with his former trade.

'When I finished I bought a season ticket at Liverpool and one at Bolton and I thought I would alternate between the two. But though I reckoned I would enjoy watching I didn't. I felt an outsider even though I suppose I wasn't really. But I didn't want to hang around the ground like some old players do.

'I thought that I couldn't live without football. I thought there would be nothing afterwards. Yet in a way I enjoy life more now because I can relax and do exactly what I want, when I want...'

*More than two years after he had left Liverpool for Bolton, Hunt returned for a record-breaking testimonial against an England side on 11 April 1972. Thousands were left outside when the gates were closed 30 minutes before the kick-off with 56,214 fans inside paying £25,000 to pay their tribute to 'Sir Roger'. Here Hunt, supported by Bill Shankly, salutes 'the magic Kop'.*

# ALF RAMSEY

**Born Dagenham, 22 Jan. 1920; Becontree Heath School and Five Elms, Portsmouth; joined Southampton as amateur in 1943–44 season after representing his army battalion against them; turned pro (on £8 per week) in August 1944, aged 24; switched from centre-forward to full-back by manager Bill Dodgin; League debut 26 Oct. 1946 v Plymouth (home, 5–1); England debut 2 Dec. 1948 v Switzerland at Highbury (6–0), but not used in next 7 games; lost place at Southampton to Bill Ellerington; refused move to Sheffield W. March 1949, but moved to Spurs in May for equivalent of £21,000; won Div. 2 and Div. 1 championship medals first 2 seasons; England recall Nov. 1949 (at Tottenham); scored 3 penalties for his country; last cap in defeat by Hungary at Wembley Nov. 1953; lost place at Spurs early 1955; appointed Ipswich manager August 1955; on shoestring budget took them to championships of Div. 3 South (1957), Div. 2 (1961) and Div. 1 (1962); succeeded Walter Winterbottom as England team manager early 1963; suffered only 6 defeats in 44 games to the World Cup final, including first 2 in charge...**

On 1 May 1974 the Football Association announced that they had sacked Sir Alf Ramsey from his position as England's manager.

The official statement was couched heavily in bureaucratic terms: 'The Committee of the Football Association, which has been considering the future of English football, has examined some aspects in detail and progress has been made.

'Following meetings, a unanimous recommendation was submitted to the Executive Committee that Sir Alf Ramsey should be replaced as the England team manager. The recommendation was accepted unanimously by the Executive Committee.

'In view of the forthcoming international matches in the Home International Championship and against Argentina and three matches in the European tour, it was decided that a caretaker manager should be appointed.

'With the approval of the Coventry City FC, Mr Joe Mercer has agreed to undertake this task. It should be stated that he does not wish to be considered for the job of permanent manager, so immediate steps will be taken to appoint the England team manager as soon as possible.

'The Football Association wishes at this time to record its deep appreciation of all that Sir Alf Ramsey has accomplished and the debt owed to him by English football for his unbending loyalty and dedication and the high level of integrity that he brought to world football.'

The man who had predicted that England would win the World Cup, and was as good as his word, had been discarded. He left behind a proud record of just 17 defeats in 113 internationals that he had supervised.

The eight subsequent years after his 1966 triumph were adjudged as relative failure. England had fumbled to third place in the European Championship of 1968, and had been losing quarter-finalists to West Germany, again, in the 1972 tournament. The collapse to defeat in León in the 1970 World Cup had been followed by a failure to qualify for the 1974 finals, following arguably the most frustrating international in the country's history, the one-sided draw against Poland at Wembley; the conversion of just one of a catalogue of chances that came England's way would have protected Ramsey's job.

Yet as he wrote at the time of his dismissal in the *News of the World*: 'That draw against Poland—a tremendous disappointment for a team that deserved to win—followed by defeat against Italy—meant I was a dead duck. Suddenly the handshakes stopped. I sensed a coldness among the FA Council.'

The mood was in stark contrast

*Modest in victory: Ramsey seems almost reluctant to hold the trophy he worked so hard to win. In three years he had revolutionised the role of the England manager, improved the international set-up and brought the country the first major honour in its history. And he had said all along that he'd do it. Eight years later, after losing only 17 of his 113 matches, he would fade even more quickly to a quiet life in Suffolk. 'I must confess that over the whole 11 years I never really enjoyed working for the FA,' he said shortly after his dismissal.*

to the cries of 'Ramsey, Ramsey' which had echoed to Wembley's rafters on 30 July 1966. After 11 years at the helm it may well have been that England's ship needed a new captain, but sadly the change took place in an atmosphere of mutiny. This came not from the players, whose loyalties even in Ramsey's later generations stood as total as those expressed in earlier chapters, but from within the game's organisers— and most notably from the media.

From the start Ramsey's relationships with the press were uneasy, regarded, it seemed on his part, as one of the unfortunate necessities of his job which distracted him from his priorities with his players. When the squad was in session, arrangements were made for the media, but these were adhered to with the strictness of prison visiting hours.

In the happy times, reporters had to live with the considerable difficulties posed by Ramsey's policies, but when the going on the field got tough that attitude rebounded in his face. In April 1972 I stood on the terraces as England wilted to that 3-1 defeat by West Germany at Wembley, but high

in the press-box the anti-Ramsey corps visibly showed their joy.

In 1981 Sir Alf Ramsey's attitude remained unbending. When I contacted him at his home in Suffolk, he declined my request for an interview. 'I'm very glad you have spoken to all the players, and I would be interested to discuss the World Cup with you. However, I have a contract with a publisher about that subject, and I would be in breach of it if I spoke to you. If you have to write about me, Martin, I think you know me quite well anyway.'

In 1974 and 1975 I spent many hours with Alf in his capacity as a football expert employed by Independent Television, where I was an editorial assistant. Certainly I know him well enough to realise that he would not submit to any amount of additional persuasion.

Ramsey's single-mindedness has been thoroughly documented—and is perhaps best illustrated by the experience of two journalists on 31 July 1966, the day after the World Cup final. Both men, highly respected in their field, had reported the competition with a genuine sense of responsibility, and had accurately apportioned credit, much of it in Ramsey's direction. But that Sunday they had to suffer the rebuff of 'Gentlemen, this is my day off' when they made their professional enquiries about Ramsey's post-victory feelings.

It was a reaction in keeping with his rejection in 1962 of an invitation from the Ipswich directors to join an impromptu party to celebrate winning the League Championship. Ramsey was approached while watching a junior match at Portman Road. 'No thank you, I'm working,' was the reply.

Yet I was present at times when he opened a door to part of his personality that he seldom revealed to strangers. A dry sense of humour surfaced when Brian Moore, lunching with him prior to a television broadcast, asked: 'Alf, did you play when England were beaten by the United States in the 1950 World Cup?'

Sir Alf responded with a grin, 'I was the only one who did.' Another television idea was to compare his choice for an England side, then under Don Revie, with that selected by Brian Clough. It made for an inter-

FAR LEFT: *Alf joined Southampton as an amateur centre-forward after playing for his army battalion against them, when he impressed despite a 10-0 thrashing.*

LEFT: *Ramsey pictured at the start of the 1950-51 season, when he helped Spurs to the League title and remained unchallenged as England's right-back.*

BELOW: *With Gil Merrick during the 6-3 defeat by Hungary at Wembley in 1953— the last of his caps.*

esting interchange of views between a man who had managed England and one who was building the credentials for the post. During the discussion, Ramsey retained his dignity, but privately he admitted afterwards: 'I think Brian Clough chose a couple of right wallies in his side.' Only the word he used was not wallies.

Ramsey's achievements made him an inevitable choice for the media, even though his clipped vowels and a limited vocabulary would never make him a 'natural'. Some journalists who had found him aloof during his England reign talked of hypocrisy as he sold his story to a national newspaper and took on a reporter's role for the 1974 World Cup. Though Ramsey may have been suspicious of the media, his lack of concern for their problems while he was England's manager was simply that. His job was to concentrate on his players, and he could never understand why anyone should think otherwise.

Roger Hunt's disenchantment with Ramsey's tactics, which led to an exchange of words at half-time in the World Cup final, is the nearest to any criticism of him by the players I spoke to during the writing of this book. Moreover, Hunt's loyalty was still unquestioned, and his commitment to Ramsey never wavered during

Ramsey with the squad that took Ipswich to the Third Division South Championship in 1957. He had joined the club, newly relegated from their only ever season in Division 2, a few months after losing his place in the Spurs side in 1955. At Portman Road he made bricks without straw; working with limited resources, both in terms of money and talent, he steered the club to the Division 2 title in 1961.

his stuttering international career.

Bobby Charlton's comments on Sir Alf epitomised the views of the other boys of '66. 'He always showed you respect as a professional player. When you were chosen for the side he never once tried to improve you as a player from a skill point of view. He had enough good players in the country to be able to say, "Right, you're the player that I want for that position. I'm not going to tell you how to play football."

'He'd tell you if you'd done something wrong, though, something professionally wrong. He'd haul you over the coals—sometimes so strongly that it was embarrassing. I remember one incident when he took Keith Newton to task after a friendly international. He'd allowed them to go through by committing himself, which he should never have done as a full-back. In front of everybody he really pilloried poor Keith.

'But when he picked you he told you the pattern the team was going to play. And he gave you the confidence that you'd been picked because you were a good player, not because your club team was doing particularly well or because of anyone else's say so, or because the press had been clam-

ouring for you to be in. Strangers used to come into the side and fit in straight away. We appreciated his professional outlook, and he made it very easy for the players.

'He found a formula that made England consistent for the first time ever. Up until Alf came anybody could beat us abroad. He stopped us being frightened of anybody, and he made us believe we were better than anybody.

'His professionalism and attention to detail showed through straight away. I recall when we went on his first real tour in 1963, which was Czechoslovakia, East Germany and Switzerland, and we won all three matches. The first game was in Bratislava, and he told everybody that when they were doing their warm-up they had to do it in the particular areas of the pitch that they were most likely to play in. I was his left-winger then, and I had to do all my warm-up down the left-side touchlines. I had to practise taking corners in case there was a difficult run-up to the ball. Across a running-track or something. Alf used to say that you might only get one corner in the match, so you should be fully prepared to make the most of it.

'But above all he made you think that you were playing because you were a good player. He took the whole responsibility, and it was marvellous.

'And because he took all that responsibility, it was, in a way, his undoing at the end. His public relations, when he went abroad, looking back now, were diabolical. But it was his way of protecting us from everything. I suppose that he realised that once the results started going the other way this would all come back on him. He did say that he didn't have the young players to replace the likes of Bobby Moore and Gordon Banks, and he forecast what was going to happen, even while he was still safely in the job.

'Unfortunately for Alf everybody used to say that he was responsible for the decline of football because he made this "terrible" 4-3-3 system of play. Now he developed that system for the international team. He didn't tell every club that this is what they should do. He had the best players to perform 4-3-3 well, which they did. Like when we beat Spain in 1965. It was perfection. But for club sides to copy it was ludicrous. You need unselfish runners like Roger Hunt and Geoff Hurst, tireless players like Alan Ball. You need unbelievably brave players like Gordon Banks, George Cohen, Ray Wilson.

'He didn't tell everybody to copy. But when we won the World Cup they thought they must. Then when everyone's complaining at having to watch 4-3-3 being played badly, suddenly it's all Alf Ramsey's fault.'

With the wisdom of hindsight, Ramsey's proclamation in 1963 that England would win the World Cup seems even more unusual than it did at the time. To the new England manager it was a product of his logical thinking, but his public image has rarely been characterised by predictions of such a forthright manner.

Between 1963 and the World Cup he not only built up an improving standard of performance on the pitch. He imposed a discipline that cannot be placed too high when it comes to analysing the reasons for England's success. In one often-recalled incident seven players, including four who would play in the World Cup final, broke a curfew in May 1964 while

the squad were preparing to fly out to play Portugal. When the guilty returned each found his passport placed conspicuously on his bed. Ramsey was making his point. Passports are only handed back to individuals at the *end* of their involvement in travelling on tour.

The discipline bred loyalty. Ramsey's concern for his players regularly earned their respect and affection. He also recognised that there were times when men needed to let their hair down, and on occasions when he did permit the alcohol to flow his was the first hand in his pocket to pay for the round.

The continuity of his thinking now appears very different to succeeding regimes. Don Revie, who was totally successful in creating a family atmosphere with Leeds United, never welded his players as tightly as Ramsey. Revie's bingo and carpet bowls sessions that passed the time in hotels have often been publicly criticised by members of his squads. Ramsey's obsession with showing cowboy films for the same reason was hardly a more highbrow form of entertainment. Yet his troops soldiered on uncomplainingly.

In the 1966 World Cup Ramsey's

*Cliff Michelmore interviews Ramsey after he had done it again in 1962—but this time in the First Division, and in Ipswich's first ever season there. Critics said that other teams had lost the title rather than Ipswich had won it — but their manager would get used to that sort of jibe in the years that followed. Only two sides won at Portman Road and runners-up Burnley were trounced 6-2. The following January Ramsey accepted the England job—after it had been turned down by Burnley's Jimmy Adamson.*

141

*ABOVE: Alf and Vicky at home in April 1970. Few other people have been privileged to get close to a man whose public image is one of a shy, difficult, often contradictory character.*

*RIGHT: Ramsey presents a silver salver to George Cohen at his testimonial in 1969, following his retirement through injury. The England boss was always fiercely loyal to his players—and they to him.*

preparation reflected his methodical approach, a detailed 11 days at Lilleshall followed by a brief weekend at home for the players. More training at the Hendon Hall Hotel was the preparation for the four-game tour, which many observers felt was too demanding so close to the tournament. He then scheduled another brief visit to wives and families—for most of the squad just a few hours—after the return to England, before the final get-together for the opening match against Uruguay.

The events of the subsequent three weeks proved the validity of the format. Ramsey retained a permanent place in the headlines: loyal to Stiles after his tackle on Simon which led to calls for the Manchester United player to be banned, unforgiving against Argentina when he stepped on the pitch to stop Cohen swapping his shirt, shortly followed by his now famous television interview when he declared: 'We have still to play our best football. It will come against the right type of opposition, a team who come out to play football and not to act as animals.'

All the players remember his inspiring talk before extra time in the final—how he told them they had won the World Cup once, now they must go out and win it again, how he took note of the Germans prostrate with the cramp being massaged out of their legs; how he ordered his players up on their feet to re-assume a business-like pose.

It was very much in character that after the presentation Ramsey refused the overtures of his players to join in the lap of honour. Instead he strode to the dressing-room, smiling but totally composed. Yet the most revealing incident came at the moment when Geoff Hurst smashed in his shot for the conclusive fourth goal.

That skilled photographer Gerry Cranham has made a bit from pointing his camera at the bench at that moment. Amid scenes of uninhibited joy from the training staff and the other members of the squad, Sir Alf sat stony-faced. During our association in television eight years later, I asked him why. 'I was watching Overath chasing back after Hurst, and admiring him for such effort and commitment in the last minute of such a match.' If ever evidence was needed to prove

ABOVE: *The full England squad pose for pictures before the defence of the World Cup in 1970.*

LEFT: *Ramsey manages a smile for his friend and rival Helmut Schoen after the Germans had avenged their 1966 defeat, at León. 'I don't think we could have played any differently if we had tried,' he said at the time—and then brought his team home early as his critics enjoyed a field day.*

143

Ramsey's detached professional approach surely that composure, when his greatest day was about to be crowned, is the most conclusive.

He approached retaining the World Cup with great optimism, often implying that he had a greater array of talent at his disposal for Mexico. Critics chipped at a number of controlled but less than thrilling performances in the interim, though not on the night of 14 March 1969. Then, Ramsey's joy at a 5-0 thrashing of France was muted by becoming another of the England party to have a burglary at his home.

The Mexican experience, in the end, only served to sharpen the knives of Ramsey's critics. There is no doubt, as Bobby Charlton confirmed, that the manager cost England any support they might have drawn from the locals. The cavalcade of cars, horns blaring, which circled the team's headquarters the night before England played Brazil symbolised Mexico's dislike of visitors who cast the public aside and rejected local provisions in favour of their own imported fare.

The disaster in León brought more criticism to Ramsey's door. Helmut Schoen, his West German counterpart, had more easily accepted the use of substitutes—not permitted in 1966. Schoen used Jurgen Grabowski as a regular replacement for Reinhard Libuda to ensure that he had a fresh attacking winger on call, and Grabowski tantalised Terry Cooper to distraction in extra time.

Ramsey, meanwhile, reached for permutations that did not work. Bobby Charlton and Martin Peters were brought off against West Germany when the result looked secure. Colin Bell and Norman Hunter found the tide of the game turning against England. In Ramsey's defence, his side were not in the habit of surrendering two-goal leads.

More than three years later that uncertainty about substitutes produced another situation which pleased only those clamouring for a new manager. As England battered away in frustration trying to crack Poland's resistance at Wembley it needed Bobby Moore, alongside him on the

*Back after an absence of three years: greeting Terry Hibbitt and the Birmingham players after taking over as caretaker manager in September 1977. Ramsey, who had been on the board since January 1976, had a good early run, winning six and drawing two of his first 10 League games, and in November he became full-time manager. Gradually results got worse and in the March, following rumours of rifts with Trevor Francis and others, he resigned because 'the board changed their mind over the transfer of Francis', whom he thought should go. It was Ramsey's last management post in England.*

bench, to urge Ramsey to throw on the Derby County forward Kevin Hector. By the time Ramsey decided only two minutes remained. Even then Hector had a header cleared from the line, inches away only from a goal which would have taken England into the 1974 finals.

In that moment Ramsey took on the fate of the condemned man. His loyalty to his players was now construed as stubbornness. His style was written off as unimaginative and unambitious, often alongside his unfortunate quote on returning from Mexico in 1970, when he declared that 'England have nothing to learn from Brazil.' Taken literally it was damning; he could only have meant that no England side would ever be able to play in the Brazilian manner, that our strengths would always lie in our physique, competitive spirit and team organisation rather than in the sunshine swagger of swerving free-kicks and loose-limbed agility.

So Ramsey witnessed the 1974 World Cup finals as an ex-England manager, still fêted by Germans who

recognised him even when he was shopping in a village supermarket. His televison work drew more from his presence than any smoothness of style—though he prophesied at the outset West Germany's eventual victory in the tournament.

There had been talk of a testimonial match for him at Wembley, against the Germans of 1966. Instead a dinner was held in his honour and 62 of the 101 players he had selected travelled to London for the occasion, including a rare gathering of the 11 boys of '66.

In September 1974 he accepted an offer to become a director of a building firm in Ipswich, and the following year he joined Gola, the sportswear manufacturers, in a consultative capacity. For almost two years small paragraphs appeared in newspapers suggesting he was returning to the game at various outposts including Uruguay and Saudi Arabia; he was linked with Ajax of Amsterdam, Anderlecht of Brussels and, nearer home, Norwich and Portsmouth.

But in January 1976 he resurfaced

*Cheers, Sir Alf. 'The silent knight' proudly displays the first pint pulled at the pub named after him in Tunbridge Wells in January 1973. The place was built by the company owned by football fanatic Sidney Brickman, who said he had been a Ramsey admirer ever since Alf put a consoling arm round his shoulders as he stood dejectedly in a train corridor following a Cup defeat at York 19 years before. Did he mind this kind of recognition? 'I had no choice...you can't say no to a friend, can you?'*

as a director of Birmingham City, clearly enthusiastic to get back into the game that he once rashly described as 'the most important human activity in the world.' In September the following year he stepped up to caretaker manager, unpaid, following the sacking of, Willie Bell. His impact was immediate. In his first match, at Middlesbrough, Birmingham won 2-1 to take their first points of the season, following four League defeats.

Two months later, when the club were on the verge of appointing Mike Smith, then the Welsh national team manager, Sir Alf changed his mind about not wanting the job on a permanent basis. His resignation from his directorship offically allowed him to be paid, though he commented obliquely at the time: 'Players do not like to confide in directors.' Birmingham again marked the appointment with a victory.

In January 1978 Birmingham City won 3-2 at Anfield, where Liverpool would not be beaten again for three years, but Ramsey's patience then began to be disturbed by his star player, Trevor Francis. The following month

he fined Francis £1,000 for speaking to the press without his permission.

Early in March, Birmingham announced Ramsey's resignation, prematurely in his own eyes. The final conflict involved a series of bad results—the last, a 4-0 defeat at Coventry, being described by Ramsey as a 'thoroughly bad performance'. The future of Francis, though, held the key to the parting of the ways. It was to be another year before Brian Clough made the Birmingham player the first million-pound footballer, but Ramsey wanted to sell him then, and tne implication was that the board changed their mind after agreeing initially to Ramsey's view. Under Sir Alf, Birmingham's record did not match his performances with Ipswich: just 24 points from 26 First Division games.

Since then his flirtations with football have been overseas. In 1979 he was linked with a lucrative post as the national team manager of Kuwait, but it did not materialise. Later the same year he was chosen by the Greek First Division club Panathinaikos as a 'technical adviser'. It lasted just over a year, something of an achievement in the highly charged atmosphere of football in that country, where not every administrator would share Ramsey's ethics. He left in October 1980, but made no public comment on his dismissal.

In 1980 Sir Alf Ramsey passed his 60th birthday, sadly distant even as an observer from England's attempts to win a trophy under Ron Greenwood. His remoteness is clearly his choice, because he never mixes easily when the topic is not his beloved football. One always felt, in fact, that he was at his happiest when he was not being recognised.

There will always be those who crossed swords with Sir Alf Ramsey, who found him rude, who christened him Old Stoneface. They would be those he would not allow to get close to him, and his privacy remains to this day.

As a public figure he was ill-equipped, but how harshly should he be judged for that. The bottom line is that the boys of '66 loved him, and they won England's only major international trophy.

And they did it for Alf Ramsey as much as for themselves.

# THE ENGLAND SQUAD

**The 1966 reserves were a balance of youth and experience, from Norman Hunter (22) to Ron Flowers, 10 years his senior. On the day of the final they could boast nearly 250 caps between them, but only four would play for England again. Just three were to become League club managers, and the interests of the 11 now range from running pubs to reporting for radio, from owning a fish and chip shop to writing novels...**

## JIMMY GREAVES [8]

In 1981 Jimmy Greaves epitomised the successful ex-footballer. His comments on the play of the new generations could be heard weekly on ATV and read in *The Sun*. With Norman Giller, a freelance writer and very good friend, he had already collaborated on five books with plans for more to come. He even found time to squeeze other business ventures into a crowded schedule.

In all, it would seem a logical development for the most famous England player *not* to take part in the 1966 World Cup final. Indeed until the teams actually strode out of the Wembley tunnel many of the public still believed he would be recalled and feared for England's goal power without him. Yet from, and partly because of, his most agonising disappointment at missing the country's ultimate triumph, the life of Jimmy Greaves started to slide. And it eventually tumbled helter-skelter towards near oblivion. No-one knew just how much it had hurt.

Greaves had always enjoyed a social drink, but gradually he grew more dependent on alcohol. It affected his playing career; it wrecked a considerable business empire he had developed during his England days; it threatened to destroy his marriage to Irene, and at the very depths of his problems they were divorced. A reconciliation with his wife has been at the hub of his remarkable battle to overcome his alcoholism.

If Greaves shocked the country when he revealed the extent to which he had sunk in a horrifying book and a most poignant television documentary, he earned the nation's respect by his strength of character as he fought back. I well remember in the mid-1970s being thrilled by an invitation to travel to Guernsey for a charity match—just because I would play alongside Jimmy Greaves. Yet at the airport, Billy Meadows, who played for Hereford United when they beat Newcastle United in that famous Cup tie of 1972 and who was then manager of Barnet, where Greaves was playing at the time, took each of us to one side and warned us not to buy our idol an alcoholic drink during our trip.

Even then Jimmy Greaves retained a public image of some propriety but his revelations, published a couple of years later and designed to help others in similar distress, made harrowing reading. His quest for drink had turned him into a bankrupt, an unrecognisable tramp who collapsed in gutters and dustbins. A hopeless case, it seemed...until a few loyal friends rekindled his fighting spirit. Today, chirpy and as popular as ever he was in the game, he will never boast or concede that the problem is totally conquered. The days since he has touched alcohol, however, have stretched into years.

Ramsey fielded the World Cup winning side for England's following three internationals, a 2-0 win over Northern Ireland in October 1966, and a 0-0 draw with Czechoslovakia and a 5-1 thrashing of Wales the following month. But Jimmy Greaves was recalled for Scotland's visit to Wembley the following April, replacing Roger Hunt. He also played, and scored, against Spain in May, and took the field for his final international in Vienna on 27 May 1967. It's interesting that in the last two games he played for the first time with both Hurst and Hunt. He had scored 44 goals in his 57 games—but it was essentially a voluntary exit.

Later that year he quietly asked Ramsey not to consider him for training get-togethers if he was not going to play. Jimmy Greaves, an instinctive goalscorer, the greatest Britain produced in the modern era, had never been one for workrate and tactical discussions. His was an idle genius. Ramsey listened sympathetically: 'There was no bitterness. No hard words. We agreed. He would just peacefully fade out of the international picture.'

The two kept their discussions confidential, though the facts filtered through to the press. It did not stop several campaigns in the media calling for Greaves' recall as England went through an ineffective spell in front of goal, with all the old arguments about flair versus functionalism. Eventually, in March 1969, Ramsey could stand it no more: 'I'm being crucified by a campaign to get Greaves back. He has asked not to be selected for England!'

A year later he was on the move from Spurs,

joining West Ham United just before the transfer deadline in the swap that sent Martin Peters to White Hart Lane. Greaves' value, after a disappointing few months (in sharp contast to his eight seasons as Spurs' top scorer) was a mere £54,000. He had established a reputation of scoring on his first appearances for clubs and country at all levels—he had done it 10 times, including debuts for Chelsea, AC Milan and Tottenham, England youth, under-23 and full—and duly obliged with two goals for West Ham at Manchester City.

Always a marvellous dribbler, with acceleration as well as control, Jimmy later added that knack of all great goalscorers—of being in the right position. And he had the temperament and the ability to finish the job. Some would question his workrate, his 'contribution'; most knew he could win a game in seconds.

Greaves attended the 1970 World Cup not as a player—like 10 others from 1966—but as a driver, finishing sixth in the London–Mexico City car rally.

Yet he played only one more full season, announcing his retirement in 1971 at the premature age of 31. 'I was losing it. I could've dropped down a division and played on but that had no appeal. The game's gone sick. The demands on players increase every season. You don't get the chance to enjoy the game like I did when I first came into football.'

Greaves' final tally was the staggering total of 357 goals in 517 League matches, all in the First Division. Those figures might have been even more impressive but for the bout of hepatitis a few months before the 1966 World Cup which he later reckoned to have robbed him of half a

*Jimmy Greaves and Geoff Hurst try one on for size at their office in 1970, when the two players were partners in a sportswear firm.*

yard of his speed. How much the World Cup disappointment robbed him of his appetite can never be gauged.

Typically he never disputed Ramsey's judgment in retaining the semi-final line-up to face West Germany. Geoff Hurst still recalls how Greaves took the time to wish him well when the team was announced, how he later said he would have done exactly the same thing had he been in Ramsey's place.

Much more pain was to lie ahead of him and many of the trappings of playing success were to be sacrificed as he sought to overcome it. But as he often did when confronted by a mass of defenders, Jimmy Greaves found a way through.

## JOHN CONNELLY [11]

Manchester United began the 1966 World Cup with three players in the England side: Stiles, Bobby Charlton and Connelly. Though Ramsey's numbering may have implied he was first choice —it was the only deviation from the line-up that beat Poland in Katowice in the final pre-tournament game—Connelly played just the one game against Uruguay before another winger, Terry Paine, was brought in against Mexico.

It was the last of his 20 caps. The first had come as far back as 1959, not long after Burnley had converted him to a winger from inside-forward. That same season he helped Burnley to the League Championship, as top scorer. In April 1964 he was transferred to Manchester United for £60,000, and in his first season at Old Trafford he played all 42 League games to win another Championship medal.

At home on either flank, Connelly suffered both from a glut of good wingers and from Ramsey's

inability to decide on a first choice. In his seven-season England career he battled with no less than 10 other players for the number 7 and 11 shirts.

Just two months after the World Cup Connelly was on the move again, sold to Blackburn Rovers for £40,000 by a United now boasting a whole array of wingers. He spent four seasons as a regular choice with Blackburn in the Second Division before moving on to Third Division Bury in June 1970—his fourth Lancashire club. Connelly eventually made the trip across the Football League complete when Bury were relegated the next season, but he was still turning it on in his final season, 1972–73, when he was the club's top scorer with 14 goals in 38 appearances. His League total was 179 goals in 567 matches.

Then nearing his 35th birthday, Connelly took over a fish and chip shop in Bury, 'Connelly's Plaice', which he still runs today.

## RON SPRINGETT [12]

Though he had made only four appearances since Gordon Banks' debut in April 1963, Ron Springett was still England's number two goalkeeper for the World Cup finals, despite losing his place to Tony Waiters for two long spells in 1964 and the impressive form of the young Peter Bonetti.

He had certainly been his country's first choice before that, missing only one of the 30 internationals between November 1959 and February 1963, and playing in all the games in the 1962 World Cup finals, after taking over from Eddie Hopkinson.

Just before the 1966 finals Springett made his last appearance at Wembley, playing in the Sheffield Wednesday side that lost 3-2 to Everton in the FA Cup final—after leading 2-0. The following May he figured in a unique transfer that took his younger brother Peter to Wednesday as he moved back to Queen's Park Rangers, who also received a small cash adjustment. Rangers had been his first club, selling him to Wednesday for £10,000 in March 1958.

Ron helped QPR to promotion in 1967–68 but the following season, due to a combination of injury and loss of form, he made only nine League appearances, and in 1969–70, still plagued by injury, he didn't play a single League game. He was then 34.

In September 1970 Springett joined Southern League Ashford Town, but his first season there ended with relegation from the Premier Division. In 1972 he left the club to run his sports shop in Shepherd's Bush, only a stone's throw from Loftus Road and not far from his Fulham birthplace, and is still there.

## PETER BONETTI [13]

It's a brutal fact that Peter Bonetti's England career of seven caps will always be blighted by blame for the 1970 quarter-final defeat at the hands of West Germany at León, when he got the nod over Alex Stepney to take over from Gordon Banks. Ramsey describes the goals as 'three defensive errors. There was panic in defence and we were made to pay for it.' But it is generally held that Bonetti must take a good deal of responsibility, not so much for Müller's killer third goal as for the Beckenbauer shot that set the Germans on their way to that astonishing comeback against their old rivals.

For Bonetti that game was sandwiched between his two winners medals—in the FA Cup final of 1970 against Leeds and the European Cup Winners Cup final against Real Madrid, both of which went to replays.

Bonetti, who had made his debut for Chelsea back in April 1960, continued playing for another eight seasons after the dramatic win in Athens, though he was not always automatic first choice after 1977. His last League appearance, his 600th, came in the 1-1 draw at home to Arsenal on 14 May 1979 at the age of 37.

Even then Bonetti was still displaying glimpses of the agility that earned him the nickname of 'The Cat' for so many years at Stamford Bridge and made him such a favourite with the fans.

A few days later he joined Dundee United in the Scottish Premier Division on a free transfer, but after only five League games in 1979–80 he lost his place and did not play again. In May 1980 he retired to run a guest-house on the Isle of Mull—a long haul from the hurly-burly of the sport in which he had made his name.

## JIMMY ARMFIELD [14]

If anyone deserved to win an honour in the game it was Jimmy Armfield, a likeable and loyal one-club man who served Blackpool from 1954 to 1971, clocking up a club record 558 League appearances.

Armfield was one of the many players in the 1966 squad who knew he would play only if his rival was injured. That, too, had been the reason for his losing the right-back spot to George Cohen in May 1964 against Uruguay—after he had played in 37 of the previous 38 internationals. Despite being only 28, Armfield could not regain his place from the adventurous and consistent Cohen, despite his usual good club form.

Just three months after becoming player-manager at Blackpool in February 1971 Armfield moved to Bolton, replacing Nat Lofthouse as team manager, and in his second season the young Wanderers side won the Third Division Championship. After earlier turning down the manager's job at Everton, Jimmy, now a target for several big clubs, moved to the Leeds hotseat in October 1974 following Brian Clough's 44-day visit, and took the club to the 1975 European Cup final.

After nearly four seasons of busy transfers and a number of good cup runs—but no trophies—Leeds sacked him in July 1978, and since then Armfield has got increasingly involved in BBC radio work and newspaper journalism. In February 1979, at 44, he was appointed chief executive at Blackburn, but the association ended at the end of the season when the club finished bottom of the Second Division.

*Applause from the England squad—and Alf Ramsey—as the team climb the steps to the royal box to receive their medals after the final. Greaves is the notable—and understandable—exception.*

## GERRY BYRNE [15]

Gerry Byrne's memories of his last competitive match at Wembley are somewhat different from those of the boys of '66. It came 14 months before the World Cup final, a dramatic clash of the two clubs, then being moulded by their managers, who would dominate English football for the next 10 years.

For Byrne it was a traumatic day. After just three minutes, hardly warmed up, he was injured in a collision—it was later found to be a fractured collar bone—and played on in great pain, as a passenger on the left wing, for another 117 agonising minutes as the game went to extra time. Just his luck; that was the first time it had been needed for 18 years. The considerable consolation was that Liverpool won.

Byrne's injury, the latest in a whole series of Cup final tragedies, prompted the Football League to sanction the introduction of sub-

stitutes at their annual meeting four weeks later, and the FA followed suit.

Gerry was fully fit for the World Cup season, but his only hope of a place was an injury or unprecedented loss of form by Ray Wilson. His single cap had come when Wilson was out of the reckoning, against Scotland at Wembley in 1963. Byrne did get one more run, in the 6-1 win over Norway in June 1966.

Like so many full-backs, including George Cohen, Gerry Byrne saw his career ended early by knee trouble following several operations. In the four seasons after the World Cup he made a total of only 38 League appearances before being forced to retire in December 1969, aged 30, when he joined the Anfield staff. He had been a good servant to the club, his only one, since gaining a regular place in 1960, and figured in all their successes of the decade.

## RON FLOWERS [17]

Though the long international career of Ron Flowers effectively finished in April 1963—he won only eight of his 49 caps in the three subsequent seasons and was most unlikely to get a game in the 1966 finals—he continued playing until 1971, 19 years after his debut for Wolves.

His fine career at Molineux, first as an at-

tacking wing-half and later as a defensive centre-back, came to an end in January 1967 after several months of trouble from a back injury sustained earlier in the season. In September he moved down a division to Northampton, and in May 1968 became player-manager. But a poor season (when he made 21 League appearances) saw the club relegated, and after only a year in charge he resigned in May 1969.

Two months later he was appointed player-manager of Telford United—later run by Geoff Hurst and Gordon Banks—and had better luck with the Southern League club, returning to Wembley after six years to captain the side that lost 2-0 to Macclesfield in the 1970 FA Challenge Trophy. The following season he made only occasional appearances but steered Telford back for a second final; this time they won, beating Hillingdon 3-2. The same season they also beat Weymouth in the Southern League Cup final, despite finishing sixth from bottom in the Premier Division.

Telford struggled at the start of the 1971–72 season and Flowers resigned as manager in the October. He left the game and now runs a sports shop in the middle of Wolverhampton—an acquisition no doubt helped by the proceeds from the testimonial granted by the club he served so long in October 1970.

## NORMAN HUNTER [18]

Only Alan Ball and Martin Peters were younger than Norman Hunter in the 1966 squad, even though he had already won four of his 28 England caps. Then, as afterwards, he was often kept out by the consistency of Bobby Moore.

Hunter, renowned equally for his tough tackling and his reliance on his left foot—though he once scored a beauty for England with his right—played a vital part in the catalogue of Leeds successes (and near-misses) in the late 1960s and early 1970s, including the club's first triumphs in the League, the FA Cup, the League Cup and the Fairs Cup.

He was in the squad for the 1970 World Cup, but his only appearance was as a substitute for Martin Peters against the West Germans at León, when he was vainly brought on by Ramsey to shut out the menace of substitute Grabowski. It was not a game for him to remember, any more than England's last game of the next World Cup, when his poor tackle led to the Poles scoring a crucial goal at Wembley.

Despite the hard image and uncompromising play that produced a stream of bookings, Hunter was rated by his fellow professionals—a fact confirmed by their vote as Player of the Year in 1974. That season he didn't miss a game as Leeds won their second League title.

On 28 October 1976, the day before his 33rd birthday, Hunter was transferred for £40,000 to Bristol City, newly promoted to the First Division—and was booked on his debut. Released after two battling seasons, he joined Barnsley, as a player under Allan Clarke in June 1979, and played 24 League games the following season—as well as being sent off for the fourth time in his career.

When Allan Clarke moved to Leeds at the start of the 1980–81 season Hunter was offered his job. Bristol City also wanted him, but he decided to stay put. A knee injury forced him to quit playing in the February, but he used all his experience to steer Barnsley to a challenging position at the top of the Third Division.

## TERRY PAINE [19]

Despite finishing his international career with the 1966 game against Mexico, Terry Paine played more than half his lengthy League life after those World Cup finals, adjusting his old style well to a new midfield role.

Though he suffered—with John Connelly and Ian Callaghan—from Ramsey's 'tinkerings', Paine had no worries about his place at the Dell. There his accurate crosses, first to Derek Reeves and later to Ron Davies and Martin Chivers, helped Southampton climb from the Third Division to seventh place in the First during the 1960s.

He stayed with Southampton, his first club, from 1957 until 1974, when after a season in which he missed only one game, but which saw the Saints relegated, Lawrie McMenemy gave him a free transfer. Paine left having missed only 26 League games in 17 years, and with the club record of 713 appearances.

Third Division Hereford appointed him as player-coach in July 1974, and he played 111 League games for them over three seasons—a period which saw him break Jimmy Dickinson's old record of 764 League appearances in October 1975. His eventual total was a staggering 824, a total unlikely ever to be surpassed. Paine, a superb striker of the ball, kept in excellent shape and always knew how to pace himself well, despite his demanding role.

After his last game in England—against Southampton in May 1977—Paine went out to the Middle East to be player-manager of Kuwaiti club Kazma, who finished second in their League under him in 1978. The following year he returned to England as player-manager of Southern League Cheltenham Town, but left after a few months, having played till the age of 40, to become landlord of the 'Prince of Wales' pub in Cheltenham. Paine, whose interests outside football have also included being a Tory councillor and owning racehorses, was awarded the MBE in 1977.

*Ian Callaghan, Norman Hunter and Gerry Byrne pause to sign autographs outside the England hotel two days before the finals. While Callaghan would have a chance of playing when the team was announced on the Monday morning (he in fact played in the third match, against France), Hunter and Byrne were only too aware that they would only get a game through injury to their rivals: Ramsey's defence picked itself by this stage. Only four players, apart from the winning side, would figure in the finals: Callaghan, Paine, Connelly and Greaves.*

## IAN CALLAGHAN [20]

If Ian Callaghan had been told, on the evening of 20 July 1966, that his next appearance for England would be over 11 years later, he could have been forgiven for a certain cynicism. But that's what happened when new manager Ron Greenwood chose the 35-year-old midfield man, along with five other Liverpool players, for the friendly against Switzerland at Wembley in September 1977.

He was retained, despite a poor draw, for another game, but then ended a remarkable international career started in Finland a few weeks before the 1966 World Cup, when he had a run in a warm-up game as Ramsey fiddled with his best approach.

Already a Liverpool regular since 1962, Callaghan stayed a feature of the side until 1978, switching from his wide role to a genuine midfield position after returning to the team after a cartilage operation in 1971—to play his best ever season, according to manager Bill Shankly. The football writers seemed to think that came in 1973–74, when he was voted their player of the year and Liverpool won the FA Cup.

Early in 1978 Callaghan lost his place in the Liverpool side and, after a club record 640 League appearances and a shoal of medals, he was given a free transfer. He joined a whole bunch of former Anfield regulars under John Toshack at Swansea the following September, and made 40 appearances to help the club into the Second Division. In January 1981, after a long spell in the reserves, he left the Vetch Field, and following a few games for Cork United signed on for the summer with Norwegian club Soudifjord. Ian received the OBE in 1976.

## GEORGE EASTHAM [22]

The subtle skills and lack of goals of George Eastham were in marked contrast to the man he covered for in the 1966 competition, Bobby Charlton, and the man who he replaced to win the last of his 19 caps, against Denmark on the pre-World Cup tour.

Though born in Blackpool, Eastham played his first football alongside his father for Ards, where his father was player-manager. He moved to Newcastle in 1956 and on to Arsenal in 1960—a transfer that wouldn't be finally settled until July 1963, when Justice Wilberforce's statement supported Eastham's contention that the regulations governing transfers were 'an unreasonable restraint of trade', and ended the 'soccer slavery' of the retain-and-transfer system. It was a big step forward, though freedom of contract would not come until 1979.

A month after the World Cup Eastham moved to Stoke for £33,000. He made few appearances for Stoke in 1970–71 but in October the next season he was recalled to the first team and the following March scored his first goal for three seasons to win the League Cup—the first trophy in the club's history.

Eastham became assistant manager under Tony Waddington in December 1972, and made his last appearance the following September, six days past his 37th birthday, and in the First Division. He stayed on as assistant and in March 1977, when Waddington resigned, he became caretaker manager. Despite relegation, Eastham was confirmed as manager in the May.

In January 1978, following a bad run, he was sacked by Stoke. He is now involved in management in South Africa, where back in 1971 his performances with Hellenic FC of Cape Town won him the Footballer of the Year award.

# THE WEST GERMANS

## HANS TILKOWSKI [1]

Already under pressure from the emerging Sepp Maier before the World Cup in England, Tilkowski lost his place to the Bayern keeper the following year. After spending most of his career at Borussia Dortmund he had a last playing season with Eintracht Frankfurt in 1969–70. He then spent eight years as coach to Werder Bremen, Nürnberg and Saarbrücken before being sacked by the Saar club in 1978.

## HORST HÖTTGES [2]

A great servant of Werder Bremen, Höttges made a record 423 Bundesliga appearances for the club before he finished playing in 1978, aged 35. He still lives in Bremen, operating as the representative for Puma in North Germany.

Höttges played in West Germany's first four matches in Mexico at left-back but missed the semi-final and third-place match. An injury to Berti Vogts brought him back for the successful 1972 European Championship, at right-back.

## KARL-HEINZ SCHNELLINGER [3]

A 19-year-old debutant in the 1958 World Cup play-off with France at right-half, Schnellinger played all four games in 1962 and all six in 1966 as left-back, then five of Germany's games in Mexico as a centre-back, often as a sweeper.

Signed from Düren by Cologne in 1959, he was sold to AS Roma in 1963, the year after helping Cologne to their first League title and being voted West German Footballer of the Year. He moved on to AC Milan for a massive fee in 1965, appearing for them in the 1968 Cup Winners Cup final (against Seeler's Hamburg), 1969 European Cup final and the 1970 World Cup Championship—all successes.

Schnellinger returned to Germany in 1974, but after a short stay with Tennis Borussia Berlin he took his wife Uschi and three daughters back to Milan, where he is an executive with an electronics firm.

## FRANZ BECKENBAUER [4]

The youngest player in the 1966 final—he was still only 20—Beckenbauer went on to become the most honoured European player of all time.

With Bayern Munich he won four Bundesliga titles, four German Cup finals, three European Cup finals (all as captain) and a Cup Winners Cup final. With West Germany, for whom he gained a record 103 gaps, he captained them to victory in the European Championship of 1972 and the World Cup of 1974. He was voted European Footballer of the Year in 1972 and came second twice and third once—in 1966.

Beckenbauer's winning ways followed him to the States after he joined Pelé at New York Cosmos on a contract too good to turn down—a controversial decision which ruled him out of his fourth World Cup in Argentina. In his first season he helped Cosmos to the NASL title, succeeding Pelé as 'most valuable player', and then won a second Championship in 1978.

In 1980 'The Kaiser', as he is known at home as well as abroad, returned to Germany, where he has a lifelong contract with Adidas, joining SV Hamburg shortly after the departure of Kevin Keegan for a huge salary—just part of his enormous income. Separated from his wife Brigitte and three sons, Beckenbauer has lived in Hamburg since 1980.

## WILLI SCHULZ [5]

Right-half in the World Cup in Chile, Schulz did not move into the middle of the German defence until the spring of 1966. In Mexico he was replaced by Schnellinger after the first game, but he reappeared as a sub for Höttges against England and retained his place for the semi-final.

'World Cup Willi' (as he was always known in Germany after 1966) stayed with Hamburg, whom he had joined from Schalke 04, until 1973. Married with two daughters, he is now a Hamburg estate agent and writes regularly for the Sunday paper *Welt am Sonntag*.

## WOLFGANG WEBER [6]

A one-club man, Weber continued playing for Cologne until 1978, the club winning the German double in his last season. He then succeeded Tilkowski as coach at Bremen, but he was dismissed in January 1980 as the side slid to relegation. Later in the year he quit the game to become a representative for Adidas. He has two children but his marriage broke up during his time in charge at Bremen.

Weber, most famous in England for his last-ditch equaliser in the 1966 final, was troubled by a back injury in Mexico and played only twice.

## HELMUT HALLER [8]

The greatest joy in Haller's life is his son Jurgen, who at 18 plays in the Second Division for Augsburg, Helmut's first club.

From Augsburg Haller signed for Bologna in 1961—a transfer delayed until after the Chile World Cup. In 1968 he continued a turbulent time in Italy with a big transfer to Juventus, and five years later he returned to Germany—to Augsburg. In 1976 he moved down to the Second Division of the regional leagues for his final season before finishing his career at 37.

More talented than popular and notorious for his histrionics after being fouled, Haller suffered a bad shoulder injury in April 1970 and appeared only once in the World Cup. Now divorced, he works with a travel agency that specialises in sports trips, and owns several homes.

## UWE SEELER [9]

'Uns Uwe'—'our Uwe'—was the idol of the Hamburg fans for 19 years from 1953, when he first appeared as a 16-year-old for the club where his father had been a star. First capped at 17, he went on to play a then record 72 times for his country, the last time in September 1970, when he scored his 43rd goal in internationals.

A brave player on the field, Seeler had an artificial achilles tendon fitted just before the 1966 finals. Out of the national side for several spells, notably then and in 1968–69, he always seemed to bounce back, figuring prominently in all six German games in a deeper role in 1970. This took his World Cup finals appearances to 21, a record he still holds.

Seeler's association with Adidas goes back to well before the 1966 competition, and he is now their head representative in North Germany. Married with three daughters, he keeps fit with a lot of tennis, as do several of the Germans.

## SIGI HELD [10]

The last of the German side to play in the Bundesliga, Held returned to the First Division for a season in 1979 at the age of 37, and is now coach at VfL Bochum.

Held played 41 times for his country, his debut coming in the 1-0 defeat at Wembley in February 1966. He helped West Germany to Mexico but played only three games—one as sub.

Most of his Bundesliga career was spent with Borussia Dortmund, who bought him from Kickers Offenbach in 1965. The following year he appeared with Tilkowski and Emmerich in the Cup Winners Cup final at Hampden against Liverpool, when he scored the first goal.

## LOTHAR EMMERICH [11]

The clown of the German side off the field, Emmerich wasn't joking when he used his lethal left foot—the main weapon in scoring 115 goals in 183 Bundesliga appearances for Borussia Dortmund before he left the club in 1969.

He then got around, playing in Belgium with Beerschot (1969–70) and Austria with Klagenfurt (1970–75) before returning to the Second Division of the German Regional League for seasons with Schweinfurt (1975–76) and Wurzburg (1976–77). Still loath to pack up at 36, Lothar then had a season in the regional Third Division with Neckargerach—as an amateur—and another as player-coach with Castell. He then became coach at Aschaffenburg, but was sacked early in 1981.

Today Emmerich lives in Zeuzleben with his wife, who runs a shop, and his two children.

## WOLFGANG OVERATH [12]

Despite his number Overath played in all the matches for West Germany in 1966, as he would do in 1970 (when he scored the goal that have gave them third place) and 1974—a unique feat.

Though he and Beckenbauer were the only survivors from Wembley to play in the Munich game, Overath didn't share his captain's European Championship success in 1972, when he was ousted by Gunter Netzer.

Hard-working yet elegant on the left side of midfield, Overath had joined Cologne in 1963, winning both his first cap and a Championship medal in his first season. He stayed with them until 1977, making 409 Bundesliga appearances, before arguments with coach Hennes Weisweiler led to his departure and the end of his career at 34. Now living in Siegburg with his wife and two sons, he is a representative for Adidas and still turns out frequently for celebrity sides.

*The visitors line up during their national anthem. Left to right: Höttges, Overath, Held, Haller, Weber, Emmerich, Schulz, Beckenbauer, Schnellinger, Tilkowski and Seeler.*

# ENGLAND'S MATCHES...THE PLAYERS' RECORDS

**GROUP 1: Monday 11 July**
**Wembley (87,148)**
**I. Zsolt (Hungary)**
**England (0) 0 Uruguay (0) 0**

| England | Uruguay |
|---|---|
| Banks | Mazurkievicz |
| Cohen | Troche |
| Charlton J. | Goncalves |
| Moore (capt.) | Manicera |
| Wilson | Ubinas |
| Ball | Caetano |
| Stiles | Viera |
| Charlton R. | Silva |
| Greaves | Perez |
| Hunt | Cortes |
| Connelly | Rocha |

**GROUP 1: Saturday 16 July**
**Wembley (92,570)**
**C. Lo Bello (Italy)**
**England (1) 2 Mexico (0) 0**

| England | Mexico |
|---|---|
| Banks | Calderon |
| Cohen | Del Muro |
| Charlton J. | Chaires |
| Moore (capt.) | Pena |
| Wilson | Nunez |
| Stiles | Hernandez |
| Charlton R. | Diaz |
| Peters | Jauregui |
| Paine | Reyes |
| Greaves | Borja |
| Hunt | Padilla |

**Scorers:** Charlton R. (37), Hunt (75)

**GROUP 1: Wednesday 20 July**
**Wembley (98,270)**
**A. Yamasaki (Peru)**
**England (1) 2 France (0) 0**

| England | France |
|---|---|
| Banks | Aubour |
| Cohen | Djorkaeff |
| Charlton J. | Artelesa |
| Moore (capt.) | Budzinski |
| Wilson | Bosquier |
| Stiles | Bonnel |
| Charlton R. | Herbin |
| Peters | Simon |
| Callaghan | Herbet |
| Greaves | Gondet |
| Hunt | Hausser |

**Scorer:** Hunt (38, 75)

**QUARTER-FINAL: Saturday 23 July**
**Wembley (90,584)**
**R. Kreitlein (West Germany)**
**England (0) 1 Argentina (0) 0**

| England | Argentina |
|---|---|
| Banks | Roma |
| Cohen | Ferreiro |
| Charlton J. | Perfumo |
| Moore (capt.) | Albrecht |
| Wilson | Marzolini |
| Stiles | Gonzalez |
| Ball | Rattin (capt.) |
| Charlton R. | Onega |
| Peters | Solari |
| Hunt | Artime |
| Hurst | Mas |

**Scorer:** Hurst (77)

**SEMI-FINAL: Tuesday 26 July**
**Wembley (94,493)**
**P. Schwinte (France)**
**England (1) 2 Portugal (0) 1**

| England | Portugal |
|---|---|
| Banks | Jose Pereira |
| Cohen | Festa |
| Charlton J. | Baptista |
| Moore (capt.) | Jose Carlos |
| Wilson | Hilario |
| Stiles | Graca |
| Ball | Coluna (capt.) |
| Charlton R. | Jose Augusto |
| Peters | Eusebio |
| Hunt | Torres |
| Hurst | Simoes |

**Scorers:** Charlton R. (31, 80);
Eusebio (83-pen)

**FINAL: Saturday 30 July**
**Wembley (96,924)**
**G. Dienst (Switzerland)**
**England (1) (2) 4**
**West Germany (1) (2) 2**

| England | West Germany |
|---|---|
| Banks | Tilkowski |
| Cohen | Hottges |
| Charlton J. | Schulz |
| Moore (capt.) | Weber |
| Wilson | Schnellinger |
| Stiles | Haller |
| Ball | Beckenbauer |
| Charlton R. | Overath |
| Peters | Seeler (capt.) |
| Hunt | Held |
| Hurst | Emmerich |

**Scorers:** Hurst (19, 100, 120),
Peters (78); Haller (13), Weber (89)

## HURST, Geoffrey Charles

**Honours:** European Cup Winners Cup winners medal 1965; FA Cup winners medal 1964; L. Cup runners-up medal 1966; MBE 1979

| Club | Season | Div | Pos | League | | FA Cup | | FL Cup | | Europe | | Inter'ls | |
|---|---|---|---|---|---|---|---|---|---|---|---|---|---|
| | | | | Ms | Gs | Ms | Gs | Ms | Gs | Ms | Gs | Ms | Gs |
| West Ham United .......1959–60 | | I | 14 | 3 | – | – | – | – | – | – | – | – | – |
| | 1960–61 | I | 16 | 6 | – | – | – | – | – | – | – | – | – |
| | 1961–62 | I | 8 | 24 | 1 | 1 | – | 2 | – | – | – | – | – |
| | 1962–63 | I | 12 | 28 | 13 | – | – | 2 | 2 | – | – | – | – |
| | 1963–64 | I | 14 | 37 | 14 | 6 | 6 | 7 | 5 | – | – | – | – |
| | 1964–65 | I | 9 | 42 | 17 | 1 | 2 | 1 | – | 9 | – | – | – |
| | 1965–66 | I | 12 | 39 | 23 | 4 | 4 | 10 | 11 | 6 | 2 | 8 | 5 |
| | 1966–67 | I | 16 | 41 | 29 | 2 | 3 | 6 | 9 | – | – | 6 | 3 |
| | 1967–68 | I | 12 | 38 | 19 | 3 | 1 | 3 | 5 | – | – | 7* | 2 |
| | 1968–69 | I | 8 | 41 | 25 | 3 | 2 | 3 | 4 | – | – | 9 | 8 |
| | 1969–70 | I | 17 | 39* | 16 | 1 | – | 2 | 2 | – | – | 11* | 3 |
| | 1970–71 | I | 20 | 39 | 15 | – | – | 2 | 1 | – | – | 4 | 1 |
| | 1971–72 | I | 14 | 34 | 8 | 4 | 4 | 10 | 4 | – | – | 4 | 2 |
| Stoke City.............1972–73 | | I | 15 | 38 | 10 | – | – | 3 | 2 | 2 | 1 | – | – |
| | 1973–74 | I | 5 | 35 | 12 | 1 | – | 4 | 1 | – | – | – | – |
| | 1974–75 | I | 5 | 35§ | 8 | 1 | – | 4 | 3 | 1 | – | – | – |
| West Bromwich Albion ..1975–76 | | II | 3P | 10 | 2 | – | – | 2 | – | – | – | – | – |
| | | | | 529¶ | 212 | 27 | 22 | 61 | 49 | 18 | 3 | 49† | 24 |

## BALL, Alan James

**Honours:** League Championship medal 1970; FA Cup runners-up medals 1968, 1972; League Cup runners-up medal 1979; [NASL Championship medal 1979]

| Club | Season | Div | Pos | League | | FA Cup | | FL Cup | | Europe | | Inter'ls | |
|---|---|---|---|---|---|---|---|---|---|---|---|---|---|
| | | | | Ms | Gs | Ms | Gs | Ms | Gs | Ms | Gs | Ms | Gs |
| Blackpool . . . . . . . . . . . . . .1962–63 | | I | 13 | 5 | – | – | – | – | – | – | – | – | – |
| | 1963–64 | I | 18 | 31 | 13 | 2 | – | 1 | 1 | – | – | – | – |
| | 1964–65 | I | 17 | 39 | 12 | 1 | 1 | 2 | 1 | – | – | 3 | 1 |
| | 1965–66 | I | 13 | 41 | 17 | 2 | – | 2 | 1 | – | – | 11 | 1 |
| Everton . . . . . . . . . . . . . . .1966–67 | | I | 6 | 41 | 15 | 6 | 2 | – | – | 4 | 1 | 6 | 1 |
| | 1967–68 | I | 5 | 34 | 20 | 4 | – | 2 | – | – | – | 7 | 2 |
| | 1968–69 | I | 3 | 40 | 16 | 5 | – | 4 | 2 | – | – | 8 | – |
| | 1969–70 | I | 1 | 37 | 10 | 1 | 1 | 3 | 1 | – | – | 10 | 3 |
| | 1970–71 | I | 14 | 39 | 2 | 6 | 3 | – | – | 6 | 3 | 6* | – |
| | 1971–72 | I | 15 | 17 | 3 | – | – | 1 | – | – | – | 2 | – |
| Arsenal . . . . . . . . . . . . . . .1971–72 | | I | 5 | 18 | 3 | 9 | 2 | – | – | – | – | 3 | 1 |
| | 1972–73 | I | 2 | 40 | 10 | 7 | 4 | 3 | – | – | – | 9 | – |
| | 1973–74 | I | 10 | 36 | 13 | 3 | – | 1 | – | – | – | 1* | – |
| | 1974–75 | I | 16 | 30 | 9 | 8 | 1 | – | – | – | – | 6 | 1 |
| | 1975–76 | I | 17 | 39 | 9 | 1 | – | 2 | – | – | – | – | – |
| | 1976–77 | I | 8 | 14 | 1 | – | – | 6 | – | – | – | – | – |
| Southampton . . . . . . . . . .1976–77 | | II | 9 | 23 | 1 | 6 | 1 | – | – | – | – | – | – |
| | 1977–78 | II | 2P | 41 | 5 | 4 | – | 3 | – | – | – | – | – |
| | 1978–79 | I | 14 | 42 | 2 | 6 | 1 | 8 | – | – | – | – | – |
| | 1979–80 | I | 8 | 26 | 1 | 1 | – | 1 | – | – | – | – | – |
| Blackpool . . . . . . . . . . . . . .1980–81 | | III | 23R | 13 | 5 | 2 | – | 3 | – | – | – | – | – |
| Southampton . . . . . . . . . .1980–81 | | I | 6 | 10 | – | – | – | – | – | – | – | – | – |
| | | | | 666 | 167 | 74 | 16 | 42 | 6 | 10 | 4 | 72† | 10 |

## CHARLTON, John (Jack)

**Honours:** Fairs Cup winners medals 1968, 1971, Fairs Cup runners-up medal 1967; League Championship medal 1969; FA Cup winners medal 1972, FA Cup runners-up medals 1965, 1970; League Cup winners medal 1968; Division II Championship medal 1964; FWA Footballer of the Year 1967; Bell's Manager of the Year 1974; OBE 1975

| Club | Season | Div | Pos | League | | FA Cup | | FL Cup | | Europe | | Inter'ls | |
|---|---|---|---|---|---|---|---|---|---|---|---|---|---|
| | | | | Ms | Gs | Ms | Gs | Ms | Gs | Ms | Gs | Ms | Gs |
| Leeds United . . . . . . . . . .1952–53 | | II | 10 | 1 | – | – | – | – | – | – | – | – | – |
| | 1953–54 | II | 10 | – | – | – | – | – | – | – | – | – | – |
| | 1954–55 | II | 4 | 1 | – | – | – | – | – | – | – | – | – |
| | 1955–56 | II | 2P | 34 | – | 1 | – | – | – | – | – | – | – |
| | 1956–57 | I | 8 | 21 | – | 1 | – | – | – | – | – | – | – |
| | 1957–58 | I | 17 | 40 | – | 1 | – | – | – | – | – | – | – |
| | 1958–59 | I | 15 | 39 | 1 | 1 | – | – | – | – | – | – | – |
| | 1959–60 | I | 21R | 41 | 3 | 1 | – | – | – | – | – | – | – |
| | 1960–61 | II | 14 | 41 | 7 | 1 | – | 4 | 1 | – | – | – | – |
| | 1961–62 | II | 19 | 34 | 9 | 2 | 1 | 3 | 2 | – | – | – | – |
| | 1962–63 | II | 5 | 38 | 2 | 3 | 1 | 1 | 1 | – | – | – | – |
| | 1963–64 | II | 1P | 25 | 3 | – | – | 2 | – | – | – | – | – |
| | 1964–65 | I | 2 | 39 | 9 | 8 | 1 | 2 | – | – | – | 5 | – |
| | 1965–66 | I | 2 | 40 | 6 | 2 | – | 1 | – | 11 | 2 | 17 | 2 |
| | 1966–67 | I | 4 | 29 | 5 | 5 | 2 | 4 | – | 7 | – | 4 | 2 |
| | 1967–68 | I | 4 | 34 | 6 | 4 | 1 | 6 | 1 | 11 | 1 | 2 | – |
| | 1968–69 | I | 1 | 41 | 3 | 2 | – | 2 | – | 7 | 4 | 3 | 1 |
| | 1969–70 | I | 2 | 32 | 3 | 9 | 1 | 2 | 1 | 7 | – | 4 | 1 |
| | 1970–71 | I | 2 | 40 | 6 | 4 | – | 1 | – | 10 | 3 | – | – |
| | 1971–72 | I | 2 | 41 | 5 | 5 | 1 | 4 | – | – | – | – | – |
| | 1972–73 | I | 3 | 18 | 3 | – | – | 4 | 1 | 2 | – | – | – |
| | | | | 629 | 71 | 50 | 8 | 36 | 7 | 55 | 10 | 35 | 6 |

● The 11 players who won the World Cup gained a total of 672 caps for England and scored 130 goals.

● They played together only six times, in consecutive matches from the quarter-final against Argentina to the 5-0 win over Wales four months later. The side won five and drew one of those games, scoring 14 goals and conceding four. One change was made for the next match, against Scotland at Wembley (Greaves for Hunt) when England lost 3-2.

● Their overall first-class career stretched over 28 years, from Jack Charlton's League debut in April 1953 to the middle of 1981, when Alan Ball was still playing in the First Division for Southampton.

● All the players spent part of their League careers outside Division 1, though Geoff Hurst played just 10 games for West Bromwich Albion in Division 2 in his last season.

## PETERS, Martin Stanford

**Honours:** European Cup Winners Cup winners medal 1965; UEFA Cup winners medal 1972, UEFA Cup runners-up medal 1974; League Cup winners medals 1971, 1973, League Cup runners-up medal 1966; MBE 1978

| Club | Season | Div | Pos | League | | FA Cup | | FL Cup | | Europe | | Inter'ls | |
|---|---|---|---|---|---|---|---|---|---|---|---|---|---|
| | | | | Ms | Gs | Ms | Gs | Ms | Gs | Ms | Gs | Ms | Gs |
| West Ham United | 1961–62 | I | 8 | 5 | – | – | – | – | – | – | – | – | – |
| | 1962–63 | I | 12 | 36 | 8 | 1 | – | 2 | 1 | – | – | – | – |
| | 1963–64 | I | 14 | 32 | 3 | – | – | 4 | – | – | – | – | – |
| | 1964–65 | I | 9 | 35 | 5 | 2 | – | 1 | – | 9 | 1 | – | – |
| | 1965–66 | I | 12 | 40 | 11 | 4 | – | 10 | 3 | 6 | 3 | 8 | 2 |
| | 1966–67 | I | 16 | 41 | 14 | 2 | – | 6 | 2 | – | – | 4 | 1 |
| | 1967–68 | I | 12 | 40 | 14 | 3 | 2 | 3 | 2 | – | – | 9 | 5 |
| | 1968–69 | I | 8 | 42 | 19 | 3 | 3 | 3 | 2 | – | – | 8 | 3 |
| | 1969–70 | I | 17 | 31 | 6 | 1 | – | 2 | – | – | – | 4* | – |
| Tottenham Hotspur | 1969–70 | I | 11 | 7 | 2 | – | – | – | – | – | – | 9 | 4 |
| | 1970–71 | I | 3 | 42 | 9 | 5 | 2 | 7 | 4 | – | – | 7 | 3 |
| | 1971–72 | I | 6 | 35 | 10 | 5 | 2 | 7 | 3 | 10 | 2 | 5† | – |
| | 1972–73 | I | 8 | 41 | 15 | 3 | 1 | 8 | 5 | 8 | 3 | 8 | 2 |
| | 1973–74 | I | 11 | 35 | 6 | 1 | – | 1 | – | 12 | 8 | 5 | – |
| | 1974–75 | I | 19 | 29 | 4 | 2 | – | – | – | – | – | – | – |
| Norwich City | 1974–75 | II | 3P | 10 | 2 | – | – | – | – | – | – | – | – |
| | 1975–76 | I | 10 | 42 | 10 | 5 | 2 | 3 | 1 | – | – | – | – |
| | 1976–77 | I | 16 | 42 | 7 | 1 | 1 | 2 | – | – | – | – | – |
| | 1977–78 | I | 13 | 34 | 7 | 2 | – | – | – | – | – | – | – |
| | 1978–79 | I | 16 | 39* | 10 | 1 | – | 3 | 2 | – | – | – | – |
| | 1979–80 | I | 12 | 40 | 8 | 3 | – | 5 | – | – | – | – | – |
| Sheffield United | 1980–81 | III | 21R | 24* | 4 | – | – | 2 | – | – | – | – | – |
| | | | | 722† | 174 | 44 | 13 | 69 | 25 | 45 | 17 | 67‡ | 20 |

## MOORE, Robert Frederick

**Honours:** European Cup Winners Cup winners medal 1965; FA Cup winners medal 1964, FA Cup runners-up medal 1975; League Cup runners-up medal 1966; FWA Footballer of the Year 1964; OBE 1967

| Club | Season | Div | Pos | League | | FA Cup | | FL Cup | | Europe | | Inter'ls | |
|---|---|---|---|---|---|---|---|---|---|---|---|---|---|
| | | | | Ms | Gs | Ms | Gs | Ms | Gs | Ms | Gs | Ms | Gs |
| West Ham United | 1958–59 | I | 6 | 5 | – | – | – | – | – | – | – | – | – |
| | 1959–60 | I | 14 | 13 | – | – | – | – | – | – | – | – | – |
| | 1960–61 | I | 16 | 38 | 1 | 2 | – | 2 | 1 | – | – | – | – |
| | 1961–62 | I | 8 | 41 | 3 | 1 | – | 2 | – | – | – | – | – |
| | 1962–63 | I | 12 | 41 | 3 | 5 | – | 2 | – | – | – | 5 | – |
| | 1963–64 | I | 14 | 37 | 2 | 7 | – | 7 | – | – | – | 9 | – |
| | 1964–65 | I | 9 | 28 | 1 | – | – | 1 | – | 6 | – | 7 | – |
| | 1965–66 | I | 12 | 37 | – | 4 | – | 9 | 2 | 6 | – | 16 | 2 |
| | 1966–67 | I | 16 | 40 | 2 | 2 | – | 6 | – | – | – | 6 | – |
| | 1967–68 | I | 12 | 40 | 4 | 3 | – | 3 | – | – | – | 10 | – |
| | 1968–69 | I | 8 | 41 | 2 | 1 | – | 3 | – | – | – | 9 | – |
| | 1969–70 | I | 17 | 42 | – | 1 | – | 2 | – | – | – | 12 | – |
| | 1970–71 | I | 20 | 40* | 1 | 1 | – | 2 | – | – | – | 5 | – |
| | 1971–72 | I | 14 | 40 | 1 | 4 | – | 10 | – | – | – | 7 | – |
| | 1972–73 | I | 6 | 42 | 3 | 2 | – | 2 | – | – | – | 11 | – |
| | 1973–74 | I | 18 | 22 | – | 1 | – | 1 | – | – | – | 1 | – |
| Fulham | 1973–74 | II | 13 | 10 | 1 | – | – | – | – | – | – | – | – |
| | 1974–75 | II | 9 | 41 | – | 11 | – | 3 | – | – | – | – | – |
| | 1975–76 | II | 12 | 33 | – | 1 | – | 3 | – | – | – | – | – |
| | 1976–77 | II | 17 | 40 | – | 2 | – | 5 | – | – | – | – | – |
| | | | | 671* | 24 | 48 | – | 63 | 3 | 12 | – | 108 | 2 |

● Between them the 11 players amassed nine League Championship medals, six FA Cup winners medals, five Football League Cup winners medals, two European Cup winners medals, three European Cup Winners Cup winners medals, two Fairs Cup winners medals, one UEFA Cup winners medal, four Footballer of the Year awards, one European Footballer of the Year award, four OBE's, two MBE's and one CBE.

● Jack Charlton took Middlesbrough up as Division 2 champions by a record 15-point margin in his first season as a manager—a feat which won him the 1974 Manager of the Year award—and steered Sheffield Wednesday to promotion from Division 3 in 1980; Nobby Stiles managed Preston to promotion from Division 3 in 1978, but to relegation back to Division 3 in 1981. Bobby Charlton had been in charge of Preston when they were relegated in 1974; Alan Ball was dismissed from Blackpool in March 1981, two months before they were relegated; Martin Peters was manager of Sheffield United when they were relegated in 1981 to Division 4; Geoff Hurst lost his Chelsea job in April 1981.

## CHARLTON, Robert

**Honours:** European Cup winners medal 1968; League Championship medals 1957, 1965, 1967; FA Cup winners medal 1963, FA Cup runners-up medal 1957, 1958; European Footballer of the Year 1966; FWA Footballer of the Year 1966; PFA Merit Award 1976; OBE 1969; CBE 1974

| Club | Season | Div | Pos | League | | FA Cup | | FL Cup | | Europe | | Inter'ls | |
|---|---|---|---|---|---|---|---|---|---|---|---|---|---|
| | | | | Ms | Gs | Ms | Gs | Ms | Gs | Ms | Gs | Ms | Gs |
| Manchester United | 1956–57 | I | 1 | 14 | 10 | 2 | 1 | – | – | 1 | 1 | – | – |
| | 1957–58 | I | 9 | 21 | 8 | 7 | 5 | – | – | 2 | 3 | 3 | 3 |
| | 1958–59 | I | 2 | 38 | 29 | 1 | – | – | – | – | – | 9 | 8 |
| | 1959–60 | I | 7 | 37 | 17 | 3 | 3 | – | – | – | – | 6 | 2 |
| | 1960–61 | I | 7 | 39 | 21 | 3 | – | – | – | – | – | 9 | 8 |
| | 1961–62 | I | 15 | 37 | 8 | 6 | 2 | – | – | – | – | 12 | 4 |
| | 1962–63 | I | 19 | 28 | 7 | 6 | 2 | – | – | – | – | 6 | 5 |
| | 1963–64 | I | 2 | 40 | 9 | 7 | 2 | – | – | 6 | 4 | 10* | 3 |
| | 1964–65 | I | 1 | 41 | 10 | 7 | – | – | – | 11 | 8 | 3 | 1 |
| | 1965–66 | I | 4 | 38 | 16 | 7 | – | – | – | 8 | 2 | 16 | 6 |
| | 1966–67 | I | 1 | 42 | 12 | 2 | – | – | – | – | – | 4 | 1 |
| | 1967–68 | I | 2 | 41 | 15 | 2 | 1 | – | – | 9 | 2 | 9 | 5 |
| | 1968–69 | I | 11 | 32 | 5 | 6 | – | – | – | 8 | 2 | 8 | 1 |
| | 1969–70 | I | 8 | 40 | 12 | 9 | 1 | 8 | 1 | – | – | 11 | 2 |
| | 1970–71 | I | 8 | 42 | 5 | 2 | – | 6 | 3 | – | – | – | – |
| | 1971–72 | I | 8 | 40 | 8 | 7 | 2 | 6 | 2 | – | – | – | – |
| | 1972–73 | I | 18 | 36† | 6 | 1 | – | 4 | 1 | – | – | – | – |
| Preston North End | 1973–74 | II | 21R | – | – | – | – | – | – | – | – | – | – |
| | 1974–75 | III | 9 | 38 | 8 | 4 | 1 | 3 | 1 | – | – | – | – |
| | | | | 644† | 206 | 82 | 20 | 27 | 8 | 45 | 22 | 106* | 49 |

## COHEN, George Reginald

| Club | Season | Div | Pos | League | | FA Cup | | FL Cup | | Europe | | Inter'ls | |
|---|---|---|---|---|---|---|---|---|---|---|---|---|---|
| | | | | Ms | Gs | Ms | Gs | Ms | Gs | Ms | Gs | Ms | Gs |
| Fulham | 1956–57 | II | 11 | 1 | – | – | – | – | – | – | – | – | – |
| | 1957–58 | II | 5 | 26 | – | 7 | – | – | – | – | – | – | – |
| | 1958–59 | II | 2P | 41 | 1 | 4 | – | – | – | – | – | – | – |
| | 1959–60 | I | 10 | 42 | – | 2 | – | – | – | – | – | – | – |
| | 1960–61 | I | 17 | 41 | – | 1 | – | 1 | – | – | – | – | – |
| | 1961–62 | I | 20 | 41 | 1 | 8 | – | 2 | – | – | – | – | – |
| | 1962–63 | I | 16 | 38 | – | 2 | – | 3 | – | – | – | – | – |
| | 1963–64 | I | 15 | 41 | 1 | 2 | – | 1 | – | – | – | 5 | – |
| | 1964–65 | I | 20 | 40 | 2 | 2 | – | 3 | – | – | – | 9 | – |
| | 1965–66 | I | 20 | 39 | – | 1 | – | 3 | – | – | – | 16 | – |
| | 1966–67 | I | 18 | 35 | 1 | 3 | – | 3 | – | – | – | 5 | – |
| | 1967–68 | I | 22R | 17 | – | – | – | 4 | – | – | – | 2 | – |
| | 1968–69 | II | 22R | 6 | – | 1 | – | – | – | – | – | – | – |
| | | | | 408 | 6 | 33 | – | 20 | – | – | – | 37 | – |

## HUNT, Roger

**Honours:** European Cup Winners Cup runners-up medal 1966; League Championship medals 1964, 1966; FA Cup winners medal 1965; Division II Championship medal 1962

| Club | Season | Div | Pos | League | | FA Cup | | FL Cup | | Europe | | Inter'ls | |
|---|---|---|---|---|---|---|---|---|---|---|---|---|---|
| | | | | Ms | Gs | Ms | Gs | Ms | Gs | Ms | Gs | Ms | Gs |
| Liverpool | 1959–60 | II | 3 | 36 | 21 | 2 | 2 | – | – | – | – | – | – |
| | 1960–61 | II | 3 | 32 | 15 | 1 | 1 | 3 | 3 | – | – | – | – |
| | 1961–62 | II | 1P | 41 | 41 | 5 | 1 | – | – | – | – | 1 | 1 |
| | 1962–63 | I | 8 | 42 | 24 | 6 | 2 | – | – | – | – | 1 | 1 |
| | 1963–64 | I | 1 | 41 | 31 | 5 | 2 | – | – | – | – | 3 | 5 |
| | 1964–65 | I | 7 | 40 | 25 | 8 | 5 | – | – | 9 | 7 | 1 | – |
| | 1965–66 | I | 1 | 37 | 30 | 1 | 1 | – | – | 7 | 2 | 13 | 8 |
| | 1966–67 | I | 5 | 39 | 14 | 3 | 1 | – | – | 5 | 3 | 5 | 2 |
| | 1967–68 | I | 3 | 40 | 25 | 9 | 2 | 2 | – | 6 | 3 | 8 | 1 |
| | 1968–69 | I | 2 | 38 | 13 | 4 | 1 | 3 | 2 | 2 | 1 | 2 | – |
| | 1969–70 | I | 5 | 17† | 6 | – | – | 2 | – | 2† | 1 | – | – |
| Bolton Wanderers | 1969–70 | II | 16 | 17 | 5 | 1 | – | – | – | – | – | – | – |
| | 1970–71 | II | 22R | 24† | 8 | – | – | 2* | – | – | – | – | – |
| | 1971–72 | III | 7 | 35† | 11 | 2* | 1 | 3* | – | – | – | – | – |
| | | | | 479¶ | 269 | 47* | 19 | 15† | 5 | 31† | 17 | 34 | 18 |

## STILES, Norbert Peter

**Honours:** European Cup winners medal 1968; League Championship medals 1965, 1967

| Club | Season | Div | Pos | League Ms | League Gs | FA Cup Ms | FA Cup Gs | FL Cup Ms | FL Cup Gs | Europe Ms | Europe Gs | Inter'ls Ms | Inter'ls Gs |
|---|---|---|---|---|---|---|---|---|---|---|---|---|---|
| Manchester United | 1960–61 | I | 7 | 26 | 2 | 3 | – | – | – | – | – | – | – |
| | 1961–62 | I | 15 | 34 | 7 | 3 | – | – | – | – | – | – | – |
| | 1962–63 | I | 19 | 31 | 2 | 4 | – | – | – | – | – | – | – |
| | 1963–64 | I | 2 | 17 | – | 2 | – | – | – | 2 | – | – | – |
| | 1964–65 | I | 1 | 41 | – | 7 | – | – | – | 11 | – | 4 | – |
| | 1965–66 | I | 4 | 39 | 2 | 7 | – | – | – | 8 | – | 16 | 1 |
| | 1966–67 | I | 1 | 37 | 3 | 2 | – | 1 | – | – | – | 4 | – |
| | 1967–68 | I | 2 | 20 | – | – | – | – | – | 7 | – | 1 | – |
| | 1968–69 | I | 11 | 41 | 2 | 3 | – | – | – | 8 | 1 | 1 | – |
| | 1969–70 | I | 8 | 9 | – | 3 | – | 2 | – | – | – | 2 | – |
| | 1970–71 | I | 8 | 17 | – | – | – | 2 | – | – | – | – | – |
| Middlesbrough | 1971–72 | II | 9 | 25 | 1 | 6 | – | 2 | – | – | – | – | – |
| | 1972–73 | II | 4 | 32 | 1 | 1 | – | 3 | – | – | – | – | – |
| Preston North End | 1973–74 | II | 21R | 27 | 1 | 1 | – | 1 | – | – | – | – | – |
| | 1974–75 | III | 9 | 19† | – | 2 | – | – | – | – | – | – | – |
| | | | | 415† | 21 | 44 | – | 11 | – | 36 | 1 | 28 | 1 |

## WILSON, Ramon

**Honours:** FA Cup winners medal 1966, FA Cup runners-up medal 1968

| Club | Season | Div | Pos | League Ms | League Gs | FA Cup Ms | FA Cup Gs | FL Cup Ms | FL Cup Gs | Europe Ms | Europe Gs | Inter'ls Ms | Inter'ls Gs |
|---|---|---|---|---|---|---|---|---|---|---|---|---|---|
| Huddersfield Town | 1955–56 | I | 21R | 6 | – | – | – | – | – | – | – | – | – |
| | 1956–57 | II | 12 | 12 | – | – | – | – | – | – | – | – | – |
| | 1957–58 | II | 9 | 31 | 1 | 2 | – | – | – | – | – | – | – |
| | 1958–59 | II | 14 | 42 | 1 | 1 | – | – | – | – | – | – | – |
| | 1959–60 | II | 6 | 41 | 1 | 3 | – | – | – | – | – | 4 | – |
| | 1960–61 | II | 20 | 32 | – | 4 | – | – | – | – | – | – | – |
| | 1961–62 | II | 7 | 39 | – | 2 | – | 3 | – | – | – | 11 | – |
| | 1962–63 | II | 6 | 33 | 1 | 1 | – | 1 | – | – | – | 6 | – |
| | 1963–64 | II | 12 | 29 | 1 | 2 | – | 4 | – | – | – | 9 | – |
| Everton | 1964–65 | I | 4 | 17 | – | 4 | – | – | – | 2 | – | 5 | – |
| | 1965–66 | I | 11 | 35 | – | 8 | – | – | – | 4 | – | 16* | – |
| | 1966–67 | I | 6 | 30 | – | 6 | – | – | – | 4 | – | 5 | – |
| | 1967–68 | I | 5 | 28 | – | 6 | – | 2 | – | – | – | 7 | – |
| | 1968–69 | I | 3 | 5† | – | – | – | – | – | – | – | – | – |
| Oldham Athletic | 1969–70 | IV | 19 | 25 | – | 3 | – | 1 | – | – | – | – | – |
| Bradford City | 1970–71 | IV | 19 | 2 | – | 1 | – | – | – | – | – | – | – |
| | | | | 407† | 5 | 43 | – | 11 | – | 10 | – | 63* | – |

## BANKS, Gordon

**Honours:** FA Cup runners-up medals 1961, 1963; League Cup winners medals 1964, 1972; League Cup runners-up medal 1965; FWA Footballer of the Year 1972; [NASL Goalkeeper of the Year 1977]; OBE 1970

| Club | Season | Div | Pos | Lge | FAC | FLC | Eur | Int |
|---|---|---|---|---|---|---|---|---|
| Chesterfield | 1958–59 | III | 16 | 23 | 3 | – | – | – |
| Leicester C. | 1959–60 | I | 12 | 32 | 4 | – | – | – |
| | 1960–61 | I | 6 | 40 | 10 | 1 | – | – |
| | 1961–62 | I | 14 | 41 | 2 | 1 | 4 | – |
| | 1962–63 | I | 4 | 38 | 6 | 2 | – | 4 |
| | 1963–64 | I | 11 | 36 | 1 | 8 | – | 9 |
| | 1964–65 | I | 18 | 38 | 6 | 9 | – | 6 |
| | 1965–66 | I | 7 | 32 | 4 | 1 | – | 14 |
| | 1966–67 | I | 8 | 36 | 1 | 3 | – | 4 |
| Stoke City | 1966–67 | I | 12 | 4 | – | – | – | – |
| | 1967–68 | I | 18 | 39 | 2 | 5 | – | 8 |
| | 1968–69 | I | 19 | 30 | 4 | 2 | – | 7 |
| | 1969–70 | I | 9 | 38 | 3 | 1 | – | 10 |
| | 1970–71 | I | 13 | 40 | 10 | 1 | – | 5 |
| | 1971–72 | I | 17 | 36 | 8 | 11 | – | 6 |
| | 1972–73 | I | 15 | 8 | – | 2 | – | – |
| | | | | 511 | 64 | 47 | 4 | 73 |

## RAMSEY, Alfred Ernest

**Honours:** League Championship medal 1951; Division II Championship medal 1950; Knighthood 1967

| Club | Season | Div | Pos | League Ms | League Gs | FA Cup Ms | FA Cup Gs | Inter'ls Ms | Inter'ls Gs |
|---|---|---|---|---|---|---|---|---|---|
| Southampton | 1946–47 | II | 14 | 23 | 1 | 1 | – | – | – |
| | 1947–48 | II | 3 | 42 | 5 | 4 | – | – | – |
| | 1948–49 | II | 3 | 25 | 2 | 1 | – | 1 | – |
| Tottenham H | 1949–50 | II | 1P | 41 | 4 | 3 | – | 7 | – |
| | 1950–51 | I | 1 | 40 | 4 | 1 | – | 6 | – |
| | 1951–52 | I | 2 | 38 | 5 | 2 | – | 8 | 1 |
| | 1952–53 | I | 10 | 37 | 6 | 9 | – | 8 | – |
| | 1953–54 | I | 16 | 37 | 2 | 6 | – | 2 | 2 |
| | 1954–55 | I | 16 | 33 | 3 | 3 | – | – | – |
| | | | | 316 | 32 | 30 | – | 32 | 3 |

\* including 1 appearance as substitute
† including 2 appearances as substitute
‡ including 3 appearances as substitute
§ including 5 appearances as substitute
¶ including 6 appearances as substitute

# INDEX

[Individual entries in bold type; italics denote picture reference]